WOMEN
and
THEOLOGY

EDITED BY

Mary Ann Hinsdale
and

Phyllis H. Kaminski

THE ANNUAL PUBLICATION OF THE
COLLEGE THEOLOGY SOCIETY
1994
VOLUME 40

ORBIS BOOKS

Maryknoll, New York 10545

The Catholic Foreign Mission Society of America (Maryknoll) recruits and trains people for overseas missionary service. Through Orbis Books, Maryknoll aims to foster the international dialogue that is essential to mission. The books published, however, reflect the opinions of their authors and are not meant to represent the official position of the society.

Queries regarding rights and permissions should be addressed to: Orbis Books, P. O. Box 308, Maryknoll, New York 10545-0308.

Co-published by the College Theology Society and Orbis Books, Maryknoll, NY 10545-0308
Manufactured in the United States of America

Library of Congress Cataloging-in-Publication Data

Women and theology / edited by Mary Ann Hinsdale and Phyllis Kaminski.
     p.   cm. — (Annual publication of the College Theology Society; v. 40 (1994)
    Includes bibliographical references.
    ISBN 1-57075-035-1 (alk. paper)
    1. Women in the Catholic Church—Congresses.   2. Woman (Christian theology—Congresses.   3. Catholic Church—Doctrines—Congresses.
I. Hinsdale, Mary Ann.   II. Kaminski, Phyllis.   III. Series: Annual publication of the College Theology Society ; v. 40.
BX2347.8.W6W65   1995
230'.2'082—dc20   95-32846
                                        CIP

To Joan Augusta Leonard, O.P. (1941-1995)

President of the College Theology Society (1992-1994)

Joan's commitment
to justice and the ideal of conversation
was evident to all who knew her.

CONTENTS

v

PART III
CHANGING THE TERMS

AFTERWORD

Acknowledgments

The editors wish to thank their colleagues whose careful reading of manuscripts assisted in the preparation of this volume.

Phyllis Kaminski thanks especially the following people from Saint Mary's College: Terence J. Martin for his critical suggestions; Linda Harrington, Tracy Hollingsworth, and Jennifer Brubaker for their secretarial help; Dan Mandell, Autumn Fields, Jen Myers, and Jean Powers from Computer Services for their technical support. Thanks are due also to Suzanne Sylvester, secretary, Religious Studies Department of the College of the Holy Cross.

Introduction:
Theology as Conversation

Phyllis H. Kaminski

"A conversation is a rare phenomenon.... It is not a confrontation. It is not a debate. It is not an exam. It is questioning itself. It is a willingness to follow the question wherever it may go. It is dia-logue."[1] When we think of theology as conversation, we recognize with David Tracy that theological inquiry aspires to a kind of discourse which is at once dialogical in process, courageous in its openness, and yet very uncommon in fact. We also recognize the fundamentally plural nature of the discursive landscape on which the theologian must operate. For as Tracy reminds us, theologians are called upon to converse in a credible and persuasive manner with interlocutors from three distinct yet related "publics"—the academy, the church, and the wider society.[2]

Construing theology as a conversation between persons with differing interests and experience is to recognize the complex, difficult, but perchance fruitful variety of interpretations of life and world that exist within the Christian tradition. It is, at the same time, to acknowledge the ideal of dialogue, where openness to differences is affirmed as something vital for the growth of theological understanding. Within this paradigm of theology, plurality is regarded as a simple fact of theological life. It is also affirmed as something to be protected and enhanced, as something good for theological inquiry. At its best, therefore, theological conversation is to be practiced pluralistically: all are to be addressed and all are to be heard. In this sense, doing theology requires a fundamental commitment to authentic conversation.[3]

In its history, however, theology has rarely included women in the dialogue; and to this day Christian theologians have not yet fully come to terms with the manifold ways in which the content and the form of theological discourse are distorted by root assumptions about gender and sexuality. On both counts, therefore, the conversation that is theology has been (and to a great extent remains) stilted. Though progress has been made on both issues, especially in the academy, much work remains. There is more to learn from women's voices if theological inquiry is truly to be a conversation in Tracy's sense; and there is more to discern about the ways in which Christian language and doctrine conceal fundamental distortions regarding the reality of women's lives and the value of women's experiences. If theological conversation is to thrive, then it must be fully opened to women and it must be cured of its systemic biases.

On the one hand, women continue to make real (though slow) headway in contributing to theological inquiry. In the past, of course, they were rarely invited to the arenas of public discourse. Spoken about and spoken to, women were consistently and successfully excluded from being active partners in theological conversation. Where they were able to participate, women were seen as outstanding exemplars, or more often branded as dissidents, heretics, hysterics or psychotics. Now, thankfully, women are less and less excluded from public domains. In fact, one of the most significant shifts in the practice of theology in the late twentieth century has been the inclusion of women's voices—at least in society and in the academy, if not yet fully in the church. Like the move toward non-European centers of theology and the inclusion of non-Christian voices, the presence and participation of women is bringing new life to the theological quest for understanding. Yet, as we approach the third millennium, it is apparent that the task of inclusion remains unfulfilled—notably in the church, where structures of exclusion persist in controlling what is talked about and who is able to talk. The presence and voices of women, therefore, still evoke some of the most hope-filled, yet also the most contested possibilities for inquiry.

On the other hand, the problems concerning theology go beyond the exclusion of women. Indeed, the absence of women is only part of the problem; simply to add women's voices does not address the more fundamental ways in which theology has been affected by unconscious bias. As Tracy reminds us, conversations skewed by systemic distortions (like racism, sexism, and classism) require a move to critical theory and argument in order to address and alleviate the distortions infecting discourse at its roots. Before a conversation can be authentically inclusive, it must be freed of such distortions.[4] Over the last two decades feminist discourse on religion has contributed precisely the kind of disciplined argument and critical perspective required for theology to come to terms with the androcentric and patriarchal assumptions resting at the very roots of Christian doctrine.

From the earliest tasks of uncovering the voices of women hidden in history, through the critique of the androcentric bias in scripture and tradition, to the construction of theological affirmations and arguments that not only reflect women's voices but also challenge the very epistemological foundations of the discipline, feminist scholarship has moved to enrich and to transform the practice of theological inquiry. In so doing, it has helped not only to include women's voices in the conversation, but also to heal all those who participate from the warping influence of inherited prejudices concerning gender.[5] Such work has contributed a great deal to the health of theological conversation. Nonetheless, the tasks of both inclusion and critique stand unfinished. Powerful forces remain—in the academy, the church and society— with vested interests in preserving skewed images of women in the Christian tradition.

Throughout its history, the College Theology Society has worked consistently to address the problem of women's exclusion and issues of gender requiring critical scrutiny. Indeed, it has regularly provided a discursive space for authentic theological conversation. Thus it is not surprising that at its fortieth annual meeting the Society chose to address the theme of Women and Theology. The papers at the conference covered an extensive range of topics—women in the biblical tradition, the tradition's treatment of women from the church fathers through the middle ages down to modern times. Convention participants discussed issues of ethics, spirituality, history, sacramental theology, religion and culture; and the relationship of theology to questions of ecclesiology, interreligious dialogue and, most broadly, to the role of the church in the world. The essays in this volume, therefore, reflect a wide spectrum of questions about women and about theology. They represent attempts to expand the horizons of theology through inclusion and to address the distortions that still skew our efforts at conversation. The authors speak as women, but they are intentionally in dialogue with all who are concerned with the integrity and relevance of theology in the academy, in the church, and in the world.

In the first part of the volume, M. Shawn Copeland sets the tone by recalling that theology done by and for women involves rhetorical strategies that call the church to recognize injustice, to heed the call to conversion, and to stand in solidarity with those still excluded from the good news. The three essays that follow highlight earlier struggles of women to enter the theological conversation. Caritas McCarthy holds up the efforts of Cornelia Connelly to develop an incarnational perspective within the historical constraints of nineteenth-century life. Dana Greene shows how Maisie Ward, early twentieth-century laywoman, author, and editor, also qualifies as theologian. Helen Ciernick discloses from more recent history the significance of the women "auditors" at the Second Vatican Council.

The essays in the second part of the volume probe the dynamic transformation of consciousness that has occurred as women explore the inclusion of their voices and the critique of hidden bias. In a series of shorter essays that reflect the implications of Nelle Morton's now famous phrase "hearing one another into speech," plenary panelists address the question of difference. Mary Rose D'Angelo speaks to ways in which hardness of hearing continues to silence the sexual, racial, or religious "other" who threatens the conversational status quo. Kwok Pui-lan addresses the radical multi-racial, multi-cultural, and multi-religious world that challenges feminist theology from Asia. María Pilar Aquino points to the unique labor of Latin American women in liberating theological discourse. Anne Patrick then articulates how all of us must move from hearing to collaboration as she outlines steps for the privileged toward a praxis of solidarity. In the essays that follow, Regina Boisclair shows how selective forgetfulness in the Catholic Sunday Lectionary perpetuates the exclusion of women in public worship. Susan Maloney points to changing historical perspectives that empower women religious to reconstruct their own history. Mary Rattigan shows how listening to women from Korea has changed her pedagogical and scholarly practice.

The third part of the volume explores future possibilities of transformation through ongoing conversation between theology and women's studies. Mary Ann Hinsdale lays out the overarching significance and implications of this dialogue. Linda Moody draws on feminist theory to suggest strategies for engaging in theological reflection across boundaries of difference. Ann O'Hara Graff argues that women's voices (and the voices of all "others") will radically alter theological understanding of revelation and the process of ecclesial decision-making. Jane Kopas points out how changed understandings of gender are redefining theological anthropology. Phyllis Kaminski suggests ways in which cultural theorist Julia Kristeva helps feminist theologians deepen their critical perspectives on language and culture in order to redefine the symbol of the cross and the power of redemptive love.

The volume contains a fitting afterword. The presidential address of Joan Leonard, published posthumously, highlights the power of memory. Joan recalls the importance of celebrating our history as she traces significant moments in the College Theology Society. More importantly, she addresses the tensions between patriarchy and feminism that still trouble the church, the academy, and contemporary society. Her look at questions of women's marginalization, connectedness, and transformed relationships points to a future of collegial collaboration among all Christians. Such mutual efforts, long fostered by the College Theology Society, are vital to the ongoing conversation that is theology and to the Christian commitment to transformation in the academy, the church and the world.

Notes

[1] David Tracy, *Plurality and Ambiguity: Hermeneutics, Religion, Hope* (San Francisco: Harper & Row, Publishers, 1987), p. 18.

[2] See David Tracy, *The Analogical Imagination : Christian Theology and the Culture of Pluralism* (New York: Crossroad, 1981), especially pages 3-46.

[3] Tracy, *Analogical Imagination*, pp. 101 ff and *Plurality*, pp. 18-21.

[4] For the need for critical theory see *Analogical Imagination*, pp. 73-74 and *Plurality*, especially pp. 28-46. For a concise introductory work, see Raymond Geuss, *The Idea of a Critical Theory: Habermas and the Frankfurt School* (Cambridge University Press, 1981).

[5] For recent examples see Ann Kirkus Wetherilt, *That They May Be Many: Voices of Women, Echoes of God* (New York: Continuum, 1994); Mary McClintock Fulkerson, *Changing the Subject: Women's Discourses and Feminist Theology* (Minneapolis: Fortress Press, 1994); and Rebecca S. Chopp, *The Power to Speak: Feminism, Language, God* (New York: Crossroad, 1991); for a feminist approach to a specific theological question and for a bibliography on theory and feminist theology, see Elisabeth Schüssler Fiorenza, *Jesus—Miriam's Child, Sophia's Prophet: Critical Issues in Feminist Christology* (New York: Continuum, 1994).

Part I

ENTERING THE CONVERSATION

Toward a Critical Christian Feminist Theology of Solidarity[1]

M. Shawn Copeland

Introduction

This essay explores some of the implications and connections between social praxis and some contemporary forms of a rhetoric of solidarity employed in styles of feminist theologies. Here, the term praxis denotes the concrete praxis of liberation, of Christian struggle for social transformation. Detached and distantiated from concrete historical, cultural, social (i.e., political, economic, technological) contexts, praxis risks becoming clichéd overused, undermined, and undermining. Here, moreover, the term praxis adverts to its "epistemological value" as well.[2] For theologies of liberation, praxis denotes an epistemological rupture—a different way of apprehending, of inquiring into, of knowing, indeed, of *doing* truth.

The term rhetoric here refers not only to the persuasiveness of the discourse of marginalized and oppressed communities, but insists upon serious attention to the historical, cultural, and social orders from within which these ignored, abused, and embodied voices arise. Moreover, focus on solidarity not only problematizes the practice of theology for Celtic, Anglo, European-American feminist theologians, but also for indigenous North American and Asian American women theologians, for *mujerista* and womanist theologians. Focus on solidarity calls for an end to facile adoption of the rhetoric of solidarity by Celtic-, Anglo-, European-American feminists, while they ignore and, sometimes, consume the experiences and voices of the marginalized and oppressed, while, ever adroitly, dodging the penitential call to conversion—to authenticity in word and in deed.

The first part of this essay outlines the context of the founding of the School of Sacred Theology at Saint Mary's College by the charismatic and formidable Mary Madeleva Wolff of the Sisters of the Holy Cross. By providing a place for women to study theology, Mary Madeleva Wolff quite directly "mothered" feminist theology to life in the United States. After this review, there follows, from the perspective of a theologian whose work primarily concerns marginalized communities, a sketch of the emergence and development of contemporary feminist theology. Here, I raise the possibility of a critical Christian feminist theology that dares unity in diversity. The second part reflects on the problematic of solidarity: probing meanings of "sisterhood," distinguishing solidarity from difference, from conformity, from imitation, and from uncritical acceptance. The third part proposes concrete steps toward getting beyond mere speech about or commonsense appeals to solidarity. It concludes with some theological observations regarding solidarity as a category and end of a critical Christian feminist theology. I am convinced that the very possibility of a future for theology as practiced by feminist theologians depends upon our abilities to accept and respect difference and to engage in authentic solidarity. I say more: the very possibility of a flourishing human future demands it.

A Review of Theology in Feminist Perspective

It is common to characterize the period in which Mary Madeleva Wolff of the Sisters of the Holy Cross founded the School of Sacred Theology as "preVatican II." With that shorthand phrase, we signal a certain theological past, our judgments on it as well as our departures from it. For in the "postVatican II" period, Roman Catholic theology in the United States as well as in so many other nations and cultures has migrated in manifold directions: toward the apprehension, articulation, analysis, and differentiated understanding of scales of human experience; toward hermeneutics, whether of tradition, of the authority of tradition, of language, or of social location; toward interdisciplinary collaboration and debate; toward interreligious dialogue; outward to map, analyze, and interpret the relation, significance, and role of religions within cultural matrices; toward meta-theoretical debates; or toward the preferential option for those who are economically poor, exploited, oppressed, and marginalized because of their gendered and/or racial-cultural-ethnic embodiment.

But, in the 1940s, the situation of theology was somewhat more tame, no less complex, to be sure, yet quite different. Recall that Bernard Lonergan, Karl Rahner, and Hans Urs von Balthasar had published only a few pieces. Hans Küng, Johann Baptist Metz, Gustavo Gutierrez, and Edward Schillebeeckx were young students; their teachers both in the classroom and on the wider intellectual scene were Marie-Dominque Chenu and Yves Congar, Etienne Gilson and Jacques Maritain, Joseph Mary Lagrange and Roland deVaux. The gift their intellectual courage and imagination made to the revitalizing of theological and ecclesial life has been termed "*nouvelle théologie*" or as some scholars suggest "*ressourcement* theology."[3]

In the 1940s, Roman Catholic theology in the United States was oriented by the magisterial work of the "Common Doctor," although the grandeur and scope of that work had been obscured by neo-scholastic eisegesis. Still, under the tutelage of Thomas Aquinas, Roman Catholic theologians took their principal intellectual coordinates from Aristotelian philosophy and science and their basic cultural coordinates from European aesthetics expressed in music, dance, architecture, painting, sculpture, and literature. And, as historian Patricia Byrne has argued, they were ultramontane in devotional practice. Celtic-Anglo-European and American, male, and overwhelmingly cleric, Roman Catholic theologians preoccupied themselves with logic, metaphysics, and epistemology; with the careful qualification and declension of sin; with the clear and distinct presentation of correct doctrine.

The founding of the School of Sacred Theology neither discounted the significance of Thomas Aquinas to Roman Catholic theology, nor did it malign white male cleric theologians. Mary Madeleva Wolff simply wanted to secure for women access to the study and practice of the sacred science. At the time, there were no women in the United States with doctoral degrees in theology, but with the support of a few bishops, Madeleva Wolff enlisted the cooperation of some white male clerics as teachers and degree advisors. But Madeleva Wolff was more than a founder, she was a subversive founder: subversive insofar as she was an educator who respected the human mind—its structures, its unity, its power. Mary Madeleva Wolff believed that women had minds and ought to use them—ought to use their minds well, seriously, rigorously. What in the 1940s could have been more exhilarating to a Catholic woman who understood herself as a serious intellectual, than the effort to reach up to the mind of Thomas Aquinas? What in the 1940s could have been more exhilarating to an intellectually serious Catholic woman, than the study and practice of theology? Madeleva Wolff made that dream and its fulfillment possible: she provided Catholic women with more than a *room*, she gave us a *school*. By inserting women into the stream of academic theology, she laid the condition of the possibility of a distinctive theological contribution emerging from women's reflection on our particular human, religious, cultural, political, and economic experiences in light of the Word of God. We honor those women who were bold explorers, pioneers in theology. Of the many women, lay and vowed religious, who studied at the School of Sacred Theology, three come immediately to mind— Betty Moslander, Margaret Brennan, and Mary Daly. Their voices have shaped and changed the situation of women in our church and in our society certainly. We owe to Mary Madeleva Wolff of the Sisters of the Holy Cross a great debt of gratitude: because of her labor, Roman Catholic women have been engaged in the study and practice of theology now for fifty years. Her labor was mother to what we recognize as feminist theology.

By now the main lines of the contemporary emergence and development of theology in feminist perspective are well known and need not be repeated in detail here. This brief review serves only as orientation to the discussion of solidarity. Theologies of liberation appeared in the latter half of the 1960s and, as Theo Witvliet has observed, the first contours could be seen roughly at the same time in passionate human hunger for freedom and liberation in various parts of the world.[4]

In a first phase, theology as an intellectual practice from feminist perspective mainly took its bearings from the concerns of the secular white women's movement and from the cultural and social (i.e., political, economic, technological) critiques leveled at the hegemony of the West by the various theologies emerging in the struggle of marginalized and oppressed peoples for liberation in Latin America, Asia, Africa, and the United States. In that nascent period, white feminist theologians and red, brown, yellow, and black male liberation theologians exposed the ideological cover stories that had permitted the collusion of Christianity in anesthetizing the liberating message of the Gospel. Moreover, the discursive practices of feminist thinkers augmented the elaboration and liberation of theology as a cognitive praxis—calling for new methodological approaches, posing new questions for inquiry, identifying new explanatory categories, and proposing new data for theological analysis and reflection. Yet, as critical as theology in feminist perspective yearned to be, it still lived and moved and thought and grew within a horizon of unquestioned privilege. Feminist theologians collapsed the meanings and consequences of social class differences among racially similar (i.e., white Celtic-, Anglo-, European American) women and simply disregarded anti-red, -brown, -yellow and -black racism as these were manifest not only in individual and private mediating practices of bias, but also in the structural, systemic legitimation of that bias. This first phase might be termed reformist insofar as it sought to include women as full participants in social and ecclesial life and in the practice of theology. Perhaps, Mary Daly's work signaled the hope (*The Church and the Second Sex*) and the raw disappointment (*Beyond God the Father*) of that period.[5]

Of course, red, brown, yellow and black women were never silent. In early essays Frances Beale and Grace Lee Boggs had analyzed the economic and psychological exploitation of black women by the dominant patriarchal capitalist societal order as well as by black men.[6] At the 1975 Detroit meeting of "Theology in the Americas," Beatriz Melano Couch was the only woman among the delegation of theologians from Latin America. Melano Couch defined herself not as a "feminist theologian, but as a liberation theologian" and noted that the other women of the conference espoused a notion of feminist liberation that aimed at the "basic transformation of society: a new order, not a new deal—political, social, economic, cultural."[7] She insisted that "racism and sexism [were] oppressive ideologies which deserve a specific treatment in the theology of liberation."[8] At the same conference, African American political essayist Michele Russell discussed sexism in the United States. Russell concentrated on the interconnectedness of global underdevelopment and the brutal incorporation of women in labor markets. She argued that "an understanding of the specific structural profile of women's participation in the economy shed some light on patterns of family life and the institutionalization of patriarchal values within a capitalist work context."[9] Moreover, Russell critiqued the competition and ranking of oppressions that resulted from "our immediate impulse as individuals fighting for self-respect to legitimize only our particular form of victimization."[10] Russell maintained that the liberation and human flourishing of red, brown, yellow and black women and consequently, of all people of darker hue, was at stake in the refusal to link rhetoric and praxis.

Poet and essayist Audre Lorde had glimpsed the promise of Mary Daly's work for illumining the conditions of red, brown, yellow and black women. In the early seventies, Daly had indicted patriarchal theology for a "methodolatry" that rendered women "nonquestions" and data about women "nondata." With *Gyn/Ecology,* she provocatively clarified the cross-cultural character of patriarchy; the historical, cultural, and societal erasure of women; and the insidious effort of colonization to induce women to participate in their own oppression.[11] Lorde was disappointed with Daly's "narrow ecology" that defined "noneuropean women as victims and preyers-upon each other" and she was repelled by Daly's silence regarding the brutal murders of twelve African American women in the Boston area not long after the publication of *Gyn/Ecology*. For Lorde and for other red, brown, yellow and black women, Daly's metaethics of radical, and putatively pluralist, feminism had turned out to be just another stop on the road of the "long and discouraging" history of white women's seeming inability to hear red, brown, yellow and black women, to dialogue with us, to see us—to bring rhetoric and action together.[12]

In a second phase, feminist theologians engaged in intellectually rigorous effort to dislodge the ideology of patriarchy and the practice of domination. While some theologians, historians, and biblical scholars abandoned the search for a usable past, others persisted, discovered, and introduced the lives of heretofore forgotten women into the scholarly canon.[13] While some theologians, historians, and biblical scholars questioned the meaningfulness of a male savior for women, others laid out persuasive accounts of the vital significance of the historical Jesus.[14] While some theologians, historians, and biblical scholars relinquished the church to crusted misogyny, others pushed forward new forms of discipleship and new ecclesial practices.[15] While some theologians and exegetes eschewed God-talk altogether and charted aprogram "beyond God the Father," still others argued the "patriarchalization of God," and revitalized Trinitarian language.[16] But, when red, brown, yellow and black applied tests of conversion and solidarity, these efforts paled.

Women attempting to do theology from within and with marginalized and oppressed communities still found their experiences ignored. As concrete as expressions of theology from feminist perspective aimed to be, they offered no differentiated interpretation of the intentional disruption of the standard of living by the biased structuring of the societal economy. That disruption is incarnated in the materially meager, but tough and resourceful lives of poor women, particularly poor red, brown, yellow and black women. It is quite true that these expressions of theology in feminist perspective insisted that the proper subject of theology is not the individual professional theologian, but the community to whom she makes a gift of her education, intellectual acumen, and moral strength. Indeed, feminist theologians employed, or rather assumed, the rhetoric of liberation—"commitment to the liberation of women" or "preferential option for the poor." Still the very use of this discourse obscured the presence of red, brown, yellow and black women and diverted attention from an examination of the specific relations between red, brown, yellow and black women and white women. The distinctive voices of red, brown, yellow and black women were silenced in the fight against racism, against economic and political dependence, against patriarchy, against heterosexism. Finally, this oversight relieved theology in feminist perspective of the obligation to reflect critically on its own sources, traditions, commitments, and horizon.

In a third phase, some white feminist theologians, particularly Beverly Harrison, Rosemary Radford Ruether, Letty Russell, and Elisabeth Schüssler Fiorenza, questioned the sufficiency of the paradigm of theology as critique of patriarchy.[17] Schüssler Fiorenza's work can provide a representative position. She proposed to treat patriarchy as a "basic heuristic concept for feminist analysis" and assigned it a normative definition that went beyond "all men dominating all women equally." She projected a critical feminist theology of liberation that would account for the previously overlooked and critical differences in relations among women and among the men who oppress women. Thus: "Patriarchy as a male pyramid of graded subordinations and exploitations [specifies] women's oppression in terms of the class, race, country, or religion of the men to whom we "belong." The definition that Schüssler Fiorenza put forward aimed for the critical "conceptualization not only sexism but also racism, property-class relationships, and all other forms of exploitation or dehumanization as basic structures of women's oppression."[18] But even this theoretical precision did not compass the cultural complexity and fulsome realities of the lived lives of red, brown, yellow and black women. This task was assumed by feminist theologians of indigenous communities in the Americas, by womanist and *mujerista* theologians, by African feminist theologians, by Asian and Asian American feminist theologians, by Latin American feminist theologians. This task has been assumed by dozens of black, yellow, brown, and red women including Katie Cannon, Cheryl Townsend Gilkes, Jacquelyn Grant, Jamie T. Phelps, OP, Emilie M. Townes, Renita J. Weems, and Delores S. Williams; by Bonita Bennett, Bernadette I. Mosala, and Mercy Oduyoye; by Chung Hyun Kyung, Virginia Fabella, and Kwok Pui-lan; by María Pilar Aquino, Ivone Gebara, Ada María Isasi-Díaz, and Elsa Tamez.[19] Their work, varied in questions, emphases, theoretical stance, method, and ecclesial relation, projects into Christian theological reflection the voices and experiences of women who have been ignored, abused, exploited, and oppressed.

Theology from feminist perspectives advanced the liberation of women from the nexus of white patriarchy and white racist imperialist discourse; yet, the background theories feminist theologians utilized (whether Marxist or socialist or gender-critical or Foucautian), continued to render the presence and experiences of red, brown, yellow and black women passive, and, sometimes, to erase these women and their experiences. *However*, if the critique and positive or constructive work of feminist theologians of indigenous communities in the Americas, of womanist and *mujerista* theologians, of African feminist theologians, of Asian and Asian American feminist theologians, and of Latin American feminist theologians along with Schüssler Fiorenza's vision for a critical feminist theology of liberation are taken into full account, we are impelled to a fourth phase. Is an inclusive critical Christian theology of liberation in *differentiated* feminist perspectives possible? Certainly and necessarily such a project would oppose dialectical cognitive praxis to the *ersatz*-epistemologies (the ideologies of domination and destruction—sexism, racism, anti-Semitism, heterosexism, political and economic exploitation) that structure the cultural and social arrangements by which women and men live so unmindfully and would uncover the gross economic mediation of the most intimate personal human relations as well as the societal whole. Such a project would stand with and engage the victims of history and embrace the oppressed as necessary partners in mutual liberation and would disclose the lineage and effects of oppression mediated through inhuman relations in a global context. Such a project would situate normative control of meaning and value in the cognitive, moral, and religious authenticity of what previously had been despised, ignored, even hated identities and realities—the identities and realities of red, brown, yellow, and black women. But, this fourth phase will require a turn, a conversion among all theologians to engage difference in the work toward authentic solidarity in word and in deed.

The Problematic of Solidarity

The English word solidarity comes from the French, *solidarité,* which is derived from the reflexive verb, *se solidariser,* which means to join together in liability; to be mutually dependent [upon], to make common cause [with]. The first definition of solidarity listed in the Oxford English Dictionary reads: "the fact or quality, on the part of communities, etc., of being perfectly united or at one in some respect, especially in interests, sympathies, or aspirations." The second definition states: "community or perfect coincidence of (or between) interests."

A *commonsense* understanding and appropriation of the notion of solidarity advert to some relation or interest or connection, but this appropriation fails to raise and to tackle questions about the cause of that relation or connection. Moreover, this understanding and appropriation of solidarity overlook the conditions of its possibility. On the one hand, mere commonsense appropriation and use of a rhetoric of solidarity may provoke expectations and hopes in a certain person or group in relation to another person or group who may or may not be able or willing to fulfill those expectations and hopes. On the other hand, merely *having* racial or gender or cultural-ethnic or sexual orientation or social class oppression in common does not ensure solidarity. In these instances, solidarity may be simply a cliché, an empty sign, signifying nothing. Such understanding, appropriation, and use result in moral idealism and, thus, lack practically intelligent, effective, and transformative praxis. Such understanding, appropriation, and use result in vacuous living and undermine the concrete eschatological future.

There is, then, a problematic or cluster of problems to be addressed if we are to think critically about the term difference which so complexifies any understanding and expression of solidarity and if we are to move beyond the rhetoric of solidarity. What does it mean to speak of solidarity as an expression of relationships *within* groups or classes? What does it mean to speak of solidarity as an expression of relationships *between* groups or classes? What do such forms of solidarity demand? What is the basis for solidarity among feminist theologies across and through the intersecting lines of class and race? Can particular feminist theologies avoid relativism and reduction in the struggle for authentic pluralism? How can feminist theologies affirm the distinct and sometimes conflictual historical experiences of divided communities of women in the quest for solidarity?

Solidarity and "Sisterhood"

For more than two decades, the notion of sisterhood has been an important organizing force in the women's movement, but that notion has a dubious origin. Elizabeth Fox-Genovese in "The Personal Is Not Political Enough" locates the roots of a notion of sisterhood in the conflicting ideals of the bourgeois revolutions of the seventeenth and eighteenth centuries and in the nurturant and reproductive roles of women within the family as well as women's feelings of attachment and loyalty to other women growing out of shared experiences of oppression.[20] On the one hand, the notion of sisterhood is aligned with the bourgeois individualism which resulted in "the passage of a few [white] middle class women into the public sphere" and which congealed the differences in social class between them and white working-class women and the differences in race between them and red, brown, yellow, and black women.[21] On the other hand, the notion of sisterhood is embedded in patriarchal familial ideology. Thus, it turns inward and lacks the "broader politics directed toward the kind of social transformation that will provide social justice for all human beings."[22] Black women have been suspicious of the notion of sisterhood, apprehending not only the subtle appeal to individualism and self-aggrandizement, but also the *de jure* and *de facto* inequality among the sisters in the family. At the same time, sisterhood as nurturant supportive feelings of attachment and loyalty to other women is not new among black women. Indeed, black women "institutionalized sisterhood in churches, organized it through the club movements that began in the late 1800s, recited it in numerous informal gatherings, and live it in extended family groupings that frequently place great importance on female kinship ties."[23] The splintering of the notion of sisterhood provides a useful starting point for this discussion of solidarity.

African American poet and political essayist June Jordan probes the commonsense dimensions of solidarity and sisterhood in an essay reflecting on her vacation to the Bahamas. From the outset, Jordan recognizes and acknowledges the ironic situation in which she and other African Americans find themselves—that is, as tourists they are part of another "weird succession of crude intruders."[24] She recognizes and acknowledges that despite limited vacation budgets, the potential and actual social (i.e., political, economic, and technological) options of visiting black Americans define them as rich in relation to those black Bahamian women and men who serve as hotel waiters, chamber maids, and maintenance workers or as sellers and traders in the local market. Settling into her hotel room, Jordan notices a card bearing the name of the maid assigned to clean her room. Thus begins Jordan's interrogation of her own consciousness of race, class, and gender identity as she distinguishes the "fixed relations" between herself and Olive, another black woman.[25]

> "Olive" is the name of the black woman who cleans my hotel room. On my way to the beach I am wondering what "Olive" would say if I told her why I chose the Sheraton British Colonial; if I told her I wanted to swim. I wanted to sleep. I did not want to be raped by anybody (white or black) at all and I calculated that my safety as a black woman alone would best be assured by a multinational hotel corporation. Anyway, I'm pretty sure "Olive" would look at me as though I came from someplace as far away as Brooklyn. Then she'd probably allow herself one indignant query before righteously removing her vacuum cleaner from my room; "and why in the first place you come down you without your husband?" I cannot imagine how I would begin to answer her. My "rights" and my "freedom" and my "desire" and a slew of other New World values; what would they sound like to this Black woman described on the card atop my hotel bureau as "Olive the Maid"? . . . . Whose rights? Whose freedom? Whose desire? And why should she [care] about mine unless I do something, for real, about hers?[26]

Jordan's analysis offers us an opportunity to explore issues of sisterhood, similarity, and hidden difference, since not all black women have exactly the same personal, religious, cultural, political, economic, social class, and educational experiences. We can only conjecture some of the differences between June Jordan and Olive—skin color and body size with its protocols and complexes of preference and affirmation, cultural appropriation and expression, schooling and education, social class status and background, as well as views on marriage and woman's role and position in a society.

Jordan identifies with the other black woman, with "Olive." Jordan knows that, to a certain and real extent, she too, is invisible, just another black woman in the crowd, subject to the brunt of sexism, sexual exploitation, political and economic manipulation. Yet, in the admission of the irony of her own angular social location as a citizen of the United States, Jordan uncovers those modes in which Olive's social location contradicts and challenges her own. Moreover, Jordan is conscious that alienation, resentment, and misunderstanding are just as possible between her and Olive as are sisterhood, keen sympathy, and understanding. Race and gender and class may serve as "indicators of concepts of connection, as elements of connection" but they are unreliable.[27] Economic advantage may impede authentic racial or gender connection and cripple social praxis; gender location may neutralize race. Jordan cautions us in our eagerness and willingness to identify with women racially like ourselves. We Indian American and Asian American, *mujerista* and womanist theologians must be willing to investigate our potential solidarity and sisterhood *with* as well as our differences *from* other Indian, Asian, Latina, Chicana, and African women. For not all red, brown, yellow, or black women have exactly the same religious, personal, cultural, intellectual, social class, and historical experiences. Complex social relations and interactions simultaneously promote coalitions and conflicts that can not always be easily anticipated. Neither race nor class nor gender can ever serve as "*automatic* [emphasis mine] concepts of connection" or of community.[28] The commonsense attempt to generate solidarity on such grounds only founders and collapses. Authentic solidarity requires something more penetrating and more profound, something, at once, more human and more transcendent.

Mere commonsense understanding and usage of the rhetoric of solidarity can and does pervade cultural, religious, and social domains. Indeed, demands for cultural, religious, and social conformity sometimes borrow the garb of solidarity. But, these demands cannot be sustained in the long-term effort required to interiorize authentic commitment of mind, heart, and work. Solidarity, as a defining quality or characteristic of a group or community, emerges from a common and/or complementary field of experience, of understanding, of judgments, of decisions, and of commitments. Solidarity emerges from the concrete unity of interests, sympathies, aspirations; common scrutiny, appraisal, and questioning; shared beliefs, values, and judgments; common decisions, commitments, and loves. Thus, solidarity is rooted in experiential, intellectual, rational, and responsible agreements and commitments to live out and live out of certain meanings.

Solidarity and Difference

In the English spoken in the United States, the noun difference denotes unlikeness, while it connotes opposition, disagreement, quarrel, and dispute. Synonyms for the adjective different, include *diverse* (suggesting conspicuous difference), *divergent* (stressing irreconcilability), *distinct* (stressing different identity and unmistakable separateness), *dissimilar* (focusing on the absence of similarity in appearance, properties, or nature), *disparate* (implying essential or thoroughgoing difference, often stressing an absence of any relationship between things), and *various* (emphasizing the number and diversity of kinds, types, etc.).[29] With the exception of various, the most common synonyms for *difference* imply negative qualities or conditions and negative relations: disagreement, dissent, discord, estrangement, dissimilarity, dissimilitude, variance, divergence, contention, dispute, disparity, inequality, unlikeness, discrimination, diversity, discrepancy.[30] The most common antonyms suggest positive qualities or conditions and positive relations: agreement, similarity, similitude, assent, consent, concurrence, accord, accordance, harmony, amity, concord, congruity, unison, and union.

If our national language is to mediate adequately national cultural, political, economic, and social class experiences then, in our usage, difference connotes suspicion, if not disdain. Difference communicates that which is and those who are to be avoided. As political philosopher Iris Marion Young observes, in the national consciousness, "the ideal of liberation" has been the "elimination of group difference."[31] We prefer and foster uniformity; we espouse what social theorist Theodor Adorno called the relentless "logic of identity."[32] This logic denies and represses the creativity and possibility of variety, variation, diversity, difference. Further, Young remarks, "the irony of the logic of identity is that by seeking to reduce the differently similar to the same, it turns the merely different into the absolutely other."[33] American culture and American people are the products of such a logic: *differently similar* Celtic-, Anglo-, European-American men and women in the United States share the similarity of skin color. That similarity is absolutized since, although those men and women have participated in and been formed by many different religious, personal, cultural, intellectual, social class, and historical experiences, their differences are reduced in the light of skin color. Thus, the different are rendered the same. On the other hand, the *merely different* in skin color—African, Latino, Chicano, Korean, Japanese, Chinese, American Indian men and women—are absolutized as *the other* and ruled out of authentic human participation in the various dimensions of life in the United States social order.

There is, as well, the temptation to dissolve difference—to ignore it or to meet it with sly or shame-faced side-long glances. Johnetta B. Cole cautions: "To address our commonalities without dealing with our differences is to misunderstand and distort that which separates as well as that which binds us as women."[34] This temptation to dissolve difference surfaces each time a white woman declares to a red, brown, yellow, or black woman: "I'm colorblind. I don't even notice your race." On the surface, the remark makes an appeal to commonalities and, in some cases, human universals. But, it is not just an appeal, it is a comforting appeal and an appeal to comfort. The white woman speaking draws upon her own conditioned frame of reference for criteria in locating, understanding and judging experiences that may well come from other and distinct frames of reference. She does not pause to consider the assumptions that undergird the situation, the experiences, the decisions, the meanings, the values of the red, brown, yellow, or black woman to whom she is speaking. Nor, does she pause to consider the assumptions that promote and undergird such facile relocation and, an ultimately, false knowledge of the other woman. The white woman speaking neither questions the understanding and knowledge she purports to have obtained, nor the judgments she has made. And this is a pity: in far too many instances, the white woman speaking risks not only her own ignorance and arrogance, but the lives and deaths of others.

The usual response that a red, brown, yellow, or black woman makes to this and other remarks aimed, whether consciously or unconsciously, to dissolve difference is not one of appreciation. The responding red, brown, yellow, or black woman recognizes the remark as the assertion of control—control of social, ceremonial, and rhetorical space. The white woman's remark directs the red, brown, yellow, or black woman to relinquish differences of social class and upbringing; to accept imputed forms of personal address, of face-to-face interaction, and contact; to surrender styles and logics of analysis that express complex meanings. No, the responding red, brown, yellow, or black woman can not be grateful, can not be appreciative; after all, given real choice, who yields individuality and distinctiveness to erasure? There is something else. With the erasure of red, brown, yellow, and black skin comes the extension of "whiteness" to those oppressed by the very structures that lend skin color privilege or pain. Red, brown, yellow, and black women perceive the dangers lurking in this dissolution of difference and so stake out, hold, and struggle to maintain their own standpoints and styles. Red, brown, yellow, and black women grasp the fallacies in the extension of whiteness. First, the extension of "whiteness" can only be temporary and *ad hoc*. It depends upon the speaking white woman, upon the level of her generosity or the level of her fear. Thus, the red, brown, yellow, or black woman is assigned a condition of dependency. Second, such "whiteness" is contextual. It is lent for the space of the encounter and can not be transferred to other situations. For, in this situation, the white woman is the arbiter, not only of "whiteness" but also of "blackness" or "yellowness," or "brownness" or "redness." Third, the "whiteness" that is extended to the red, brown, yellow, or black woman can never be evoked or assumed by her *on her own* or *for her own*. This extended "whiteness" is patently artificial. It is not for her, it is a device for someone else's comfort. This "whiteness" is given and taken back at a white woman's whim. This "whiteness" can not undo the social and historical harm a red woman shoulders; it can not insure a black woman's life against the violence of white supremacist hate groups, it can not defend a brown woman's body against insinuation and innuendo, it can not guarantee the spiritual solace for a yellow woman's heart.[35] This artificial "whiteness" estranges potential allies from each other, for it rejects the authentic possibility that *differences might enrich rather than divide*.

It is possible, then, that "the politics of difference," while aiming to problematize and pluralize the experience of women in feminist analysis could instigate the isolation of African, African American, Asian, Chicana, Chinese, Latina, Korean, Japanese, and indigenous American women. Afro-British literary critic Hazel Carby warns that the "category of difference" ought not be used as if it were an *absolute*, thus denying the complexity of the presence of difference. Moreover, too often, when social, racial, and cultural-ethnic differences are absolutized, the response of so-called "liberal whites" is silence. Thus, these women and men absent themselves from the moral obligation of conversation and dialogue, of self-criticism and conversion. Furthermore, because these women and men are members of the so-called dominant racial group, even if their silence emerges from anger or guilt, from sadness or shame or frustration, the net result "is indistinguishable from not having to take any . . . position whatsoever in relation to. . . . the other. [And] if one does not have to take a position, then difference has been preserved as absolute and so has the dominant social order."[36] Any advance toward concrete change of the social order is achieved only by critically intelligent confrontation with ideologies of power and domination which sustain and suffuse the social order.

Getting beyond the Rhetoric of Solidarity

In the Western European intellectual tradition, the art of rhetoric has had an ambiguous history. Since its inception, around the fifth century B.C.E., the meaning of rhetoric has oscillated *between* concern with specific techniques of communication *and* the sense that persuasion has a larger ethical orientation, between ornamentation and moral obligation. The long-standing debates generated by Platonic and Aristotelian notions of rhetoric give rise to the qualification—*mere rhetoric* which adverts to the most debased meaning of rhetoric as "artful sometimes fanciful lying."[37] Thus the exhortation to move beyond rhetoric, not only acknowledges this qualification, it raises the question of moral obligation of speech in relation to action, in relation to praxis.

Marginalized and oppressed communities employ a rhetoric of protest to provoke a conversion and/or transformation that is to be realized concretely in practices of solidarity. That is to say, the goal of the rhetoric of protest as employed in theology is the concrete realization of religious, moral, and intellectual transformation in church, in society, in history. With a rhetoric of protest, marginalized communities critique the facile and liberal character of the rhetoric of solidarity which privileged communities embrace. Thus, we theologians who are red, brown, yellow, and black women challenge white feminist theologians to conversion, to solidarity.

African American poet and political essayist June Jordan recounts the following interaction with one of her graduate students:

> I praised the excellence of her final paper; indeed it had seemed to me an extraordinary pulling together of recent left brain/right brain research with the themes of transcendental poetry. I praised the excellence of her final paper. . . . She told me that . . . she'd completed her reading of my political essays.
>
> "You are so lucky!" she exclaimed.
>
> "What do you mean by that?"
>
> "You have a cause. You have a purpose to your life."
>
> I looked carefully at this white woman; what was she really saying to me?
>
> "What do you mean?" I repeated.
>
> "Poverty. Police violence. Discrimination in general."
>
> (. . . I thought: Is this her idea of lucky?)
>
> "And how about you?" I asked.
>
> "Me?"
>
> "Yeah you. Don't you have a cause?"
>
> "Me? I'm just a middle-aged woman: a housewife and mother. I'm a nobody."
>
> For a while I made no response.
>
> First of all, speaking of race and class and gender in one breath, what she said meant that those lucky preoccupations of mine, from police violence to nuclear wipe-out, were not shared. They were mine and not hers. But here she sat . . . beaming good will or more "luck" in my direction.
>
> In the second place, what this white woman said to me meant that she did not believe she was "a person" precisely because she had fulfilled . . . traditional female functions. . . .
>
> If she believed me lucky to have regular hurdles of discrimination then why shouldn't I insist that she's lucky to be a middle class white Wasp female who lives in such well-sanctioned and normative comfort that she even has the luxury to deny the

power of the privileges that paralyze her life?

If she deserts me and "my cause" where we differ, if, for example, she abandons me to "my" problems of race, then why should I support her in "her" problems of housewifely oblivion?[38]

This white female graduate student seems to lack any sense of the moral obligations that the privilege of study enjoins upon her. This student seems to lack any comprehension of the concrete meanings and implications of solidarity with the victims of history, of a notion of the common human good. Poverty, police violence, discrimination are not her problems, nor are they the problems of her group. Oppression, misfortune, and fear are not her problems. Or, at least, so she thinks. As Jordan remarks elsewhere, "In America, you can segregate the people, but the problems travel."[39] This woman seems to fail to recognize that each and every one of us living in the United States has been constructed as a racialized subject: *if blackness is invented, so is whiteness.* She seems to fail to grasp the implication of whiteness in the construction of blackness. Hence, she perceives racism and its concomitant violence, police brutality, and discrimination as the problem of Indian and Black and Latino and Chicano and Korean and Japanese men and women. Thus, the white female graduate student seems to overlook just how systemic violence is embedded in the unquestioned standards, symbols, habits, patterns, and practices which compose a society as well as in the epistemological, moral, and religious assumptions which underlie not only the performance of prescribed social (including political, economic, and technological), cultural, and religious roles and tasks, but also the individual and collective consequences of following, or not, approved social, cultural, and religious codes and rules.[40]

I pause briefly on the bias of racism. Racism is prejudice augmented, inflated, promoted, and sustained by structural power: racism permeates and sustains religious, cultural, political, economic, social class structures in order to stigmatize, ostracize, stereotype, and control segments of a population for the benefit and privilege of all those who collude with supremacists. Evelyn Brooks Higginbotham notes:

Like gender and class, then, race must be seen as a social construction predicated upon the recognition of difference and signifying the simultaneous positioning of groups vis-à-vis one another. More than this, race is a highly contested representation of relations of power between social categories by which individuals are identified and identify themselves.[41]

The racial embodiment of gender is further captured when Higginbotham states that:

> in societies where racial demarcation is endemic to their sociocultural fabric and heritage—to their laws and economy, to their institutionalized structures and discourses, and to their epistemologies and everyday customs—gender identity is inextricably linked to and even determined by racial identity.[42]

The white female graduate student with whom Jordan is speaking seems to fail to grasp or understand the benefits she derives from racist structures. She does not appear to grasp or understand the damage these structures and the ideologies that support them wreak on herself as well as others. She does not appear to grasp how her own gender identity is linked and determined by her own racial identity. This white female graduate student does not seem inclined to draw out the connections between the structural ordering of society and personal locations within that social order. Race is not her problem; violence is not her problem; and, it seems that gender oppression is not really her problem either. This graduate student seems to have failed to find any connection in the oppression of black (and red, brown, and yellow) women and that of white women. Does race obscure the similarity? Or perhaps, this woman thinks that adopting a critical feminist stance will betray her own mother and her own blood sisters? At the same time, she seems to overlook what traverses the borders of race, culture, ethnicity, history, religious confession, gender, sexual orientation, economic and social class status, political affiliation, nationality—*humanity*.

Further, insofar as the white female graduate student seems to insist that Jordan is "lucky to have regular hurdles of discrimination," she trivializes the historic and bloody struggle so many women and men have fought to exercise the most basic freedoms and rights of citizenship in the United States. Her conversation discloses a carelessly romantic and romantically careless attitude toward an historic and ongoing struggle that has meant death and loss for so many.

Quite poignantly, the student is mired in a discourse of helplessness, of powerlessness, of self-diminishment. "I'm just a middle-aged woman: a housewife and mother. I'm a nobody." The political seems, for her, not so much personal as *other*; and if that is the case, solidarity is not even a possibility. This white woman seems unwilling to risk the cold light of self-criticism, unwilling to perceive the deeper implications of so quickly a formed assessment. She seems to have missed or disregarded opportunities for growth, for change. She seems to have failed to put herself in the way of *conversion—intellectual, moral,* or *religious.*

The white female graduate student seems to have swallowed whole the epistemological myth that knowing is the equivalent of taking a look; that objectivity is established by seeing what is already-out-there-now to be seen.[43] Of course many readers will recognize this formulation as Bernard Lonergan's criticism of the confusion of the world of immediacy with the world mediated by meaning. The result is a picture-thinking mentality. In this instance, black must be aligned with black, white with white; suffering, discrimination, and subjugation are correlated with black; middle-class, normative, dominant are correlated with white. The female graduate student resists the implicit, but persistent, invitation in Jordan's political essays *to be attentive, to be intelligent, to be reasonable, to be responsible!* The student employs, not only a dichotomous logic, but cuts off further questions and thus fails to make an adequate judgment. The simultaneity and interlocking character of oppression are occluded. For this white female graduate student, the political is not so much personal as *other*; solidarity is not even an authentic human possibility.

Insofar as solidarity with others is not an option, the student lacks moral conversion. Living out of a picture-thinking mentality obscures moral choice and response: if the student cannot *picture* herself literally or implicitly in a given situation of oppression or marginalization, no moral choice or response to the situation is necessary or required. She takes her bearings by the standard a picture-thinking mentality provides: blinded by bias to her own psychic diminishment and to ethnocentrism. Authentic social praxis is subverted by individualism.

Like every African American who deals intimately with non-African Americans, perhaps, Jordan feels sadness. This woman, her student, does not grasp her complicity as a racially privileged woman in the creation of her teacher's own compound-complex situation. Like every African American who deals intimately with non-African Americans, perhaps, Jordan is disappointed. Yet, in that disappointment, Jordan's examen illuminates the negative option also available to red, brown, yellow, and black women. If we have uncovered the white woman's logic and cavalier pose, why not take up a similar stance? Shouldn't we red, brown, yellow, and black women insist that white women are lucky to be middle class, lucky to live in "such well-sanctioned and normative comfort," lucky to have the "luxury to deny the power of the privileges that paralyze" their lives? Jordan's option and her subsequent challenge to us are to analyze and evaluate our own enmeshment in and with difference. We too are summoned to *be attentive, to be intelligent, to be rational, to be responsible.* In analysis, criticism, and evaluation, we can uncover possibilities and opportunities for our own intellectual and moral conversion, for our own commitment to social transformation. Rigorous analysis and critique can expose those of us from within marginalized communities to the risks inherent in forgetting that race and class and gender are historicized and contextualized. Moreover, self-criticism is an important prelude to practical, theoretical, and theological self-determination. If we theologians who are red, brown, yellow, and black women challenge white feminist theologians to conversion, to solidarity we must challenge ourselves as well. We must deepen and complexify our knowledge of human reality. We must uncover and eliminate nascent or incipient forms of bias within ourselves and within our communities. We must expose and eliminate instances and elements of decline, consider carefully adverse criticism and protest. If solidarity is to be an authentic possibility for us, it can not come at the expense of our selves or of the selves of others. Indeed, any loss or assimilation of self is "antithetical to solidarity, for solidarity presumes mutually affirming, autonomous others."[44] To repeat, solidarity presumes human persons who are willing to place themselves in the way of conversion. Yet, conversion cannot be willed, neither can it be manipulated. It *is* possible when we place ourselves in the way of change's possibility, when we open ourselves to difference. Still, conversion is always tenuous, always precarious; while difficult to achieve, it is even more difficult to sustain. Conversion stands as another condition of the possibility of moving beyond the mere rhetoric of solidarity; that possibility is realized in Christian social praxis.

Getting beyond Clichéd Rhetoric

How do we get beyond the naive, "politically correct," clichéd rhetoric of solidarity? Not difference, but indifference, ignorance, egoism, and selfishness are the obstacles to solidarity. We must push through our own personal indifference, ignorance, egoism, and selfishness; we must push through the indifference, ignorance, egoism, and self-ishness of our society. These obstacles to solidarity can be understood comprehensively as failures in authentic religious, intellectual, and moral living; they can be expressed compactly as bias. By the term bias, I do not mean unswerving commitment to personal preferences, even in the face of contrary and contradictory evidence; nor do I refer to personal temperament. Rather, by bias I mean the more or less conscious decision to refuse corrective insights or understandings, to persist in error. Bias, then, is the arrogant choice to be incorrect.[45] Thus, anti-Semitism, racism, sexism, homophobia, class exploitation, and cultural imperialism are explicit concrete forms of individual and group bias. Moreover, anti-Semitism, racism, sexism, homophobia, class exploitation, and cultural imperialism are forms of consciousness that, at once, sustain the hegemony of the patriarchal, white supremacist ordering of the society in which we live, and undermine our efforts to critique that consciousness, to participate in personal and social transformation and thus move authentically beyond mere rhetoric about solidarity.

How do we get beyond naive, "politically correct," clichéd rhetoric about solidarity to Christian social praxis? A first step calls for active and attentive listening. Polite nods of the head may indicate hearing, but not authentic listening. Lynet Uttal expresses the sentiment so many red, brown, yellow, and black women feel about dialogue and conversation with white women, when she writes

I am tired of polite silences and the lack of response or requests for clarification. I am tired of feeling that my words were given space, but they might as well have not been said because they didn't get built upon or incorporated into the conversation. I can feel the polite bridge built from the speaker before me, over my words, to the next speaker—a useless bridge because the ideas under it are already dried up by the silence from the banks.[46]

On the part of white women, such active listening will require them to reject postures and stances of guilt. For white women such listening constitutes half of the condition of the possibility of authentic social praxis. To negotiate the borders of race and social class, ears, minds, and hearts must become attuned to vocabularies, grammars, syntaxes, scales, and tones. It is obvious that attuning oneself to the distinctiveness of these several voices calls for practice; equally obvious is an understanding that practice calls for a new and bold expression of the virtue of humility. For white women such practiced, humble, active, and attentive listening is the beginning of authentic participation in conversation.[47]

As for red, brown, yellow, and black women, speaking will require us to reject postures and stances of manipulation. For us such speaking constitutes half of the condition of the possibility of social praxis. To negotiate the boundaries of race, gender, and social class, our voices must mediate the experiences, understandings, meanings, values, and worlds of our peoples authentically. It is obvious that such negotiation summons us to attune ourselves to the differentiated voices within our own communities; here also practice and the virtue of honesty are necessary.

This distinction between speaking and listening is heuristic rather than determinative; these roles are to be exchanged. Yet, those who have so enjoyed the fruits of privilege ought not quickly seize the silence. With rapid unmindful ease, white women as members of the dominant race and/or social class can negate and dissolve the speech of marginalized red, brown, yellow, and black women. Those who adopt "monological languages cannot dialogue." Such languages are "self-enclosed, self-consistent, and self-sufficient." At the moment of critical conversation and dialogue, a monological language will define its partner as either illogical or an epiphenomenon of itself; at the moment of critical conversation and dialogue, a monological language will swallow its interlocutor whole, thus eliminating any rationale for confrontation or debate.[48] The knowledge of when and how to keep silent is not acquired by speaking; the knowledge of when and how to speak is not acquired by silence. Other virtues are required here: on the one hand, resolve and sacrifice or relinquishment; on the other hand, courage and self-criticism. Certainly, these rules for speaking and listening oblige both parties to patience and restraint; they enjoin both parties to an ethics of respectful listening and an ethics of thinking before speaking. Moreover, this speaking and listening is radical, insofar as it is rooted in the liberatory mode of the Gospel which recounts the gracious speaking and sending of the Word and the unexacted gracious self-expression of the Word on our behalf. Thus, such speaking and listening is the condition of the possibility of authentic shared Christian social praxis.

How do we get beyond naive, "politically correct," clichéd rhetoric about solidarity to Christian social praxis? A second step is social analysis. Although women share an oppression as women with one another, "what they share as sexual oppression is differentiated along class and racial lines in the same way that patriarchal history has always differentiated humanity according to class and race."[49] Social analysis affords one way of critically understanding the interstructuring of the oppressions of gender, race and class. It is the attempt to attain a more thorough, comprehensive, and critical understanding of a social situation through examining those historical and structural relationships that buttress that situation. Change or transformation of that situation follows from social analysis.

In the context of solidarity as a theological category for a critical Christian feminist theology of liberation, social analysis is distinguished by five moments: first, horizon analysis; second, description; third, analysis; fourth, theological reflection; and fifth, response and evaluation.

First, conversion, as I have pointed out earlier, is the transformation of an individual and the individual's world. Conversion is a turn in direction. Conversion occurs within a horizon. The analogue for horizon is the field of vision—what can be seen from a particular standpoint. Any field of vision or horizon is determinate, limited by standpoint; the same may be said of the horizon of a woman, a class, a group, a race. Horizons are contexts or worldviews; they are conditioned by culture, by society, by history. Shifts in horizon may be the process of deepening, extending, enriching a present horizon. There is also the process of dramatic movement in which a woman or a man changes horizon, in which she or he moves intellectually and/or morally and/or religiously *from* one worldview *to* another. Horizon analysis exposes difference. Criticism of our own horizons illustrates how objective differences in work experience, social class status, gender, race, sexual orientation, cultural-ethnic origin, family life can be sources of different perspectives and worldviews. Thus, we uncover incongruities in society.

The second moment in the process is to make a general description of the intersection of gender, race, and class in the situation. A comprehensive approach to collecting information will include questionnaires to determine demographic and physical data, the social (i.e., political, economic, and technological) configuration, the religious and cultural milieu, as well as formal interviews. In the third moment of social analysis, we identify and interrogate patterns that emerge in the description of the situation. In the fourth moment, we begin the task of theological reflection. By taking the actual situation in all its complexity as the starting point for theological reflection, we are compelled to judge the material and religious incongruities we encounter. The criterion for this judgment is the Gospel. This reflection establishes the ground for the fifth moment, decision and commitment to social praxis. The decisions and commitments we make, however, are open to change, to revision, to evaluation. The process of social analysis aims to assist us to meet actual needs and to heal alienations within community. When one or more of these actual needs are met, this change affects other needs or issues. Thus, social analysis is often described as circular. Christian social praxis is one way of speaking humanly, critically about our active concrete commitment to the Gospel in our own time of cultural, social, and moral upheaval. It is one way of speaking about our own commitment to the concrete realization of a common human good, about the new orientation and change in us signified by created grace.

Theological Implications of Solidarity

Solidarity is not a novel or topical addendum to the theological agenda; it is an integral part of theology as careful reflection on the doctrines of the Trinity and the Incarnation reveals. Yet, the Eucharist with its precise denotation of the meaning of the Incarnation of the Second Person of the Trinity as Jesus of Nazareth and his sacrifice for us illustrates in a most striking and accessible way the meaning of solidarity for Christians. Recent attention to solidarity, however, emerges from the refusal of the various theologies of liberation in their encounters with one another "to reduce the other to an epiphenomenon of itself or to be reduced by the other as such."[50] Moreover, in the "movement toward an ever more interrelated world," these theologies have begun to understand that insidious multidimensional forms of oppression rule out any ranking or comparison of suffering. If solidarity is to mediate the struggle for liberation, it must also be recognized as its end. This understanding will have methodological, doctrinal, practical, and spiritual consequences for the various particular theologies of liberation.

What are some theological implications of solidarity for a critical feminist theology of liberation? A *first implication regards method in theology.* In the "movement toward an ever more interrelated world," a critical feminist theology strives to understand concretely how insidious forms of oppressions experienced in so many different ways by different women are harnessed into one oppression—"a system of death that operates everywhere, at every level of life."[51] A critical feminist theology acknowledges the interconnection of oppressions; they impinge on each other and mutually condition each other. Further, these oppressions cannot be reduced or collapsed into one another. A critical feminist theology will employ the human and social sciences to understand the interstructuring and autonomy of these oppressions and to uncover patterns of coercion and domination. Such study enlarges the theoretical horizon of a critical feminist theology; illumines that theology's analysis of social theories of power and hegemony; and supports that theology's opposition not only to totalitarian and utopian schemes, but to the acquisitive individualism of the market economy as well. This means, of course, that a critical feminist theology is an interdisciplinary exercise.

A *second implication regards anthropology.* The turn toward solidarity as a theological category recognizes the need for a more adequate answer to the question, What does it mean to be a human person in the context of modernity's turn away from the human person as social and political by nature? Modernity's dominant notion of persons depicts them as egoistic, isolated, passive, individualistic, acquisitive. The mass society modernity generates is "glutted by sensate gratification, ordered by benevolent governors, populated by creatures who have exchanged spiritual freedom and moral responsibility for economic psychic security."[52] Solidarity invites a response that retrieves and affirms the notion of the person as a dynamic acting human achievement, rather than as a passive consuming being who is the product of this or that external change. For to be human is to be more than a mass of howling biological, psychological, emotional drives and needs; more than a bundle of desires, more than a consumer. To be human is to engage in the project of one's own life as a struggle for solidarity—the concrete personal and public realization of the moral obligation of speech, to do and be what we pledge and promise.

In its appeal to self-transcendence as immanent in human existence, solidarity does not substitute what is substantive of human nature for what is merely accidental and biological, although never insignificant, i.e., gender or race or social class or group or ethnic-cultural heritage. To substitute gender or race or social class or ethnic-cultural heritage for what is substantive of human being is to surrender reason's power; but, to dismiss or dissolve or ignore gender or race or social class or ethnic-cultural heritage as irrelevant is to disregard concrete, differentiated human persons, to render them invisible. Such substitution and disregard are tantamount to a blatant refusal to understand. That refusal exposes the derailment of intelligence by the biases that spawn economic and political exploitation, elitism, imperialism, homophobia, anti-Semitism, sexism, racism, ethnocentrism.

A *third implication concerns community.* Solidarity is an achievement of community. For a critical feminist theology, "solidarity as a community of mutually affirming, autonomous selves, is a project antithetical to the monological premises of the dominating status quo."[53] Moreover, as a critical Christian theology, solidarity is grounded in the confession of Jesus as Lord.

When the gift of the Spirit leads a group of men and women to confess Jesus as Lord, the community we call church comes into being. This confession founds and realizes a common world of experience, understanding, judgment, decision, and commitment. This confession transforms patterns of human interaction and action; it evokes a new reality—transhistorical, transpolitical, transcultural. Prerogatives rooted in socially constructed disparities are deconstructed. Perhaps, this is much too simplistic. In the concrete, we find ourselves striving to realize concretely the fruitful insights of intelligence and rectitude. More profoundly, we find ourselves standing before the Cross of Jesus of Nazareth yearning to grasp the enormity of suffering, affliction, and oppression; to apprehend our complicity and collusion in the suffering, affliction, and oppression of others.

Solidarity is a wrenching task: to stand up for justice in the midst of injustice and domination; to take up simplicity in the midst of affluence and comfort; to embrace integrity in the midst of collusion and co-optation; to contest the gravitational pull of domination. We need grace for solidarity and for community. We are in need of the grace of interruption: to change our course, to accept fully the challenge of transformation in the concrete. We are in need of the grace of liberation: to free us from the gravity that impedes the human spirit and anesthetizes our deepest desires for more fruitful, more creative living and loving. We are in need of the grace of risk. This grace opens us to the promptings of the Spirit, to respond to the Word that calls, to speak and to listen to one another. This grace nudges us to dis-ease and discomfort with whatever obscures the sight of the glory of God on the face of another human being.

A *fourth implication concerns Eucharist.* "Solidarity presumes a common ground."[54] Too frequently, that ground has been the bodies of the marginalized, oppressed, and poor—especially the bodies of marginalized, oppressed, and poor red, brown, yellow, and black women. A broken body and broken bread is a powerful mediating symbol of Eucharist. With great feeling, Ruy Costa writes of this relation:

> A hurting body has been the symbol of solidarity for Christians since the institution of the Holy Communion: "This is my body, ... This is my blood." The celebration of this body was perceived as a threat to the status quo, the Roman totality, and so became a *sacramentum,* that is, an underground encounter in which people made and renewed their solidarity with each other unto death.[55]

Eucharist is at the heart of Christian community, but it is an empty gesture, a mere routine or *pro forma* act, if we have not confessed our sins; repented of our participation and/or collusion in the marginalization of others; if we have not begged forgiveness from those whom we have offended; if we have not pledged firm purpose of amendment; if we have not moved to healing and creative Christian praxis.

The Eucharist is at the heart of the Christian community. Participation (*koinonia*) in the Body and Blood of Christ is a communion with the whole Christ: the suffering Christ, the exalted and risen Lord, the body of believers. Eating the bread and drinking the cup involve something much deeper and more extensive than consuming the elements of this ritual meal. *Women and men must do what they are being made:* there are social as well as sacramental consequences to the Eucharist. For to be one in Christ Jesus is to reject those systems of living that deprive women and men of human and political rights, that oppress the poor, that suppress women, that authorize racism, that promote discrimination against men and women because of fear of their sexual orientation, that obstruct the self-determination of the peoples of the world. We cannot live authentically—that is, attentively, intelligently, reasonably, responsibly—under the aegis of the Reign of God, while we continue to sleep through the deformation and distortion of the whole people of God. Johann Baptist Metz reminds us that "the faith of Christians is a praxis in history and society that is to be understood as hope in solidarity in the God of Jesus as the God of the living and the dead who calls all people to be subjects in the divine presence."[56] Thus, we are called to be active members of the Body of Christ, living as Jesus lived subordinating our personal and collective, social and cultural decisions to the coming Reign of God. We are called to follow Jesus to those who are broken, abused, dispossessed, and marginalized. These are the women and men whom we must seek out: they require our solidarity. These women and men are our comrades in the work of justice; these women and men are the partners with whom we must struggle to find out what it means to live authentically; women and men with whom we have a future, without whom we have nothing. And when we stand and speak and live in solidarity with them, we realize ourselves as the community of the Resurrected Lord. In this is our service, in this is our love, in this is our salvation.

Conclusion

This essay assumes a fourth phase of feminist theology; crucial to that phase is the notion and practice of concrete and authentic solidarity. A critical Christian feminist theology will be grounded in the experience and thought of Native American theologians, of womanist theologians, and *mujerista* theologians, of African feminist theologians, of Asian and Asian American feminist theologians, of Latin American feminist theologians. A critical Christian feminist theology will never neglect the experience and thought of white feminist theologians, yet such a theology will emerge only in the attentive, humble listening *and* honest speaking—the collaboration of red, brown, yellow, black, and white women.

Such a theology adopts a social analysis that will read "the signs of the times" in the light of the Gospel. That theology makes a *fundamental option* for the oppressed and marginalized poor—especially poor red, brown, yellow, black, and white women. A critical Christian feminist theology is identical with its theologians insofar as these thinkers submit their cognitive, affective, moral, and religious consciousness to explanatory differentiation in the mode of interiority. A critical Christian feminist theology is identical with its theologians insofar as these thinkers consciously recover the course and immanent intelligibility of the drive for authentic direction in their own lives and ground their theology in discoveries they have made and verified in that drive. Critical Christian feminist theologians read, not only "the signs of the times," but their own inner lives and horizons as well. Self-criticism is a lifelong process, an ongoing commitment. Critical Christian feminist theologians draw, not only on research and data from other disciplines, but think, work, and theologize from within an *ethics of collaboration.*

It follows, then, that such a theology advances a radical form of Christian social praxis, but without any reckless or romantic or idealist call to *mere* activism. A critical Christian feminist theology functions as an "integrating wisdom capable of being practiced cooperatively in reversing dehumanizing injustices."[57]

A critical Christian feminist theology recognizes and embraces women and men of all races and classes *in their particularity.* Each human person is of inestimable worth. Each is a singular work of divine creation; each bears the unmistakable stamp of the Creator's image and likeness. Each one is valuable in her or his unique embodied personhood; each one is necessary to the other. But, solidarity transcends interdependence and enables each one to apprehend the "other," not as an instrument or a commodity or an object, but as "sister," "brother," "neighbor." For, together, and *in* our togetherness, by the grace of the Eucharist, we are made one in Christ. Together and *in* our togetherness, we are made the community of the Resurrected Lord. Together and *in* our togetherness, we constitute the mystical Body of Christ.

By focusing on solidarity as a theological category I have hoped to call attention to the gap between rhetoric and Christian social praxis in expressions of feminist theology. Moreover, I have hoped to encourage diffuse, halting, yet, unfulfilled efforts toward a critical Christian feminist theology that aims for "the basic transformation of [the whole of] society: a new order, not a new deal . . . [but] . . . a *new humanity*."[58] That theology thinks and works, hopes and struggles for the flourishing of the one humanity that God created. By focusing on solidarity as a theological category I hope to have contributed to the full emergence of the fourth phase of theology in critical Christian feminist perspective.

Notes

[1] This chapter is an elaboration of themes of the plenary address I gave at the 1994 annual meeting of the College Theology Society, Saint Mary's College, Notre Dame, Indiana. Conference organizers designated the address to honor the memory of the women who studied in the School of Sacred Theology established at Saint Mary's College in 1944 by Sister Mary Madeleva Wolff of the Sisters of the Holy Cross.

[2] María Pilar Aquino, *Our Cry for Life: Feminist Theology from Latin America* (Maryknoll, NY: Orbis Books, 1993), 12; see also, Clodovis Boff, *Theology and Praxis: Epistemological Foundations* (Maryknoll, NY: Orbis Books, 1987); Enrique Dussel, *Philosophy of Liberation* (1985; Maryknoll, NY: Orbis Books, 1990); cf. Bernard Lonergan, "Theology and Praxis," pp. 184-201, in *A Third Collection: Papers by Bernard J. F. Lonergan, S.J.*, ed. Frederick E. Crowe, S.J. (New York/Mahwah: Paulist Press, 1985).

[3] See Claude Geffré, *The Risk of Interpretation: On Being Faithful to the Christian Tradition in a Non-Christian Age* (New York/Mahwah: Paulist Press, 1987), especially, pp. 250-268.

[4] See Theo Witvliet, *The Way of the Black Messiah: The Hermeneutical Challenge of Black Theology as a Theology of Liberation* (Oak Park, IL: Meyer Stone Books, 1987).

[5] Mary Daly, *The Church and the Second Sex* (Boston: Beacon Press, 1968), *Beyond God the Father: Toward a Philosophy of Women's Liberation* (Boston: Beacon Press, 1973).

[6] Frances Beale, "Double Jeopardy: To Be Black and Female," pp. 90-100, and Grace Lee Boggs, "The Black Revolution in America," pp. 211-223, in *The Black Woman: Anthology*, ed. Toni Cade (New York: New American Library, Inc., 1970).

[7] Beatriz Melano Couch, "Statement by Beatriz Melano Couch," p. 374, in *Theology in the Americas*, ed. Sergio Torres and John Eagelson (Maryknoll, NY: Orbis Books, 1976).

[8] Ibid., p. 375.

[9] Michele Russell, "Women, Work, and Politics," p. 345, in *Theology in the Americas*.

[10] Ibid., p. 350.

[11] Mary Daly, *Gyn/Ecology: The Metaethics of Radical Feminism* (Boston: Beacon Press, 1978).

[12] Audre Lorde, "An Open Letter to Mary Daly, " pp. 66-71, in *Sister Outsider: Essays and Speeches by Audre Lorde* (Trumansburg, NY: The Crossing Press, 1984).

[13] For some representative works see Caroline Walker Bynum, *Fragmentation and Redemption, Essays on Gender and the Human Body in Medieval Religion* (New York: Urzone, 1991), Eleanor McLaughlin and Rosemary Radford Ruether, ed., *Women of Spirit* (New York: Simon and Schuster, 1979), Rosemary Radford Ruether, ed., *Religion and Sexism: Images of Women in the Jewish and Christian Traditions* (New York: Simon and Schuster, 1974), Phyllis Trible, *God and the Rhetoric of Sexuality* (Philadelphia:Fortress Press, 1983), Idem., *Texts of Terror: Literary-Feminist Readings of Biblical Narratives* (Philadelphia: Fortress Press, 1984), Elisabeth Schüssler Fiorenza, *In Memory of Her: A Feminist Theological Reconstruction of Christian Origins* (New York: Crossroad Publishing Company, 1983), Beverly Wildung Harrison, "The Power of Anger in the Work of Love," *Union Seminary Quarterly Review* 36 (1981): 41-57, Anne Carr, "Is Christian Feminist Theology Possible?" *Theological Studies* 43 (1982): 279-297, Rosemary Radford Ruether, "Feminism and Patriarchal Religion: Principles of Ideological Critique of the Bible," *Journal for the Study of the Old Testament* 22 (1982): 54-66.

[14] For some representative works see Caroline Walker Bynum, *Jesus as Mother, Studies in the Spirituality of the High Middle Ages* (Berkeley: University of California Press, 1982), Carter Heyward, *The Redemption of God, A Theology of Mutual Relation* (Lanham, MD: University Press of America, 1982), Eleanor McLaughlin, "Christ My Mother: Feminine Naming and Metaphor in Medieval Spirituality," *Nashotah Review* 15, 3 (Fall 1975): 228-248, Rosemary Radford Ruether, *Sexism and God-Talk: Toward a Feminist Theology* (New York: Crossroad Publishing Company, 1983), Patricia Wilson-Katsner, *Faith, Feminism, and the Christ* (Philadelphia: Fortress Press, 1983).

[15] For some representative works see Rosemary Radford Ruether, *Women-Church: Theology and Practice of Feminist Liturgical Communities* (San Francisco: Harper and Row, 1985), Letty Russell, *Church in the Round: Feminist Interpretation of the Church* (Louisville, KY: Westminster / John Knox Press, 1993).

[16] For some representative works see Catherine Mowry LaCugna, *God for Us: The Trinity and Christian Life* (San Francisco: Harper, 1991), Elizabeth Johnson, *She Who Is: The Mystery of God in Feminist Theological Discourse* (New York: Crossroad Publishing Company, 1993).

[17] For some representative works see Beverly Wildung Harrison, *Making Connections: Essays in Feminist Social Ethics* (Boston: Beacon Press, 1985), Letty Russell et al., ed., *Inheriting Our Mothers' Gardens: Feminist Theology in Third World Perspective* (Philadelphia: Westminster Press, 1988), Elisabeth Schüssler Fiorenza, *Bread Not Stone: The Challenge of Feminist Biblical Interpretation* (Boston: Beacon Press, 1984).

[18] Schüssler Fiorenza, *Bread Not Stone*, p. xiv.

[19] This list is not meant to be exhaustive, but rather suggestive of black, yellow, brown, and red women engaged in the practice of theology with a commitment to the analysis of interstructured oppressions and solidarity. Their works include Katie Cannon, *Black Womanist Ethics* (Atlanta: Scholars Press, 1988), Cheryl Townsend Gilkes, "Going Up for the Oppressed: The Career Mobility of Black Women Community Workers," *Journal of Social Issues* 39 (1983): 115-139, Idem., "The 'Loves' and 'Troubles' of African-American Women's Bodies: The Womanist Challenge to Cultural Humiliation and Community Ambivalence," pp. 232-249, in *A Troubling in My Soul: Womanist Perspectives on Evil and Suffering*, ed. Emilie M. Townes (Maryknoll, NY: Orbis Books, 1993); Jacquelyn Grant, *White Women's Christ, Black Women's Jesus: White Feminist Christology and Womanist Response* (Atlanta: Scholars Press, 1989), Jamie T. Phelps, OP, "Joy Came in the Morning Risking Death for Liberation: Confronting the Evil of Social Sin and Socially Sinful Structures," pp. 48-64, in *A Troubling in My Soul*, Idem., "Caught Between Thunder and Lightning: A Historical and Theological Critique of the Episcopal Response to Slavery," pp. 21-34, in *Many Rains Ago: A Historical and Theological Reflection on the Role of the Episcopate in the Evangelization of African American Catholics* (Washington, DC: USCC, 1990); Emilie M. Townes, *Womanist Justice, Womanist Hope* (Atlanta: Scholars Press, 1993), Idem., *In a Blaze of Glory: Womanist Spirituality as Social Witness* (Nashville, TN: Abingdon Press, 1995), Renita J. Weems, *Just A Sister Away: A Womanist Vision of Women's Relationships in the Bible* (San Diego: Lura Media, 1988), Delores S. Williams, *Sisters in the Wilderness: The Challenge of Womanist God-Talk* (Maryknoll, NY: Orbis Books, 1993); Bonita Bennett, "A Critique on the Role of Women in the Church," pp. 169-174, in *The Unquestionable Right to Be Free: Black Theology from South Africa*, ed. Itumeleng J. Mosala and Buti Tlhagale (Maryknoll, NY: Orbis Books, 1986), Bernadette I. Mosala, "Black Theology and the Struggle of the Black Woman in Southern Africa," pp. 129-133, in *The Unquestionable Right to Be Free*, Mercy Amba Oduyoye, *Hearing and Knowing: Theological Reflections on Christianity in Africa* (Maryknoll, NY: Orbis Books, 1986), Mercy Amba Oduyoye and Musimbi R. A. Kanyoro, eds., *The Will to Arise: Women, Tradition, and the Church in Africa* (Maryknoll, NY: Orbis Books, 1992); Chung Hyun Kyung, *Struggle to Be the Sun Again: Introducing Asian Women's Theology* (Maryknoll, NY: Orbis Books, 1991), Virginia Fabella and Sun Ai Lee Park, eds., *We Dare to Dream: Doing Theology as Asian Women* (Kowloon, Hong Kong: Asian Women's Resource Centre for Culture and Theology; Manilla, Philippines: EATWOT Women's Commission in Asia, 1989), Virginia Fabella and Mercy Amba Oduyoye, eds., *With Passion and Compassion: Third World Women Doing Theology* (Maryknoll, NY: Orbis Books, 1989); Kwok Pui-lan, "Discovering the Bible in the Non-Biblical World," pp. 270-282, in *Lift Every Voice: Constructing Theologies from the Underside*, ed. Susan Brooks Thistlethwaite and Mary Potter Engel (San Francisco: Harper and Row, 1990); María Pilar Aquino, *Our Cry for Life: Feminist Theology from Latin America*, Ivone Gebara, "Option for the Poor

as an Option for the Poor Woman," *Concilium* 194 (1987): 110-117, Idem., "Women Doing Theology," in *Through Her Eyes: Women's Theology from Latin America*, ed. Elsa Tamez (Maryknoll, NY: Orbis Books, 1989): 37-48; Ada María Isasi-Díaz, *En La Lucha = In the Struggle: A Hispanic Women's Liberation Theology* (Minneapolis: Fortress Press, 1993), Elsa Tamez, *Against Machismo* (Oak Park, IL: Meyer-Stone Books, 1987).

[20] Elizabeth Fox-Genovese, "The Personal Is Not Political Enough," *Marxist Perspectives* 2 (Winter 1979-80): 94-113; see also Nancy A. Hewitt, "Beyond the Search for Sisterhood: American Women's History in the 1980s," pp. 1-14, in *Unequal Sisters: A Multicultural Reader in U. S. Women's History*, ed., Ellen Carol DuBois and Vicki L. Ruiz (New York: Routledge, Chapman & Hall, Inc., 1990).

[21] Fox-Genovese, "The Personal Is Not Political Enough," pp. 97-98.

[22] Ibid., p. 112.

[23] Bonnie Thorton Dill, " 'On the Hem of Life': Race, Class, and the Prospects of Sisterhood," p. 175, in *Class, Race and Sex: The Dynamics of Control*, ed. Amy Swerdlow and Hannah Lessinger (Boston: G. K. Hall, 1983).

[24] June Jordan, *On Call: Political Essays* (Boston: South End Press, 1985), p. 40.

[25] Ibid., p. 41.

[26] Ibid.

[27] Ibid., p. 46.

[28] Ibid., pp. 46-47. Adrienne Rich makes this same point when she writes "The mere sharing of oppression does not constitute a common world," p. 203, in *On Lies, Secrets, and Silence: Selected Prose, 1966-1978* (New York: W. W. Norton & Company, Inc., 1979).

[29] *Webster's New World Dictionary of the American Language*, 2nd College Edition (New York: Simon and Schuster, 1982).

[30] See Joseph Devlin, *A Dictionary of Synonyms and Antonyms* (1938; New York: Popular Library, Inc. 1961).

[31] Iris Marion Young, *Justice and the Politics of Difference* (Princeton, NJ: Princeton University Press, 1990), p. 157. It is important to point out that recent social movements of oppressed groups have challenged this ideal, arguing that a positive self-definition of group difference and self-determination are more authentically liberating.

[32] Ibid., p. 98.

[33] Ibid., p. 99.

[34] Johnetta B. Cole, ed., *All American Women: Lives that Divide, Ties that Bind* (New York: Free Press, 1986), p. 1.

[35] Indeed, scholarship on the social construction of race can not bring an immediate and unqualified halt to racially motivated assaults, patent discrimination, bigotry, or ridicule; nor can scholarship on the gendered oppression of women bring an immediate and unqualified halt to the structured discrimination, repression, sexual harassment, rape, battering, or murder of women because they are women. Change in the concrete behavior of concrete human beings is required.

[36] Hazel V. Carby, "The Politics of Difference," *Ms. Magazine* (September/October 1990): 84.

[37] Richard A. Lanham, *A Handlist of Rhetorical Terms: A Guide for Students of English Literature* (Berkeley: University of California Press, 1968), p. 88.

[38] Jordan, *On Call*, p. 43.

[39] Ibid., p. 27.

[40] Young, *Justice and the Politics of Difference*, pp. 40-42.

[41] Evelyn Brooks Higginbotham, "African-American Women's History and the Metalanguage of Race," *Signs: Journal of Women in Culture and Society*, vol. 17, no. 2 (1992): 253.

[42] Ibid., p. 254.

[43] See Bernard Lonergan, *Method in Theology* (New York: Herder & Herder, 1972), pp. 262-263. For a discussion of the relation of Lonergan's work to feminism, see the collection by Cynthia S. W. Crysdale, ed., *Lonergan and Feminism* (Toronto: University of Toronto Press, 1994), especially the excellent essay by Paulette Kidder, "Woman of Reason: Lonergan and Feminist Epistemology," pp. 33-48. For some works treating the critique made by feminist thinkers and philosophers against dominant sexist objectivist and relativist epistemologies, see Sandra Harding and Merrill B. Hintikka, eds., *Discovering Reality: Feminist Perspectives on Epistemology, Metaphysics, Methodology, and Philosophy of Science* (Dordrecht, Boston, and London: D. Reidel Publishing Company, 1983), Linda Alcoff and Elizabeth Potter, eds., *Feminist Epistemologies* (New York and London: Routledge, 1993), Allison M. Jaggar and Susan R. Bordo, eds., *Gender/Body/Knowledge: Feminist Reconstructions of Being and Knowing* (New Brunswick and London: Rutgers University Press, 1990), and Sandra Harding, *Whose Science? Whose Rationality? Thinking from Women's Lives* (Ithaca: Cornell University Press, 1991); see also, Iris Marion Young, "Abjection and Oppression: Dynamics of Unconscious Racism, Sexism, and Homophobia," pp. 201-213, in *Crises in Continental Philosophy,* ed., A. B. Dallery and C. E. Scott (Albany: SUNY Press, 1990).

[44] Ruy O. Costa, "Introduction," p. 17, in *Struggles for Solidarity: Liberation Theologies in Tension*, ed. Lorine M. Getz and Ruy O. Costa (Minneapolis: Fortress Press, 1992).

[45] See Bernard Lonergan, *Insight: A Study of Human Understanding* (New York: Philosophical Library, 1958), chaps. 6 and 7.

[46] Lynet Uttal, "Nods That Silence," p. 319, in *Making Face, Making Soul: Haciendo Caras: Creative and Critical Perspectives by Women of Color*, ed. Gloria Anzaldúa (San Francisco: An Aunt Lute Foundation Book, 1990).

[47] For a sound, serious, and complex analysis of racism and feminism, see Barbara Hilkert Andolsen, *Daughters of Jefferson, Daughters of Bootblacks: Racism and American Feminism* (Macon, GA: Mercer University Press, 1986); for a critical analysis of the meaning of "whiteness" as a social construct and which critically addresses "white guilt," see Jeanne Perrault, "White Feminist Guilt, Abject Scripts, and (Other) Transformative Necessities," *West Coast Line*, 13/14

(Spring-Fall 1994): 226-238.

[48] Costa, "Introduction," p. 17, in *Struggles for Solidarity: Liberation Theologies in Tension.*

[49] Zillah R. Eisenstein, "Some Notes on the Relations of Capitalist Patriarchy," pp. 46-47, in *Capitalist Patriarchy and the Case for Socialist Feminism,* ed. Zillah R. Eisenstein (New York: Monthly Review Press, 1979).

[50] Costa, "Introduction," pp. 15, 16, in *Struggles for Solidarity: Liberation Theologies in Tension.*

[51] José Míguez Bonino, "The Dimensions of Oppression," p. 34, in *Struggles for Solidarity: Liberation Theologies in Tension.*

[52] T. J. Jackson Lears, *No Place of Grace* (New York: Pantheon Books, 1981), p. 300.

[53] Costa, "Introduction," pp. 15, 16, in *Struggles for Solidarity: Liberation Theologies in Tension.*

[54] Ibid., p. 20.

[55] Ibid., p. 21.

[56] Johann Baptist Metz, *Faith in History and Society* (New York: Crossroad Press, 1979), p. 76.

[57] Matthew Lamb, "Political Theology," p. 778, in *The New Dictionary of Catholic Theology,* ed. Joseph Komonchak et al. (Wilmington, DE: Michael Glazier, Inc., 1987).

[58] Beatriz Melano Couch, "Statement by Beatriz Melano Couch," 374.

"In this flesh"—Cornelia Connelly and the Incarnation

Caritas McCarthy

In April, 1879, an American woman lay dying in England. Seventy-year-old Cornelia Connelly was being cared for in her convent at St. Leonards-on-Sea by her Sisters of the Holy Child Jesus for whom she had been foundress and superior for thirty-three years. The children of the school to whom she had endeared herself waited anxiously with the sisters for news of her. For over a month, this woman, always noted for her beauty, had been covered by a virulent eczema caused by severe nephritis. The sisters noted that she who had had "a face of Paradise" now had "the appearance of one scalded from head to foot, of a leper." Internal and external irritation was so intense as to cause periods of delirium and unconsciousness. Suddenly, the day before her death on April 18th, the nursing sister heard her exclaim with great decision: "In this flesh I shall see my God!" This she repeated three times, each time striking one hand with the other.[1]

"In this flesh I shall see my God!" Although Cornelia is here witnessing to her real kinship with Job in suffering (cf. Job 19:26), far more is she witnessing to her union with Jesus manifested to her in the Gospels as "Word made flesh" (Jn 1:14), through whom she had already "seen" her God, whose earthly life had given meaning to her life "in the flesh." Her life had been unusually eventful and challenging, including marriage and motherhood before her vowed celibate life with its ministry of foundress and educator. Her powerful faith-witness in her death agony can be seen as a final contemplative utterance, crowning a life of affective, imaginative contemplation of Jesus in the Gospels which, through all vicissitudes, had integrated her prayer and life, led her to union with her God.

What has struck this writer, through many years of studying and writing about Cornelia's history and spirituality and that of her Society of the Holy Child Jesus, is the degree to which she used her demanding and fulfilling, her sometimes tragic, life experiences to relate to her God whom she discovered in the Gospels—a God-man also deeply involved in demanding and fulfilling human life experiences. This resonance, this intersection of experiences, and the graced insight it gave her on the Incarnation will be the focus of this paper. Much more can be written, and has been written about her in book-length studies of her life and spirituality.[2] For Cornelia, "Incarnation" meant both the whole Paschal Mystery of God become human, and the more restricted sense in which she often used the term—the mystery revealed in the Infancy Narratives of the Gospels. It was with regard to this latter mystery and its relation to the whole Gospel that she showed profound insight.

The focus of this paper both springs from and, hopefully, will promote ongoing awareness of the distinctiveness of women's experiences and the need to retrieve and utilize the theological reflection that stems from their integration of prayer and life. Rahner has said that just as we need Christ to understand humanity, so we need humanity's experience [and this must include feminine experience] to understand Christ and the salvation he brings.[3] David Stanley underscored this need in treating contemplation of the Gospels;[4] and now, in one way or another, a host of biblical scholars with philosophical and literary-critical approaches have affirmed the value of bringing the reader's/pray-er's life experience to bear on the mystery being studied/contemplated.[5]

We shall first review Cornelia's extraordinarily eventful life, rich in joys and achievements, but also full of immense sufferings, even persecutions; her life, even as Job's, witnesses to the vulnerability of life "in the flesh." We shall consider briefly how contemplation assumed a central role in her very active life, and then present a series of citations (necessarily short) from her prayer journals, letters, instructions, and her Rule for her congregation, which illustrate the focus of this paper.

Cornelia left no lengthy treatises or "revelations" like other contemplatives in her tradition. But so deep was her union with God in the midst of daily activities that she has left a steady stream of "spiritual footprints" throughout the considerable body of her writings of every kind. This study can only begin to indicate the vitality of these numerous "footprints."[6] They trace the journey of a woman for whom the experience of both the ecstasy and the "bite" of life "in the flesh" was made salvific by her God who had also chosen to share with her both the ecstasy and "bite" of life "in the flesh." Although the reader may find some of her language, style and imagery too typical of nineteenth-century devotional literature, she/he will also find expressions in which Cornelia broke free of stereotypes.

Cornelia's life[7] began with a privileged youth in Philadelphia, 1809-31. She was raised first as a Presbyterian, then, from the age of fourteen, as an Episcopalian. At the age of twenty-two she married an Episcopalian priest and went with him to Natchez, Mississippi, where she bore two children. After four years of marriage, the couple converted to Roman Catholicism, she in New Orleans in 1835, he in Rome in 1836. In Rome she revealed to an American priest her anguish over her husband's efforts to continue in the Catholic Church the priesthood to which he had been ordained in the Episcopal Church: "Is it necessary for Pierce Connelly to make this sacrifice and to sacrifice me?—I love my husband and my darling children!"[8]

When Pierce agreed to a ministry as a layman in America, she rejoiced in a respite from impending sacrifice and, despite financial insecurity, was happy in raising her family and in teaching in a Sacred Heart School on the frontier in Louisiana. Although her husband taught in an adjoining Jesuit school, she was the principal breadwinner. Sorrow struck again, first in 1839 when her seven-week-old baby girl died in their lonely prairie home, and the following year when a tragic accident claimed the life of her two-year-old son who had been born in Europe. In October 1840 Pierce asked her to consent to his making renewed efforts to become a Catholic priest and eventually to separate from her. She agreed on condition that continuing discernment prove his vocation authentic. Their last child was born six months after this consent.

Within four years Pope Gregory XVI himself affirmed the authenticity of Pierce's vocation and the following year he was ordained in Rome where Cornelia and the children were also then situated. Meanwhile, Cornelia's own discernment led her to accept a call from the Pope and English Catholic leaders to found a congregation of sisters to minister to the women and children of England's Catholic revival, and from there to extend her work to America. Her mission included an agreement that her children would remain under her care. A letter to her husband at the time she founded her congregation reveals the cost of her sacrifice: "You have not the violent temptation that I have in thinking of the little Bethlehem room [their former bedroom], nor have you gone through the struggles of a woman's heart. No! you never have."[9]

Cornelia had scarcely three years to experience the joy of her growing congregation when Pierce apostasized from the Catholic Church and priesthood, kidnapped their children and tried to force her to return to married life. Though anti-Catholicism prevailed in England and English marriage law was misogynist, Pierce was ultimately unsuccessful in the courts. However, he kept the children from Cornelia and caused trouble for her young Society of the Holy Child Jesus. Cornelia experienced much enduring achievement and happiness during thirty-three years of leading her congregation and schools, but also suffered much from an oppressive English hierarchy and from a betrayal within her own congregation. Yet the unfailing testimony of those who knew her was to her strong, loving presence, her vitality, even to her joy. What role did prayer play in her life?

To the foregoing cursory survey of Cornelia's eventful life must be added an event crucial to the subject of this paper. In December 1839 she was introduced by the Jesuits of Grand Coteau, Louisiana, to the *Spiritual Exercises* of St. Ignatius of Loyola; major emphasis was placed on affective imaginative contemplation of Jesus in the Gospels. Although Cornelia's sparse writings prior to this introduction indicate that she had long found the Gospels a source for inspiration, there is strong evidence that the *Spiritual Exercises* were crucial in fostering her contemplative graces, and, later, in giving her a vehicle for fostering the growth of her sisters in prayer.[10]

In her years as superior of her congregation she was to learn how deeply this prayer was rooted in Christian tradition from the medieval Church onwards, and she was to include some of its exponents—Bernard of Clairvaux, Francis of Assisi, Gertrude of Helfta and Teresa of Avila—in the spiritual reading of her community. She may not have known the route, through the Pseudo-Bonaventure and Ludolph the Carthusian, by which the tradition came to Ignatius, but she drew heavily on Jesuit continuators of the tradition.[11] However, long before that time, as a young wife and mother helped by the *Exercises*, she gave herself wholeheartedly to this kind of prayer to which she felt a natural affinity. She was able to identify her journey with Christ's journey from conception through infancy, youth, public life, passion and resurrection.

Detailed studies indicate that Cornelia's appropriation of the *Exercises* as a whole was one of the most decisively positive factors in her life leading her to spiritual maturity and freedom. Extraordinarily for her times, they seem to have been presented to her in a way that enabled her to affirm the validity of her own spiritual experience, and her sisters to affirm theirs; they provided further an authoritative document (necessarily, in her time, masculine and traditional) by which they could validate their prayer life for ecclesiastical authorities. Cornelia used the *Spiritual Exercises* as she said, as a "syllabus," a "bulwark" and "the groundwork" of the spiritual life, and as a "bulwark" to her Constitutions. She seems quite easily to have situated herself and her sisters, not on the Ignatian battlefield, but in the home, the garden and the school. Elements of the *Exercises* recognized today as inappropriate and even negative for women were apparently, in her misogynist era, overshadowed by their clearly positive effects.[12]

When we turn to Cornelia's writings we see that they spell out the essential elements of the prayer she practiced. She wrote a Rule for her congregation in a period of great hope for its future, balanced by intense personal suffering from her husband and the sudden death of her eldest son. At the head of her Rule was the call to her sisters "to seek in the mysteries of the life of this Divine Lord all that can serve to their greater perfection and the good of their neighbour"; "to contemplate the Eternal Wisdom in the lowliness of His Humanity"; "to be filled with the waters of this heavenly fountain";—that is, to go in faith to the Gospels as the privileged place of salvific encounter with the risen Jesus who had shared our life in the flesh. Cornelia continued with fruits of this contemplation: "What more sublime teaching can we find among these mysteries than that of the Incarnation! Here it is God manifests to us in the most wonderful manner the treasures of His mercy and His boundless love." She called the sisters to be truly present to the scene contemplated, to see the Divine Child born in a stable, to feel him "exposed to bitter cold."[13]

In instructions on prayer apart from her Rule, she issued the same call to seek, and to be present to Gospel mysteries, to feel, to listen and to speak—for instance, to Jesus in his Passion. On Ash Wednesday Cornelia called her sisters to "unite ourselves to the Passion of Our

Lord, . . . placing ourselves on Mount Calvary, remembering that the past, present and future are equally present to Our Lord." She continued with some suggestions for this prayer: "I will now begin. Yes, my Jesus, I will in spirit follow Thee to Calvary and feel the stripes they laid on Thee, . . . that on the Cross I may die with Thee in all my daily obedience, and little sacrifices be one with Thee. . . ."[14]

Cornelia spoke in the same experiential terms when guiding a certain Sr. Clare whom she knew to be suffering, and whom she invited to taste a personal experience of union with Jesus and Mary: "Now there stood by the Cross of Jesus, Mary, His Mother. May two stand by your Cross—your Mother and yourself—Mary and Clare!"[15] The strength of Cornelia's expression of union with Jesus in suffering is at its best in her personal journal notes. In the midst of difficulties with English bishops, she wrote: "Walk on steadfastly in your sorrows to meet Jesus in Jerusalem."[16] In the same way her letters to her sisters sometimes conveyed depth in a pithy style. To console a sister, she wrote of "humiliations sent to you straight from His own humble heart—Christmas will show you!"[17]

Contemplation of Jesus led Cornelia to close familiarity with Mary: she wrote to a sister: "I never quarrel with Our Lord and Our Lady at the same time; if I'm out with Our Lord, I stay in with Our Lady."[18] To a bishop who had made impossible demands, she wrote that she had read his letter to Our Lady of Sorrows, "and the interior answer I got was 'burn the letter and tell the Bp to forget what he wrote & come and tell you what more you can do than you have done.' I have burned it, my Lord, & now will you come down & tell me what more I can do than I have done."[19] Clearly, Cornelia integrated prayer and life!

Jesus' Gospel companions became Cornelia's friends. On a matter very crucial to her Society, she wrote a prayer in her journal: "All America for our own! Ah, St. Peter who walked upon the waters, take us to America. . . ."[20]

The above citations are, of course, primarily Cornelia's instructions on preparation for prayer, the heart of which is the unitive experience, the experience of presence which God alone can give; this is often ineffable. For purposes of instruction she tried to give some expression to this unitive experience: "that kingdom of peace within where the soul's whisperings are answered by the king himself giving abundantly that jubilee of heart . . . not bargained for in this life of accepted suffering."[21] But even more expressive of her experience of union is an entry in her own personal spiritual journal at the time of one of the most tragic and decisive events of her life: the death of her two-year-old son in Grand Coteau in 1840. It takes us back to her married life.

When 1840 commenced, Cornelia was a happy wife and mother, rejoicing especially in the steady growth of her second son, John Henry, her two-year-old "Pretty Boy," the darling of her heart. While playing with the family dog in the yard of his home in the isolated Louisiana frontier country, this child was accidentally pushed into a vat of boiling sugar cane. Cornelia held her agonizing baby son, scalded from head to foot, in her arms for forty-three hours, until, on February 2, Feast of the Presentation of the Child Jesus in the Temple, she presented her son to the Lord. Her spiritual notebook reveals an extraordinary mystical identification of herself and her son with Mary and Jesus: "Fell a victim on Friday, suffered forty-three hours and was 'taken into the temple of the Lord' on the Feast of the Purification."[22] In the midst of unimaginable suffering, by what must have been an extraordinary grace, she was able to identify her son with Jesus who was *the* Friday victim, to identify herself with Mary who had held her crucified son on Calvary and had, years before, "taken" her infant son "to the temple of the Lord" as an offering to the Father. Elizabeth Mary Strub has written:

> Cornelia's . . . thoughts as she records them are carried backwards from Good Friday to the Purification—from Jesus' adulthood and passion to his infancy. John Henry became for her the sign that Jesus' passion would always lead her back to the Child. In fact, Cornelia came to the Holy Child as the center of her Society's devotional life by way of suffering and separation—by way of her own Calvary. . . . Her personal tragedy was illuminated and transposed by the passion of Jesus explicating the infancy of Jesus. . . . Cornelia went beyond personal grief, and, through the compassionate holding of the little body in her arms, received the grace of suffering with Christ and of knowing his sorrowing mother as an alter ego. . . . In John Henry . . . she saw Jesus . . . in Jesus she saw everyone, especially the poor, as her own child in his need. There was a very physical base to her understanding of this mystery by which Christ identified himself with humanity. It is not surprising that the Incarnation came to be the mystery she pondered most deeply.[23]

Both before and after her decisive experience of John Henry's death, Cornelia had other experiences of the utter vulnerability, the total dependence—"lowliness" as she said—of the human baby, and of the mother who gives birth. She bore her five children far from traditional helpers—the women of her own family. John Henry had been born in Vienna, among people whose language she did not speak, and only one month after she had made the arduous journey by coach from Rome to Vienna, with her "sight-seeing" husband. Two children were born in her isolated prairie home in Grand Coteau, her baby girl dying at the age of seven weeks. Her youngest son was born after his father had told her he wished a separation so that he might become a priest.

It is against the background of her experiences as mother that we must read the Rule she wrote for her congregation more than a decade after the death of John Henry. She spoke with feeling of "that Divine Child enclosed for nine months in the womb of his creature, born in a stable, exposed to bitter cold, flying into Egypt, then hidden for thirty years in a carpenter's workshop . . . a humbled God." She testified to the fruit of this kenosis: "Here it is that God manifests to us in a most wonderful manner the treasures of His mercy and of His boundless love."[24]

Cornelia's striking term, "a humbled God," is at the center of a passage in an early draft of her Rules and Constitutions, expressing her understanding of the salvific love manifested in Jesus' *kenosis* from crib to cross and resurrection:

> As the Society of the Holy Child Jesus is spiritually founded on the virtues of poverty, suffering [Cornelia's term for "chastity"?] and obedience, which our most blessed Redeemer came down to practice in the grotto of Bethlehem, and thence through his whole life to Calvary, so all ought to begin life again with the most sweet and holy and loving Child Jesus—a humbled God—walking with him step by step in the ways of the child, in humility and poverty mortifying their senses, their imaginations, passions, whims, inclinations and aversions, so that they may finally be united to the Man God, and that through his sacrifice on Mount Calvary they may look forward to a glorious eternity.[25]

This passage, recapitulating much from previous citations, adds significant emphases. The incarnate God—the humbled God—offers companionship in all stages of life, above all, in suffering. Of the latter Cornelia had abundant experience. The child also offered an image of growth, and the divine child an assurance of spiritual growth—growth through the communication of God's own life to us, growth through the company of Jesus as model. Her faith in the dynamism of growth, for which her own children gave her vivid images, was apparent in her own life, in her letters about her own children; that faith continued all through her life to invigorate the spiritual formation and education she gave in her convents and schools. An invitation to the children of her schools to contemplate the Child Jesus in his home in Nazareth emphasizes the call to "grow as he grew":

> You must follow him [Jesus] as he worked with St. Joseph, as he went on his many and troublesome errands, as he helped his Blessed Mother in her household labours. You must learn then, how he looked, how he acted, and how he prayed, . . . growing as he grew. . . . And when you grow up may you so love and follow the Man Jesus.[26]

Just as the students of her schools, so her sisters, too, would find God in and through their human experiences, because God had become human: "As you step on through the muddy streets, love God with your feet; and when your hands toil, love Him with your hands; and when you teach the children, love Him with His little ones."[27]

One final citation will be given to indicate how important it was to Cornelia and her sisters to ground prayer and life in sound theology, a soundness which seems to have been lacking in at least one bishop and canonist who tried to "improve" her Society's Rule. A few years after her death, these clerics tried to add to her Society's statement of its devotion to the Holy Child Jesus, the statement "and to the Infancy of Mary." Dismayed, Holy Child sisters insisted on the removal of this addition, writing emphatically "there is not and never has been . . . devotion to the Infancy of Mary . . . it was never in our own Rule as written by our foundress."[28] Cornelia had recognized the utterly transcendent, gratuitous gift of God revealing himself as God in the "Word made flesh," even in the utterly vulnerable flesh of the child in the womb and in the arms of his mother. Her whole life was centered on her relationship with God. Her giftedness lay in her total openness to divine transcendence while drawing on all the resources of her humanity to know and to respond to the God who shared it. It was through those experiences which were hers particularly as a woman, that she gained most profound insight into the mystery of the "Word made flesh." This insight seems to have saved her from the Jansenism in her milieu which devalued her because she was a married woman. The devaluation becomes apparent when one reads in the prayer journal of one of her oldest and closest sister companions that, as much as she admired Cornelia she imagined another foundress "higher" in heaven "on account of her virginity!"[29] As theologians continue to wrestle today with the mystery of God fully human as well as divine, we do well to retrieve the insights of women contemplatives who found, as they allowed their human experiences to be illumined by the Gospel, a place of vital encounter with the "Word made flesh."

Notes

[1] *Documentation Presented by the Historical Commission for the Beatification and Canonization of the Servant of God, Cornelia Connelly* [hereafter referred to as D]. Society of the Holy Child Jesus [hereafter referred to as SHCJ], Archives, Rome, Italy. D 71:57. See also Caritas McCarthy, SHCJ, *The Spirituality of Cornelia Connelly* (Lewiston: Edwin Mellen Press, 1986), p. 198; and pp. 209-22 for detailed information on the sources for Cornelia Connelly.

[2] McCarthy, *Spirituality*, including bibliography. Most comprehensive is Elizabeth Mary Strub, *Informatio*, vol. 4 of Positio for the Canonization Process of the Servant of God, Cornelia Connelly, 1809-1879, printed for the Sacred Congregation of the Causes of Saints, Rome, 1987.

[3] Karl Rahner, *Theological Investigations, 1* (Baltimore: Helicon Press, 1961), pp. 166-68, 183-85. Justin Kelly, "Prayer and Incarnation," *Way Supplement*, 14 (1978): 3-25.

[4] "Contemplation of the Gospels, Ignatius Loyola, and the Contemporary Christian," *Theological Studies,* 29 (1968): 417-43.

[5] Brendan Byrne, " 'To See with the Eyes of the Imagination . . .': Scripture in the Exercises and Recent Interpretation," *Way Supplement*, 72 (1991): 7-19, with bibliography, to which should be added Sandra Schneiders, *The Revelatory Text* (San Francisco: HarperCollins, 1991).

[6] McCarthy, *Spirituality*, pp. 209-17.

[7] Radegunde Flaxman, *A Woman Styled Bold* (London: Darton, Longman and Todd, 1991), is the most recent and authoritative biography. McCarthy, *Spirituality*, gives biography in conjunction with spirituality, and, pp. 223-24 indicate the contribution of previous biographies.

[8] "Synopsis: Notes Compiled by Mrs. Mack [Cornelia's niece]," Jan. and Feb., 1911, SHCJ Archives, Rome, CCTc53.

⁹ *The Writings of the Servant of God*, Cornelia Connelly [hereafter referred to as CC], SHCJ Archives, Rome; CC 1:12.

¹⁰ McCarthy, *Spirituality*, pp. 52-53, 136-43.

¹¹ McCarthy, *Spirituality*, pp. 143-48.

¹² McCarthy, *Spirituality*, pp. 52-53, 136-43.

¹³ Caritas McCarthy, SHCJ, *A Study of the Constitutions of the Society of the Holy Child Jesus as Developed under Cornelia Connelly*, privately printed as Source 4, by the SHCJ, Rome, 1975; this reproduces all the stages of the SHCJ Rules and Constitutions to 1880. Texts cited here are found on pp. 77-80; also in McCarthy, *Spirituality*, pp. 114-115a.

¹⁴ CC 8:97.

¹⁵ CC 28:11.

¹⁶ CC 22:17.

¹⁷ CC 7:29.

¹⁸ D 63:66.

¹⁹ CC 13:81.

²⁰ CC 22:28-29.

²¹ Cornelia's "Preface" to J. Rigoleuc, *Walking with God*, trans. Mary Ignatia Bridges SHCJ (London: Richardson, 1859).

²² CC 21:5.

²³ Strub, *Informatio*, pp. 109-13.

²⁴ McCarthy, *Spirituality*, pp, 109-115a, reproduces these texts in their context.

²⁵ McCarthy, *Spirituality*, pp. 108-11.

²⁶ Cornelia's "Preface" to Meditations as a Preparation for Whitsuntide [author unknown], trans. Emily Bowles, SHCJ (London: Richardson, 1851), pp. 2-3.

²⁷ CC 8:87.

²⁸ D 58:119, 135-37; also Source 4, 149.

²⁹ Manuscript notes of Mother Maria Joseph Buckle, SHCJ, in the Archives of the Society of the Holy Child Jesus, Mayfield, England.

Maisie Ward as "Theologian"

Dana Greene

There *is* one dangerous science for women—one which they must indeed beware how they profanely touch—that of theology. Strange, and miserably strange, that while they are modest enough to doubt their powers, and pause at the threshold of sciences where every step is demonstrable and sure, they will plunge headlong, and without one thought of incompetency, into that science where the greatest men have trembled, and the wisest erred.[1]

So wrote John Ruskin. That Ruskin should even raise this question is a tribute to the Protestant women who by virtue of their educations had begun to reflect on theological issues by the late nineteenth century. Although progress was slow, by the middle of the twentieth century their achievement was noteworthy. John Macquarrie, in his survey of twentieth century religious thought, cites three women—Evelyn Underhill, Georgia Harkness, and Simone Weil—as having made a contribution to theology. Although not at the center of theological inquiry, their contributions to spirituality and mysticism were significant.[2]

Catholic women, excluded more systematically from higher education until well into the twentieth century and barred completely from clerical life, could not contribute to "the queen of the sciences" which was a totally clerical preserve. Not until the opening of The School of Sacred Theology at Saint Mary's College in 1944, were women able to study theology as it was traditionally defined. Yet unwittingly, Catholic women were reshaping the meaning of theology itself.

While none would be called a theologian—Dorothy Day, Jessica Powers, Sister Madeleva, Caryll Houselander, and Maisie Ward—each made a contribution to broadening the concept of the study of God. As Day and Houselander found God in the poor, and Powers and Madeleva found God the subject of poetry, Maisie Ward, publisher, writer, street preacher and social activist, found God in the lives of great writers and saints, in the Gospel preached and doctrines proclaimed, and in the ordinary circumstances of twentieth century life. Under the aegis of the Catholic Evidence Guild she reinvigorated the doctrines of the Catholic Church by explaining them on the outdoor speaking platform. For almost half a century she and her husband, Frank Sheed, published for educated readers in the English-speaking world the best writing by the Catholic mind. As a writer and author of more than two dozen books, Ward showed how belief shaped human life. As an advocate for social reform issues she illustrated how belief impelled to action.

The achievements of Maisie Ward are disparate and unsystematic. In this sense her work is symptomatic of a woman's life; she had no formal higher education or training; she perceived the needs of others easily and responded fully; and she lived by her wits. Hers was not a life of contemplation, but an active life that brought into play her intelligence and self-confidence. The titles of Ward's two autobiographies, *Unfinished Business* and *To and Fro on the Earth*,[3] give some sense of her self-understanding as an engaged and committed person. What is unique in Ward's various contributions is the importance she gives to intellectual powers as a means of bending the will toward God. "I don't see how the ordinary person who hasn't some special mystical insight can do otherwise than use his mind with a steady effort that in its very feebleness must increase humility and dependence as well as faith."[4] The intellectual study of God, theology, was for Maisie Ward a means to deepened faith.

Maisie came from the family of William George Ward who converted to Catholicism with John Henry Newman. Her father, Wilfrid Ward, was a prominent Catholic biographer and editor of the *Dublin Review*. Her mother, Josephine Ward, was a Catholic novelist who was related to the Duke of Norfolk, first among Catholic peers. Maisie's childhood was lived in the insular world of nineteenth century English Catholicism. She was influenced in her youth by Newman and Chesterton—her father knew both of them—and Browning, as well as the preachers Fathers Maturin and Robert Hugh Benson.

In 1919 she joined the Catholic Evidence Guild and for more than four decades, whether in London, New York or Sydney, she lectured as a Catholic evangelist. In 1926 she co-founded the British publishing firm Sheed and Ward, under whose sponsorship the Catholic intellectual revival was stimulated first in England and then in America. Sheed and Ward not only translated continental Catholic writers but encouraged English-speaking ones, many of whom were converts. It published biography, essays, philosophy, poetry, novels, sociology, history, devotional writing, but not much theology, at least initially. The aim of these books, as Frank Sheed said, was "right above the middle of the brow," meaning they were not scholarly or esoteric works but provocative ones for educated lay Catholics and clergy who liked to read.

Besides the out-of-doors platform, Maisie and Frank lectured indoors all over the world to Catholic audiences at hundreds of Catholic colleges, Newman centers, communion breakfasts, and parish gatherings of every sort. This lecturing was apologetic in nature and triumphalistic in tone, reflecting the Catholicism of the time. However, inherent within it were the beginnings of an apostolic world view which was increasingly willing to be engaged with the world.

Maisie Ward was herself a writer who edited or wrote twenty-nine books—biographies, histories, lives of the saints, essays, and scholarly and devotional works. Several of these were spiritual writings.[5] She did an edition of *The English Way: Studies in English Sanctity from St. Bede to Newman*, in which she wrote a chapter on Mary Ward, the seventeenth century founder of the Institute of the Blessed Virgin Mary whose convent school she had attended. During World War II she wrote *This Burning Heat*, which showed the valiant efforts of civilians helping one another during the Blitz. *The Splendor of the Rosary* explained the rosary as a vehicle for linking doctrine and devotion. In *France Pagan?*, written right after the war, she chronicled the postwar efforts of evangelization by Abbé Godin, a priest-worker among poor French youth. In *Be Not Solicitous: Sidelights on the Providence of God and the Catholic Family* she gave spiritual guidance to the family. In *Saints Who Made History* she studied the contributions of the Church fathers of the first five centuries, and in *They Saw His Glory: An Introduction to the Gospels and Acts* she explored the Good News as revealed by the evangelists. In commenting on a lecture Ward gave from this book on the Gospel of Mark, Sister Madeleva wrote, "That was the high hour of my life with Maisie Ward, unforgettable, luminous, to be compared with very few hours of my life."[6]

Besides this spiritual writing Ward also wrote three short biographies of saints—Anthony of Egypt, Catherine of Siena and Jerome, and a longer book, her first, on St. Bernard of Siena, the people's preacher.[7] Although she began with a stereotyped and pietistic idea of the saints, she slowly came to see the great variety among them. Each emerged to meet the particular needs of a historic time. Through their sanctity they claimed an authority to shape something new in the midst of chaos. They were manifestations of the divine in the world and through them Christ's work was done.

Maisie Ward is probably best known for her biographies of Chesterton, Newman, Robert Browning, Caryll Houselander, and her family history of the Wilfrid Wards.[8] Each of these was a voluminous study based on extensive scholarly research. In writing her two-volume study of Browning she consulted over six hundred sources. Ward claimed that "biography is my craft and my passion." These books demanded prodigious work and commitment on her part. Commenting on her contribution as a biographer, Anne Freemantle wrote, "Maisie Ward is the rarest of combinations, an accurate, serious historian and biographer who wears, not blue stockings, but rose-colored spectacles, that enable her to see the best in every character she confronts, without mitigating or excusing what she cannot approve."[9] Irrespective of Freemantle's play on colors, she gets at a central insight about Ward as a biographer. Ward viewed her subjects sympathetically; seeing through the lens of love, she was able to penetrate to their core. However, she was also generally uncritical of them and defensive on their behalf.

The contributions of Maisie Ward both as a publisher who stimulated the Catholic literary revival and as a writer who forwarded it were captured by Sister Madeleva in a perceptive piece entitled "Maisie Ward: A Shepherdess of Sheep." She wrote that Maisie "has kept spiritual ward over millions through the avenues of the spoken and the written word for half a century. The reading world has become her flock."[10] She was pastor, in short, to educated Catholics.

Maisie believed that "God mattered"; that is, that if one believed, one lived that belief. Toward the end of her life she wrote, "It is my business, a) to pass on the Good News and b) to feed the hungry and harbour the harbourless. And in twenty-four hours to the day there is not time to accomplish the essential if one involved oneself in the inessential—even if it is in its own way important."[11] Maisie spent a good piece of her life harboring the harborless and championing their cause. She wrote on the priest-worker movement and the Canadian maritime cooperatives. She raised money for land reform in India, begging support from wealthy friends and making appeals to Catholic parishes. She was a strong supporter of the Catholic Worker movement and of Friendship House. In her earlier days she supported the Catholic Land Association, operating several farms with unemployed boys or refugees. She lent money to those who needed it, like those in the Marycrest community in Nyack, New York, to build a Catholic community. But most importantly she founded the Catholic Housing Aid Society in mid-1950. Forty years later, it remains a resource for those needing low income housing in Britain.

Maisie Ward's life was remarkable for the variety of these achievements, for her flexibility and ability to change over time, and for the sense of self-empowerment which drove her forward. Her drive and energy came from an inner life that was shaped and disciplined by the Catholic Church. Frank Sheed said of her that she had an "instructed heart," one formed by a Church that offered her the daily discipline of the sacraments and devotion.[12] It was the mass that was the mainstay of her devotional life. As early as 1928 she and Frank Sheed built a chapel in the countryside and drew a congregation to it. They began a sung mass, a dialogue, which diminished the distance between the congregation and the priests they imported from London. She loved the mass and would assist at several if possible. For her it was a universal prayer that covered all the needs to adore, to thank, to ask forgiveness, to intercede. It united one with the sick, those in prison, the lonely all over the globe.[13]

Although the doctrine of the Mystical Body was only officially promulgated in the 1940s, it had captured Ward's imagination early in her life. As a young girl in a convent school in Cambridge she was introduced to the preaching of Robert Hugh Benson, the convert son of the Archbishop of Canterbury, who at the beginning of this century did more than anyone else in England to reinvigorate the notion of the Mystical Body.

Maisie's understanding of the doctrine grew slowly—first in seeing the church as the Mystical Body of Christ on earth, second, in the implications of the Mystical Body for its members, third, for the importance of the Eucharist as the means by which one deepened one's participation in the Body of Christ. Maisie spent her life living into the implications of this doctrine. She wrote:

> Slowly we realized our immense responsibility. God, becoming incarnate, worked through a human nature. He used that nature to heal and to bless, He gave pardon through His human lips, He gave Himself with His human hands. In that human nature He suffered and died for the world. When, at the Ascension, that human nature left the earth, God incarnate continued to act, through a multitude of human beings. We, His Church, are the Incarnation continued.[14]

It was the doctrine and sacramental life of the church which shaped Ward's activist orientation. She grounded herself in the prayer of the church—the mass, rosary, the divine office—and dedicated herself to doing God's work in the world. But she never considered herself to be of a contemplative bent. In a speech she gave on prayer, she began by pointing out the absurdity of being chosen to lecture on this topic.[15] She was convinced, however, that everyone could learn how to pray and that the more one did it, the more prayer would improve. By getting "our day into prayers," one more easily "get(s) prayer into our day," she said. She was also aware that "the zeal for action swamps prayer" and that there were perils in the active life. "We must somehow draw back from a *Vita Activa*," she wrote, "become only mechanical and sterile, to something that should resemble that other side, recognized by the philosophers as well as the mystics."[16] She critiqued modern Catholicism for its "neglect, almost the fear, of the deep mystical content of Christianity."[17]

In her later life Maisie became more interested in the mystical tradition. Julian's *Showings* was one of the books she kept beside her bed for many years. (The others were probably by Dickens, whom she loved and read until the time of her death.) She also was fascinated by Dag Hammarskjold's *Markings* and Teilhard de Chardin's *The Divine Milieu*. She saw that they were aware, as few others were, of the deeper, wider dimensions surrounding a brief human life. She juxtaposed Teilhard's obsession with the world's vastness with Julian's vision of God in all creation, in the little thing like the hazelnut.[18]

In evaluating her own life Ward noted "with a certain anxiety that my life's curve has been other than that of most of those chosen out by the Church for our imitation: nearly all of them begin with love and service of neighbour, proceeding onwards and upwards to an almost exclusive world of worship, solitude, adoration."[19] Her life followed a different course; it continued to be marked by great activity, and this, she explained, resulted from her need to respond to suffering in her world.

Suffering is a common vehicle for driving one inward to a deeper mystery at the heart of life. But for most of her life Maisie Ward experienced little of it. Her childhood was sheltered, marred only by the death of a younger brother. She worked in an English hospital during World War I, but unlike her contemporary Vera Brittain, who was transformed by the experience of war, Maisie was not. When she was thirty-eight, however, she gave birth to her first child and almost died in the process. In gratitude for life, she opened a community chapel in Surrey. During World War II she lived safely outside Philadelphia, but the ravages of the war, communicated to her by friends and relatives in Britain, began to affect her. It is during that time that she became friends with Caryll Houselander. This friendship was very important to Ward; Houselander remained her most intimate female friend outside her family.

Ward saw in this strange and sometimes eccentric friend a spiritual vitality that she found in no other. She was for her a "divine eccentric." After Houselander's death in 1954 Ward wrote a biography of her and published a collection of her letters. In these she reveals the importance of Houselander's life and writing. As a lay woman writing on theology and mysticism, Houselander was unique. As Ward suggested, one had to go back to Julian of Norwich to find an English Catholic lay woman writing on these subjects. As a self-proclaimed neurotic, Caryll had an ability to relate to human suffering. This, combined with her natural genius for psychology, made her particularly helpful to those with mental problems.

Ward and Houselander came together as publisher and writer during the years of World War II. Both had a heightened concern for human suffering because of the war and both published books on that subject. But it was Houselander's understanding of the meaning of suffering and the means to overcome it that resonated with Ward. Although suffering must not be sought, it must be accepted as part of life and central to the redemptive process. Its power to destroy could be defused only by charity, not by asceticism.

Houselander understood that she, unlike most Catholic writers including Ward, began with a different assumption about the human condition. She laid out this telling difference to her friend:

I think that the difference between most Catholic writers and myself is that they seem to start with the idea of preserving the good in people, they have, as a rule, personal traditions which lead them to think of goodness as something already there and to be kept radiant, but I, who have a very dark background, start with the idea of everything being in ruins, and having to get back to goodness, I do not expect to find people good, but I expect to find Christ wounded in them, and of course that is what I do find.[20]

Ward was especially impressed with Houselander's book *Guilt*. Beginning with the belief that all persons are sinners, Caryll derives the conclusion that there is no great gulf between the "well-balanced" and the "neurotic." Once shared human sinfulness is acknowledged, one should set sinfulness aside and focus on God's forgiving love. It is only when one ceases to resist this continual love of God that healing can begin in a life.

Houselander provided the enormously optimistic Ward with a way to understand the suffering and evil of their time. But she also helped her come to appreciate a fundamental aspect of the doctrine of the Mystical Body. Houselander claimed that as each person had a particular vocation, each had a general one too: to be Christ in the world, to enter into the world's suffering, and to help heal it, not through asceticism, but through love.

Although Ward's methodology was always to focus on the needs of others, be it the need for meaning in the lives of non-believers or the need of educated believers to nourish their minds and spirit, it was only through the experience of the war and her friendship with Houselander that she came to deepen her concern for the suffering of others and begin to understand the social limitations of the "old spirituality." "I realized more and more," she wrote:

that God who had made the order of nature meant it not to be abolished but consecrated and widened by the order of grace . . . And while it is easy to love in general terms a world remote from us, the effort to like the neighbour whom we are obliged to help is an essential element in Christian love. If vitality is to be there it must be in a framework of reality.[21]

This framework of reality for liking and loving she found in the small faith communities which worked with real social needs and came alive as "a branch of the True Vine, as a limb of the Mystical Body." She saw the work of these communities as going beyond individual compassion. For decades she had worked to help friends buy homes—twice she had bought farms to sustain young Scottish boys or Polish war refugees—but the work of the small faith communities was work of compassion and creativity. "Creation is at work everywhere," she wrote, "on a large scale occasionally, but more significantly in small-scale achievements by the hundred, by the thousand. All over the world I have found small groups who are guiding a new world in the shell of the one crumbling around us."[22]

At the end of her life Ward saw the real work of the spirit being carried out in these small communities. Her last autobiography, *To and Fro on the Earth*, is a chronicle of the many groups which worked for the good. It is prophetic in seeing that the vital future of religious life would come not from large, wealthy, centralized institutions, but from small groups living at their periphery. "Evil is large and loud, indeed raucous," she wrote:

> It destroys easily, quickly, on a vast scale—and always gets the front page. Good is quiet, slow perhaps, for to build takes longer than to destroy, but (it is) steadily, perpetually creative. Because it is personal it must be small in scale. Almost everything that grows large grows too large, ceases to do its work and dies of swollen heads and swollen purses. But all over the world small scale groups that work at a thousand valuable things are coming into existence.[23]

Maisie applied the same criteria of simplicity, smallness, and connectedness to meaning to the church she loved. "The main and tragic failure of the church in the modern world," she wrote, "is that it has grown rich, forgotten its own teaching and, like all the wealthy, measures out even its charity with careful moderation."[24]

Maisie Ward's faith undergirded all her works. She labored at the juncture where faith and life intersect, expanding the subject matter of theology. Through the Catholic Evidence Guild she presented the faith as a unified system of belief and thought which realized itself in transformed human beings. As a publisher she showed the Catholic mind engaged with the questions of modernity. As a writer of biography and history she illustrated how belief is lived out in particular times and places. In her own mind she saw her contribution specifically tied to the teaching of theology: "In my lifetime I have heard the stirring call to Catholic Action by Pius XI, have witnessed the immense share borne by laymen in the intellectual apostolate, have received from my Bishop authority to teach theology on the street corner, sharing . . . in the Church's commission, 'Go ye and teach all nations.' "[25]

As she expanded the field of what could be considered theology, she also believed that theology, as traditionally understood, was an aid to prayer and social action. She wrote to Dorothy Day, "Frank and I have both found that the most valuable time of our lives was that given to simply deepening our doctrinal knowledge. You are a much better pray-er than either of us, but I think you, also, would find that it helps both one's prayers and one's social thinking."[26]

As intellectual and activist, Maisie Ward's life chronicles the vast changes in Catholicism over the last century. She emerged from an insular, defensive, and triumphalistic English Catholicism to be a spokesperson for a church willing to interact with the modern world. The daughter of Wilfrid Ward became at eighty the defender of conscientious objectors in the Vietnam war. In the end her reach was global. She not only traveled to and fro on the earth to lecture—in the Philippines, India, Australia, and all over the United States—but her concern was with people very different from herself—those without housing in London, Harajan in Kerala, and orphans in Mexico and Peru. Her Catholicism was universal; it had grown to include the world. But she did not merely reflect these changes, she helped cause them through her writing, lecturing indoors and out, publishing, and social activism. It is the totality of these achievements—in short it is the life itself that is significant and causative.

Maisie's achievements are remarkable—the fact that they were achieved by a Catholic lay woman makes them the more extraordinary. Gender played a role both to enhance and limit her achievement. The fact that she was a woman restricted her impact, but also allowed her to say things others could not say. Because her influence was not bestowed but earned, she had nothing to protect. Hence her freedom. Her social class also had positive and negative implications. As the granddaughter of William George Ward and the daughter of Wilfrid and Josephine Ward she carried with her the status of an upper-class intellectual by virtue of birth. This was particularly helpful in America where class was supposed to be irrelevant, but was not. On the other hand, the fact that she was a foreigner of a certain lineage meant that she was always the outsider. She might be able to inspire, but she could not lead.

As biographer, historian, preacher, teacher, social critic and activist Maisie Ward was Vesuvius-like—erupting in many directions, dynamic because she was connected through subterranean routes to a center which was vital. Like a volcano Maisie Ward changed a theological landscape and bedded down a rich lava soil from which new life and thought could grow.

Notes

[1] John Ruskin, "Of Queen's Gardens," in *Essays and Letters Selected from the Writings of John Ruskin,* ed. Mrs. Louis G. Hufford (Boston: Ginn and Company, 1894), p. 87.

[2] John Macquarrie, *Twentieth-Century Religious Thought: The Frontiers of Philosophy and Theology, 1900-1980* (London: SCM Press LTD., 1983), pp. 408-09.

[3] *Unfinished Business* (N.Y.: Sheed & Ward, 1964), and *To and Fro on the Earth* (N.Y.: Sheed & Ward 1975).

[4] Maisie Ward, "Journal," Archives of the University of Notre Dame (AUND), Sheed and Ward Papers, (SWP), CSWD 13/19, p. 139.

[5] *The English Way: Studies in English Sanctity from St. Bede to Newman,* ed. Maisie Ward (London: Sheed & Ward, 1933); *This Burning Heat* (N.Y.: Sheed & Ward, 1941); *The Splendor of the Rosary* (N.Y.: Sheed & Ward, 1945); *France Pagan? The Mission of Abbé Godin* (London: Sheed & Ward, 1949); *Be Not Solicitous: Sidelights on the Providence of God and the Catholic Family* (N.Y.: Sheed & Ward, 1953); *They Saw His Glory: An Introduction to the Gospels and Acts* (N.Y.: Sheed & Ward, 1956); *Saints Who Made History: The First Five Centuries* (N.Y.: Sheed & Ward, 1959).

[6] Sister Madeleva, "Maisie Ward: A Shepherdess of Sheep." AUND, SWP, GSWD 001/ll. n.d.

[7] *Saint Anthony of Egypt. Saint Catherine of Siena. Saint Jerome* (N.Y.: Sheed & Ward, 1950); *San Bernardino: The People's Preacher* (London: Manresa Press, 1914).

[8] *Gilbert Keith Chesterton* (N.Y.: Sheed & Ward, 1943); *Young Mr Newman*

(N.Y.: Sheed & Ward, 1948); *Robert Browning and His World: The Private Face—1812-1861* and *Robert Browning and His World: Two Robert Brownings?* (N. Y.: Holt, Rinehart and Winston, 1967, 1969); *Caryll Houselander: The Divine Eccentric* (N.Y.: Sheed & Ward, 1962); *The Wilfrid Wards and the Transition: The Nineteenth Century* and *The Wilfrid Wards and the Transition: Insurrection versus Resurrection* (London: Sheed & Ward, 1934, 1937).

[9] Anne Freemantle, "Dealing with the Springs of Life," AUND, SWP, GSWD 001/11, p. 10.

[10] Sister Madeleva, "Maisie Ward: A Shepherdess of Sheep."

[11] Letter from Maisie Ward to unknown person, Dec. 30, 1958, AUND, SWP, CSWD 3/04.

[12] Frank Sheed, *The Instructed Heart* (Huntington, IN: Our Sunday Visitor, 1979).

[13] For her view on the Mass see "Changes in the Liturgy: Cri de Coeur," *Life of the Spirit* (October, 1961), pp. 127-36 and "Life and Liturgy," a speech by Maisie Ward. AUND, SWP, CSWD, Box 15.

[14] Maisie Ward, "Maisie Ward," in *Born Catholics*, assembled by F. J. Sheed (N.Y.: Sheed and Ward, 1954), p. 141.

[15] Maisie Ward, "Notes on Prayer." AUND, SWP, CSWD 13/17.

[16] *To and Fro on the Earth*, p. 10.

[17] Ibid., p. 173.

[18] Maisie Ward, "Notes on Julian of Norwich," AUND, SWP, CSWD 13/10; "Dag Hammarskjold and Teilhard de Chardin" *Catholic World*, 210 (January, 1970), pp. 159-164.

[19] *To and Fro on the Earth*, p. 10.

[20] Letter of Caryll Houselander to Maisie Ward, 7 July 1945, AUND, SWP, CSWD, 12/12.

[21] *Unfinished Business*, p. 195.

[22] Quoted by Frank Sheed in *The Instructed Heart*, p. 38.

[23] *To and Fro on the Earth*, p. 175.

[24] Ibid., p. 17.

[25] Maisie Ward, "Postscript," AUND, SWC, CSWD 15/04.

[26] Letter. Maisie Ward to Dorothy Day, May 31, 1944. Marquette University Archives. Dorothy Day Catholic Worker Collection. Series D-1, Box 6.

Cracking the Door:
Women at the Second Vatican Council

Helen Marie Ciernick

Introduction

At the 1987 Roman synod on the "Vocation and Mission of the Laity in the Church and in the World," Patricia Jones, a theologically trained parish worker from Liverpool, England, was one of the first spokespersons to address the bishops. Only a quarter century earlier at the Second Vatican Council, the council leaders denied women the right to address the bishops on their own behalf. It is often forgotten how recently in the history of the church this injustice took place. In the drive to move the church forward on questions surrounding the place and role of women, scholars often ignore the historical perspective. Rather than explore the church's past, the advance of women in the church is measured by the rapidly progressive changes in the roles of women in society. Patricia Jones's speech placed within the perspective of women's history warrants little notice, but placed within the perspective of church history it illustrates significant progress.

That women were present at the Second Vatican Council is a little known fact among historians. At the beginning of the third session, the leadership of the council invited twenty-three women to join the men auditors, already present. Outside the council hall numerous women had been working as lobbyists, experts, and staff members of organizations. While the work of these women is important and warrants an indepth study, this paper will focus on the developments that led to the invitation and evaluate the results of the auditors' presence at the council.

The following reconstruction opens with a survey of American Catholic periodicals to discern women's expectations prior to and after the opening of the council. Did they have particular hopes for changes in the place of women in the church? Who was lobbying for women to be present at the council? Why were women finally invited? The story closes with the arrival of the women auditors and an examination of their achievements and frustrations. The paper concludes with a discussion of the importance of reconstructing the women's presence at the Second Vatican Council.

Although the invitation was recognized by some women as an important event, few contemporary publications allotted more than a paragraph to the occasion. Research in American journals and books uncovered few references to the women. Of these, only two were written by female auditors. By necessity, then, this paper draws upon a broad range of sources that includes *La Documentation Catholique*, materials from the archives of the National Council of Catholic Women, and the popular Catholic periodical *Ave Maria*. The breadth of sources permits voices to be heard which may have been excluded from mainstream sources. The dearth of secondary literature attests to the fact that the significance of the women's presence at the council has been largely overlooked. In the thirty years since the council, only three articles have been published which focus solely on the women of Vatican II and their activity. While all three articles were written by women, it is still disappointing that women historians and theologians are equally responsible for overlooking the significance of women at Vatican II.[1]

Availability is only one part of the problem of uncovering sources in women's history. An examination of church history reveals that the role of women in the church as officially prescribed by the hierarchy and ascribed by tradition often stands in contrast to the activism of women in the church. Since documentation has not always readily testified to this fact, old sources need to be revisited and challenged to reveal instances when women may have moved beyond their prescribed and ascribed roles. New sources need to be uncovered which document women not as passive persons on the periphery, but as active agents of change. The women of Vatican II are an example of women moving beyond the role assigned them by the church.

Catholic Women and the Second Vatican Council

When Pope John XXIII, on January 25, 1959 at St. Paul's Outside the Walls, announced his intention of convening an ecumenical council, Catholic women were ready for change. Through higher education, participation in various forms of Catholic Action, such as the Young Christian Workers and Christian Family Movement, and entry into the work force, women had been outgrowing the role assigned them in Catholic domesticity. Yet, at the opening of the council, while many European women were armed with petitions, few American women had expectations for change. Only as the council proceeded did American women begin to perceive the council as possibly affecting their lives.

A survey of popular Catholic periodicals revealed that during the first two sessions the topic of women was nearly ignored among the laity's questions for the council. In October 1961, *The Sign* published a two-page article of nine interviews with Catholic lay leaders from around the world. Only two women were interviewed, Margaret Mealey, executive director, National Council of Catholic Women (NCCW), and Rosemary Goldie, executive secretary, Permanent Committee for International Congresses of the Lay Apostolate in Rome (COPECIAL). They criticized the church for failing to recognize that women were a vital force in the laity who were ready to contribute more if they were given the opportunity.

Mealey's request of the council stemmed from her experience as the executive director of the NCCW. In her work, she witnessed the discrepancy among dioceses regarding the activism of women in the church. She called upon the council for recognition of the work women do within the church. There existed a "need [for] explicit directives delineating women's work in the lay apostolate."[2] Too often dioceses wasted the talents of women in tasks that belied the spiritual formation and education they received in college. However, Mealey did not ask for women to be admitted to the council, she was only asking that consideration be given to the capabilities and needs of women.

Goldie placed Mealey's concerns regarding women within the context of the emerging ecclesiology and theological anthropology of the time. She expressed hope for a broader, more contemporary understanding of "the layman" in which laywomen, particularly church professionals, were acknowledged for all they had to offer the church. She stated, "When we speak of 'the layman,' we may hope that the term will include a mid-twentieth-century version of 'women's place,' not only in the home and in society, but also in the church."[3] In a 1964 interview with *The Month* she explained that such changes regarding the perception of women would be in keeping with John XXIII's call for *aggiornamento*.[4] A renewed inclusive ecclesiology would develop from a sharpened perception of women which draws upon developments in psychology and theology. Understanding women in their own right would engender changes in the church leading toward a more equitable ecclesiastical society. She explained:

> I should like to suggest a simple factual statement: There does not exist a 'Church' and alongside it, a problem of 'woman', but a Church of men and women. Since the Church is a human society—and just in so far as she is a human society—she cannot develop normally without a certain balance and integration of the respective contributions of these men and women who are her members.[5]

She criticized the council's failure to include even one mother general in the Preparatory Commissions; despite the attention given the question of women religious in the council hall, women religious remained absent.[6] Indeed, their views were not even sought in consideration of the prospective agendas. Goldie concluded that the church had yet to recognize the value of women's work in the church, much less perceive their potential as Catholic layleaders.

While Mealey did not call for women to be present at the council in her 1961 interview with *The Sign*, in the fall of 1962 the NCCW was critical of the omission of women from the council. The November 3, 1962 issue of *America* included an unsigned article in its "Current Comment" column entitled, "Women in the Church." The author reported that the 1962 biennial congress of the NCCW had invited reflection upon the fact that the council was composed exclusively of males. They asked, "What of women in the church?" The author posed the same question with acerbity:

> Was there a subtle irony in the fact that the first heroic size statue of a saint to meet the eyes of most bishops, as they filed into St. Peter's to begin their labors, was that of St. Teresa of Avila?[7]

It appears that women were not to draw comfort, but rather were to see additional irony in the opening prayer. The anonymous author admitted that while Saint Teresa may not have been an advocate of women's rights herself, the irony should not be overlooked. A more "direct and explicit" form of participation must be granted to women. She/he looked to a future council for this injustice to be rectified, despite the multitude of works generally acknowledged that women perform in the church. The article closed on a cryptic note:

> Meanwhile, the ladies [sic] at Detroit and elsewhere can draw comfort from the fact that the first act of the bishops, in their opening statement of October 20, was to proclaim that they met "united in prayer with Mary, the mother of Jesus."[8]

Again it appears that women were not to draw comfort from this invocation of Mary, but rather were to see additional irony in the statement. By the fall of 1964 women's exclusion from the council and their limited role in the church were drawing more attention.

Ave Maria published the third of a ten part series of interviews with a panel of ten women in September of 1964.[9] The interviews, conducted by a team of the magazine's editors, confirmed the increasing popularity of Goldie's and Mealey's concerns regarding the role of the "emancipated woman" in the church. The editors summarized the women's concerns when they wrote that "the cry of the true modern revolutionary is for [her] growth, spiritual growth and growth in a creative self-service to the world and the Church."[10] Women, they asserted, possessed the qualities of intelligence and compassion, qualities needed if the church was to move effectively into the modern world. One woman expressed it clearly:

> It was Lenin who said that the success of any mass movement is dependent upon the participation of women. If there is to be a "new Pentecost" in the life of the Church today, we can't afford to ignore the possible contributions and responsibility of 50 percent of the "people of God."[11]

The women on the panel were deeply alienated by the exclusion of women from the council. They believed that half the population of the church lacked representation at a council explicitly called to move the church into the modern world. Rather than garnering the respect of the modern world with which it desired to enter into dialogue, the council only succeeded in making itself "a laughing stock in the world."[12] One panelist explained:

> To those outside the Church, the lack of female representation in anything so important as the Council, and the whole theme of updating, of moving with the times where possible, and of retaining only those institutions and customs which have their roots in necessity, is further proof of the Church's intransigence. Half the Church is unrepresented in the halls of holy renewal. To a large segment of "emancipated" women, this is a scandal.[13]

The church needed to hear women's voices if it was to achieve its goals. Their hopes for the council included the presence of recognized Catholic women leaders, and failing that, at least Catholic women religious who had achieved leadership roles.

The panelists were not the only ones to perceive the incongruity of no representation for the majority of activists in the church. Before the American women even criticized the exclusion of women, European women and male leaders of the council were taking action to rectify the situation.

Eva-Maria Jung, the wife of a lay auditor at the third session, portrayed the atmosphere at the first two sessions as cold, even bordering on hostile for women.[14] At the first session, no women were permitted in the council hall except for the rare woman journalist.[15] This prompted Jung to make the same observation as the *America* writer in a harsher tone:

> Only the stone images of some saints and queens looked down from the walls of St. Peter's, silent and unwanted witnesses upon the assembled Council Fathers.[16]

The first recognition of women came not from the bishops but from the men of the press corps who wrote in protest of the council's policy of barring women from liturgies and other events. During the second session, the lay auditors rose to women's defense. They set up an office for meetings and discussions and invited women from lay organizations to run it. While the men were working within the council walls, outside women were launching their own offensive drive for participation.

Women came to Rome during the first and second sessions to petition for their concerns and the admission of women to the council. Theresa Muench, a German speaking journalist holding a degree in theology, set the stage for women's arrival during the preparatory stages of the council. She intentionally backed the Vatican spokesman into a corner by asking, "Have women also been invited to the Council?"[17] Among the various responses came the patronizing reply from Auxiliary Bishop Walter Kampi, the director of the council's German press center, "No, but be comforted; at the Third Vatican Council women will certainly be present."[18] Muench was not "comforted." She launched a campaign on behalf of women; she submitted two petitions that called for changes in church rhetoric, canon law, and liturgy. She received support from Dr. Gertrud Heinzelmann, a Catholic lawyer from Switzerland, who challenged the church's implicit Thomistic argument for banning women from the priesthood.

European Catholic women's organizations pelted the Vatican with petitions for recognition of women's presence in the church. The Saint Joan's International Alliance, an English organization, which for over thirty years had been fighting for equal rights for women in the church including ordination, had turned its attention to the council at its 1963 general meeting. Its third petition requested that women be invited to the council as experts.[19] Two earlier petitions of 1959 and 1961 reiterated their concern for a larger role for women in the church. The Central Union of Catholic Women's and Mothers' Communities, located in West Germany, sent an eleven-page letter entitled "Wishes of Catholic Women, Mothers and Married Couples Addressed to the Ecumenical Council." Pilar Bellosillo, President of the World Union of Catholic Women's Organizations (WUCWO), after learning that laymen were to be invited as auditors to the council requested the same honor for women. She argued that men could not represent women in a male dominated church that perpetuated this imbalance through the practice of convening all male councils. Instead, women must present their own viewpoints on such issues as birth control, the family and the training of priests.

As mentioned earlier, American women were less active than European women. While the articles in *Ave Maria* and *America* and the work of the NCCW archives illustrated that the absence of women from the council was a vital issue for American women, no evidence has been found of any concerted action. In 1964 Katherine Burton, a columnist for *The Sign,* noted that "it was rather odd that, in this republic [U.S.A.] of ours, no such plea [for women's presence] was heard."[20] She attributed this, in part, to the fact that the role of American Catholic women in their church has been chiefly one of charity and "yes, Father."

Calls for the presence of women began to have an impact in the council's second session during debates on the schema regarding the laity and religious. The arrival of the male lay auditors made the absence of women from the council more conspicuous. "Now people in the Council spoke, not only of the 'separated brothers'. . . , but also of the 'separated sisters,' meaning the wives and colleagues of the lay auditors who were not allowed to accompany them to the Council."[21] Theologian Karl Rahner, who had come under fire for his comments on the feminization of the church, now spoke on woman's behalf. Acknowledging the current and future work of women, he called for their full recognition as members of the lay apostolate: "Theoretically, this position of equality is no longer being disputed, but in practice much still remains to be desired. For example, although laymen were admitted to the Council, there were no women."[22]

He stressed that priests and bishops needed to respect women and not view their work and position in the church as subordinate. The full independence, dignity, and responsibilities of women must be recognized by the church.

At a press conference on October 4, 1963 the Archbishop René Stourm of Sens, France, announced that a proposal to admit women as auditors was currently under consideration by the Commission on the Lay Apostolate. Two days later journalist Henri Fesquet was questioning the absence of women but from the position of a gradualist. He wrote, "There is no reason women can't be at the Council, but we must let things mature. They will perhaps be invited to the third session or another Council. In any event, male auditors were invited to be spokesmen for women's organizations as well."[23] Fesquet was overly pessimistic in his assumptions. Just over two weeks later on October 22, 1963 at the end of the second session, Cardinal Leo Suenens of Malines-Brussels made the final push for the presence of women at the council. Father Placid Jordan, O.S.B., of the NCWC news service explained that Suenens's recommendation was "understood to be the result of a joint initiative taken by laymen now auditing council sessions. The auditors had officially approached the cardinal moderators of the council and suggested that the time had come to give serious consideration to the admission of women."[24] Suenens made the appeal in a speech on the laity and the church:

> In order to demonstrate in a concrete way the Council's conviction in this area, we hoped that the number of lay auditors would be increased and the ways of recruiting them broadened; that, among them, women might be appointed because they represent half of humanity; and finally that representatives of men religious who were not priests and of women religious be appointed.[25]

Suenens knew that as long as women and male religious were excluded, the council would not be representative of the whole church. Three days after Suenens's speech Jordan reported that Bellosillo was expected in Rome later that month to discuss the question of women auditors with council authorities. The results of that meeting were not evident until ten months later.

On September 12, 1963 Pope Paul VI announced his intention to invite women. His announcement was unexpected. As late as two days before the pope's speech, spokesmen for ecclesiastical circles in Rome stated, "There will be no women at the Council." In light of *L'Osservatore Romano*'s silence on the decision and the absence of a list of women, the news services doubted that women would be invited.[26] Pope Paul VI had no doubts. He explained his intentions at the time of the announcement, "These measures were taken so that women will know how much the church honors them in their human dignity and in their Christian and human mission . . ."[27] Reflecting on the invitation, Burton provided a distinctive perspective on this event: "When we keep saying that women are half the church, as well as half the world, don't forget that it is men—the Pope, the more forward-looking among the prelates, the understanding laymen—who are making our breakthrough a fact."[28]

Burton's rather deferential statement implies that the fate of women's presence at the council was in the bishops' hands. If these men had not chosen to listen to and act on behalf of the women, then women would have remained outside the council and voiceless. Women, Burton pronounced, would now see the pope as their pope and his action as a validation of women's viewpoints.[29]

As the bishops submitted the names of lay and religious women to be considered, the names of auditors were released gradually. As a result of the meeting with Bellosillo, the leaders of national and international associations were invited in order to avoid charges of discrimination among the religious orders and local organizations. Originally fifteen women were invited and as the council continued eight more women received invitations. *The Tablet* published the names of the original fifteen women: Alda Micelli of Italy, president general of the Regalita di Cristo Missionaries; Pilar Bellosillo of Spain, president of the World Union of Catholic Women's Organizations; Rosemary Goldie of Australia, executive secretary of COPECIAL; Marie-Louise Monet of France, president of the International Middle Class Movement; Anna Maria Roeloffzen of the Netherlands, secretary of the International Federation of Young Catholic Women; Amalia Cordero Lanza Montezemolo of Italy, president of the Organization for the Spiritual Assistance to the Armed Forces; Iduccia Marenco Grillo of Italy of the Women's Union of Italian Catholic Action; Mother Sabine de Valon of France, superior general of the Dames du Sacre Coeur and president of the Union of Superiors General; Mother Mary Luke [Tobin] of the United States, superior general of the Sisters of Our Lady of Lorreto and head of the Conference of Major Superiors of Women Religious in the United States; Mother Marie de la Croix Khouzam of Egypt, superior general of the Egyptian Sisters of the Sacred Heart and president of the Egyptian Teaching Sisters' Union; Mother Marie-Henriette Ghanam of Lebanon, superior general of the Order of the Sacred Hearts of Jesus and Mary and president of the Assembly of Superiors General; Mother J. Julian of Germany of the Poor Handmaids of Jesus Christ and secretary general of the Union of German Superiors General; Mother Guillemin of France, superior general of the Daughters of Charity; Mother Estrada of Spain, superior general of the Handmaids of the Sacred Heart; Mother Constantina Baldinucci of Italy, superior general of the Institute of Maria Santissima Bambina and president of the Italian Sisters Union.[30] Two women invited late in the third session were Mother M. Claudia Feddish of the order of Saint Basil the Great of the Mount Saint Marcia and Catherine A. McCarthy of the United States, the 1963 delegate to the World Union of Catholic Women's Organizations and president of the NCCW.

Two days after his announcement, Pope Paul VI presented his welcoming speech to an empty *auditrices'* box.[31] The sequence of events regarding the announcement and invitations is unclear. Rosemary Lauer stated that the pope had first considered inviting women when the list of men auditors was compiled. McEnroy reported that he had been disappointed by the absence of women. According to Alice Curtayne, the decision to invite women was made early in the second session. She contended that the *auditrices'* box was empty because Rome had moved slowly in contacting the women. At the time of the pope's speech most had not received official confirmation of their appointment. She explained that many of the women proceeded to Rome as soon as they were notified of their status and despite the delays in putting their names on the list and sending formal invitations. She speculated on the reason for the lag.

> The conclusion was inescapable that not all the Roman authorities read the signs of the times with equal enthusiasm. The women's presence therefore represented a significant victory over narrow-minded anti-feminist conservatism.[32]

Even with the delays, women were pleased with this limited achievement. Tobin, having acted upon Suenens's earlier urging for women religious to come to Rome, was already in transit when she received word of her invitation. The news was "thrilling" to her:

> This door, swinging open to admit fifteen women from different parts of the Roman Catholic world, represented an unexpected sign of hope. It signaled at least a minimal awareness of the questions women were asking and some recognition of their secondary status in the church. True, fifteen women among twenty-five hundred bishops was hardly a "quota," but it was a beginning.[33]

Aggiornamento had opened the church not only to the world but to all the people of God.

Unfortunately the door had not swung fully open. Restrictions had been placed upon the women. The limitations reflected their marginal status at the council and in the church. They would attend only those general congregations at which questions regarding women were being debated, meet with council members between meetings, sit beside and not with the male lay auditors, and frequent only the women's coffee bar.

Gradually the women overcame their marginal status and moved closer to the center of the council with the help of the men. The men invited the women to their weekly meetings that entailed theologians discussing the currently debated schema. They worked with the women to ensure that interventions made by the auditors represented them all, and supported some of the council leaders' complaints that the women religious were not being given an adequate voice in the writing of the document on religious life. These men did not believe that it was enough to allow the women to speak freely in subcommission meetings; they held that women should speak in their own voices on the council floor. The council leaders could not expect the women to sit quietly and watch men discuss women's problems. During the debate on Schema 13, "The Church in the Modern World," the lay auditors requested that Bellosillo speak before the council members on the question of women in the world. To the dismay of the men auditors and some of the bishops, their proposal was rejected by the secretary general of the council. The fact that this decision was not reversed by the pope implies that he was in favor of the prohibition.

Despite the set backs there were advancements. The women's and men's efforts wrought change. Tobin wrote of how the women attended those general sessions they wanted to attend and not just the sessions on women. Bellosillo in an open letter published in the NCCW's publication *Word* reported that between the third and fourth sessions the women and men auditors studied the issues in order to be prepared to contribute to the commission on Schema 13, and religious and laywomen auditors created their own study group to examine issues pertaining to women.[34] The most important change can be attributed, in part, to Cardinal Prefect Emilio Guano and Coordinating Secretary, the Redemptorist moral theologian, Bernard Haring. They stated openly that they believed if the women were to be present then they should be members of the document commissions. Consequently Goldie, Guillemin, Bellosillo, Monnet, Vendrik and Tobin attended the mixed commission meetings on Schema 13 as full voting members.[35] Tobin stated that once there, "we were allowed to speak as freely as we wished and in whatever language we chose; and each of us did speak."[36] Women were also active in the commission on the laity and influenced the drafts of most documents still in committee. However, they remained banned from the Committee on Religious Life until the end.

Progress also occurred outside the council walls. The women auditors were invited to attend the daily press conferences. On two occasions, Tobin was asked to sit with the theologians and experts and to speak as the expert on women religious.[37] This achievement, added to those gains attained within the council, brought the women closer to a realization of their goal of general recognition.

Women auditors were determined to gain respect for women's full status as members of the human family and of the church, and recognition of their ability to speak on their own behalf. Periodic setbacks reminded them that they still had far to go to overcome centuries of discrimination. Tobin recounted a patronizing attempt by the bishops to counter the discrimination shown women. A "flowery" passage of praise for women was read for the auditors upon which they were to comment. Surprised by the women's lack of response, the author asked why the women were not pleased with it. Tobin recalled Goldie's reply and her own reaction:

> Pressed for a response, Rosemary answered: "You can omit all the flowery adjectives, the pedestals and incense, from your sentence. All that women ask for is that they be recognized as the full human persons they are, and treated accordingly." I do not believe that to this day [1985] the bishops who were present then have understood what Rosemary meant to convey. This episode represents to me the state of ignorance of the problem at the time of Vatican II.[38]

Tobin and Goldie realized that the aspirations of the women remained a fundamental problem for the council "fathers." Tobin's reflections on the council's closing ceremonies illustrated how far the council members had come in the course of the council and how much farther they had to go toward understanding the needs and desires of women:

> On the last day of the Council, a great outdoor Mass was celebrated in front of Saint Peter's. At its conclusion, part of the program involved the presentation of certificates of honor to distinguished persons in various categories. Four philosophers, for example, were so honored; they walked across the platform and received from the hands of the Pope some special insignia of recognition. Then four literati, four musicians, and so on, were

singled out for praise. Finally, four women walked across the stage. And the announcer proclaimed that "women should be honored for their contribution to the Church."

I turned to my nearest neighbor in the bleachers, [Father Godfrey Diekmann, O.S.B.], and said, "But women are not a *category* in the church. They should not be honored as women more than men should be honored as men. Men and women are the church, aren't they?"

Father Godfrey looked at me and said, "You're right, Sister; you women need to help us see this."[39]

Tobin must have been ready to ask him if men were deaf and blind. Had they not heard the cries of the women and not seen the work of their hands? At the Second Vatican Council, the bishops recognized women, but through the lens of tradition. Consequently, it was not the recognition envisioned by Mealey and Goldie in 1961. As Tobin told Diekmann, women are not a *category* in the church, they are full and equal members. At the council, women moved beyond the role assigned to them. They were expected to be like the statues of female saints, *silent and unwanted.* But, they came to life and within the walls of the council hall began to rewrite the roles prescribed and ascribed to women.

Conclusion

Tobin's experience at the council gave her hope regarding the future of women in the church. "No woman has spoken, not yet. This is something for the future if ever. It is wonderful that we got here at all."[40] Twenty years later she still saw it as a significant advancement, but not in such optimistic terms:

For me, in regard to the status of women, Vatican II was an opening, although just a tiny crack in the door, to a recognition of the vast indifference to women and the ignoring of their potential for the whole body of the church.[41]

Advancement has not come as quickly as Tobin expected in 1965. The full church membership envisioned by the women of the 1960s is still sought by the women of the 1990s—that of a full and equal membership in which *woman* is not a *category*. Most women today understand that as long as men have sole voice in the church, and seminarians are educated apart from women, women will remain merely a *category*. Today, changes are coming, albeit slowly, but they are coming.

Dolores R. Leckey, executive director of the Committee on the Laity for the National Conference of Catholic Bishops, shortly after the 1987 synod on the laity, published her reflections on the changes that had taken place in the church since the Second Vatican Council. Four of the seven observations pertained directly to the status of women in the church. What they revealed is that the question of *woman* had shifted from the debate as to whether or not there is a question worth considering, to the individual questions surrounding the situation of women in the church.

Within the course of the Second Vatican Council women moved from barely receiving any recognition to recognition as a *category* still largely dependent upon the power of men. Leckey's reflections conveyed the fact that the church changes in barely detectable increments. When looking at councils and synods for signs of change the final documents cannot be the only evidence examined. Conciliar documents on the questions of women are disappointing to read. The advances made at Vatican II and since are not found in the statements but in the actions behind the documents.

The Second Vatican Council offers an example of the discrepancy which can exist between woman's official role and woman's actual role in the church. At the council women moved beyond their limited role as auditors—silent submissive observers. The women worked with the men auditors on interventions, they participated in study sessions, met with council members, spoke at press conferences, and were full and voting members of commissions and subcommissions. They helped shape conciliar documents which continue to shape the church today. While all these achievements may not be officially recognized by the church and are limited at best, Catholic women must reclaim and proclaim them as vital developments in church history.

Elisabeth Schüssler Fiorenza, in her work *In Memory of Her: A Feminist Theological Reconstruction of Christian Origins*, stressed the importance of reconstructing women's history. She turned to Judy Chicago's play *The Dinner Party: A Symbol of Our Heritage*, in order to illustrate her point: "All the institutions of our culture tell us through words, deeds, and even worse silence that we are insignificant. Our heritage is our power."[42]

The reconstruction of women's history enables women to define their identity, gain a sense of power, and shape their future. Schüssler Fiorenza wrote, "if history in general, . . . is one way in which androcentric culture and religion have defined women, then it must become a major object for feminist analysis."[43] Feminist church historians must reject heuristic concepts which limit their perception of women to biological function or sociological cast. Androcentric heuristic models prevent feminist historians from seeing women's lives outside the traditionally prescribed spheres and permit women to view themselves only as objects of oppression. When this happens, women forfeit their right to claim an active role in history and help to perpetuate the image of themselves as powerless children. The task of historians is to recover instances when women have been not only victims, but also agents by seeking "instead for heuristic models that explore women's historical participation in social-public development and their efforts to comprehend and transform social structures."[44] Locating times when women challenged and moved beyond their roles enables the historian to move women's history from the periphery of church history and closer to its center. Thereby, women's roles in shaping the church are more fully recognized and "woman's" history is no longer a special category. Women's history, as does men's history, becomes "man's and woman's" history.

Elizabeth Johnson's work also illustrates the significance of the Second Vatican Council for women. In her book, *She Who Is: The Mystery of God in Feminist Theological Discourse*, she stated clearly that symbols function.[45] She stressed that women need to search church history and theology for the means by which to redefine those symbols which are used to limit women. The events of Vatican II offer the means by which to reconfigure the potentially destructive symbols of the council: the title of "auditor"; the delays in sending the invitations; the restrictions placed upon the women auditors; and the prohibition against them speaking on the council floor. Most council members may have intended for the women's presence to be merely symbolic. The women were to be simply silent observers—auditors; to hold an empty position in order to quiet women's plea for change.

By reconstructing—not recreating—women's history at Vatican II, we see that the council becomes more fully an empowering moment in church history. It offers women a means by which to appropriate the symbol of the Second Vatican Council as a moment of *aggiornamento* for women and the church. The power of an ecumenical council as a symbol of woman's subordination is diminished. At the Second Vatican Council, the women moved beyond the roles prescribed for them by the council leaders. They spoke within the commissions with their own voices and influenced the shape of the documents and their future. They were active agents and not just passive victims. The women and their activity are symbols that may be used to support the movement for the full participation of women in the church. The movement can draw strength from the fact that women spoke in their own voices at an ecumenical council.

Notes

[1] M. Carmel McEnroy, R.S.M., who is in the process of completing a book on women at Vatican II deserves much credit for recognizing the significance of the topic. She has conducted the very important work of interviewing the surviving women auditors, and the friends and associates of those women who have died. Her book, expected out shortly, is entitled, *Guests in Their Own House: The Women of Vatican II.* She has already published an essay based on her early interviews, "Women of Vatican II: Recovering a Dangerous Memory," in *The Church in the Nineties: Its Legacy, Its Future*, ed. Pierre Hegy (Collegeville: Liturgical Press, 1993), pp. 149-57.

[2] "Nine Lay Leaders Suggest More Ideas for Vatican Council," *The Sign* 41 (October 1961): 14.

[3] "Nine Lay Leaders," 15.

[4] Although this article was published in February of 1964, I have placed it in the period prior to the invitation, because its contents suggest that it was written and printed prior to Pope Paul VI's invitation.

[5] Rosemary Goldie, "Women in the Church," *The Month* 31 (February 1964): 79.

[6] Goldie, working in Rome since 1958, was in a position to make this criticism. Executive Secretary of COPECIAL, "she was directly involved, though unofficially, in conciliar preparations." See McEnroy, 152.

[7] "Women in the Church," *America* 107 (November 3, 1962): 972.

[8] "Women in the Church," 973.

[9] The panel consisted of well-educated women who were active in the church. Of the ten, eight had earned bachelor degrees and three had earned advanced degrees, one of which was a medical degree. The panel: Virginia Beck Smith, Rose Lucey, Merope Kersten, Mary Holub, Mary Houck, Pat Somers Cronin, Helen

Youngpeter, Sally Leighton, Dr. Lena Edwards, M.D. (an African-American), and Sr. Jacqueline Grennan, S.L.

Ave Maria did not publish the author's name. In "the editor's desk" column for the September 19, 1964 issue, John Reedy, C.S.C., the editor and publisher explained that "Our editors raised questions and assembled answers." Assuming that the editors were only those listed for that issue, no women were among the interviewers or the writers. The editors: John Reedy, C.S.C., William J. Jacobs, Kenneth W. Peters, Thomas Hoobler, Justin Soleta, and Robert Griffin, C.S.C..

[10] "The Woman and the Council: Will Her Voice be Heard?" *Ave Maria* 100 (October 3, 1964): 26.

[11] "The Woman and the Council," 26.

[12] "The Woman and the Council," 26.

[13] "The Woman and the Council," 26.

[14] The differences in perceptions of council atmosphere raise further questions regarding the events leading to the inviting of women to the council. The tone of Ms. Jung's article was at times near angry and bitter. A stridency was not represented in the comments of Goldie, Tobin and Bellosillo.

[15] During the first two sessions, the women journalists were not received on equal footing with their male counterparts. Michael Novak relayed the story of one woman journalist who attempted to receive communion at a council mass. "As about twenty of them rose to join the lay auditors at communion, a young American woman, Miss Eva Fleischner, a member of the Grail and a correspondent for *Ecumenical Notes*, was the last in line on her way toward the communion rail. A male functionary motioned emphatically that she should stop. He motioned again, violently. Since the other members of the press, all men, were approaching the rail, she tried to hurry forward. The man physically restrained her; he would not let her receive communion." Women journalists were not allowed in the council hall after this incident. Novak reports from "good sources" that this decision came from Pope Paul VI. The explanation offered for this scandalous behavior of depriving women of the Eucharist was that the pope was being besieged by sister superiors, asking that nuns be allowed in the council. To avoid giving them further ground for argument, the pope sacrificed recognition of other women. Michael Novak, *The Open Church, Vatican II, Act II* (New York: The Macmillan Company, 1964), 202-3.

On the other hand, McEnroy, in her article, offered an amusing story about a woman journalist which illustrated the changed atmosphere between the first two and last two sessions.

[16] Eva-Maria Jung, "Women at the Council: Spectators or Collaborators?" *The Catholic World* 200 (February 1965): 277.

[17] Jung, 277.

[18] Jung, 277.

[19] Jung, 279.

[20] Katherine Burton, "Women Get Inside the Council," *The Sign* 44 (November 1964): 43.

[21] Jung, 280.

[22] Karl Rahner, "Equality for Women in the Church," *U.S. Catholic* 30 (September 1964): 62.

[23] Henri Fesquet, *The Drama of Vatican II, The Ecumenical Council, June, 1962-December, 1965*, trans. Bernard Murchland (New York: Random House, 1967), 147.

[24] Floyd Anderson, ed., *Council Day Book, Vatican II Session 1, October 11 to December 8, 1962, Session 2, September 29 to December 4, 1963* (Washington, D.C.: National Catholic Welfare Conference, 1965), 217.

[25] "Cardinal Suenens (Malines-Bruxelles)," *La Documentation Catholique* no. 1413 (December 1963): 1565. Translated by editor.

[26] Fesquet, 296-97.

[27] Fesquet, 296-97.

[28] Burton, 43.

[29] Burton, 43.

[30] "The New Men and Women Auditors," *The Tablet* 218 (October 3, 1964): 1123.

[31] The pope welcomed the women with these words: "And we are delighted to welcome among the auditors our beloved daughters in Christ, the first women in history to participate in a conciliar assembly." Floyd Anderson, ed., *Council Daybook, Vatican II, Session 3* (Washington, D.C.: National Catholic Welfare Conference, 1965), 10.

[32] Alice Curtayne, "The Council and Women," *Christus Rex* 20 (October, November, December, 1966): 270.

[33] Mary Luke Tobin, S.L., *Hope Is an Open Door*, (Nashville: Abingdon, 1981), 19-20.

[34] Pilar Bellosillo, "Auditors, Active, Effective," *Word* 2 (February 1965): 12-13.

[35] McEnroy, 154-5.

[36] Mary Luke Tobin, S.L., "Women in the Church: Vatican II and After," *The Ecumenical Review* 37 (July 1985): 296.

[37] Curtayne, 270.

[38] Tobin, "Women in the Church," 296.

[39] Tobin, *Hope*, 30-1.

[40] Adolph Schalk, "The Church and Women," *U.S. Catholic* 31 (September 1965): 22.

[41] Tobin, "Women in the Church," 296.

[42] Elisabeth Schüssler Fiorenza, *In Memory of Her: A Feminist Theological Reconstruction of Christian Origins*, (New York: Crossroad Publishing Co., 1985), xiv.

[43] Schüssler Fiorenza, xix-xx. Schüssler Fiorenza presents her methodology for reconstructing woman's history in the first part of *In Memory of Her.*

[44] Schüssler Fiorenza, 86.

[45] Elizabeth A. Johnson, *She Who Is: The Mystery of God in Feminist Theological Discourse* (New York: Crossroad Publishing Company, 1993).

Part II

ADDING VOICES

Hardness of Hearing, Muted Voices:
Listening for the Silenced in History

Mary Rose D'Angelo

When I was invited to contribute to this session named with Nelle Morton's phrase, "hearing one another into speech," my thoughts were drawn to areas of feminist exchange in which the relationship of hearing and speaking continues to be interrupted by silences that impoverish feminist theological discourse. The issue of silence is a particularly acute one for me. Listening for the remains of "lesser lives" in the ancient world requires an effort to undo many centuries of silence, misrepresentation and ignorance.[1] Attempting to hear the voices or even the echoes of women in the origins of Christianity means listening for resonances of those who were unheard in the past, and who have been further silenced not only by design but also by neglect. This enterprise is made more difficult by the ways in which silences and silencing function in our present.

An incident that took place at a feminist theological conference I participated in some years ago gave me a heightened consciousness of the ways that silence operates in my own historical thinking. As is so often the case at feminist meetings, the conversational interludes of that gathering were occupied with a running evaluation of the conference. One continuous thread consisted of complaints that lesbian voices had been silenced at the conference and the issue of lesbians in theology was being suppressed; a continuous counter-thread dismissed these complaints. Knowing the organizers of the conference, I was inclined to discount, or at least evade these discussions.

The panel in which I was a presenter was a response to a stirring plenary presentation by Phyllis Trible on texts from the Hebrew Bible; it took place in the basement of Riverside Church, and, not too surprisingly, did not touch on the issue of lesbianism in any way. During the discussion that followed the presentations, a young woman minister from Maine stood up and, gesturing at the buttresses, arches, and whatevers flying over our heads, began a rambling question that touched on lesbians, anonymous cathedral builders, difference, silence, history and biblical interpretation. As I struggled to find the thread, the chair of the panel responded, "Let me see if I can repeat what I hear you saying. You're saying that, that when I'm preaching in my church in midtown Manhattan, you want me to think about how what I'm saying about the Bible would be heard by someone, say, a Nicaraguan coffee picker."

Of course, that was what the questioner wanted, except that what she wanted the preachers, readers, commentators and so on to think about was how a *lesbian* would hear the Bible itself, interpretation of the Bible and the multitudinous traditional and novel readings of Christian history. She wanted to know where the lesbians were, both in the history and among the historians.

The sudden appearance of a Nicaraguan coffee picker in a mainline Protestant church in midtown Manhattan during the Sandinista years gave me the jolt I needed to recognize the operation of the silence I had heard so much about. Unlike me, the panel chair had understood the question. The coffee picker had come on the scene partly because she had put thought and energy into the concerns of Nicaragua, and partly, I fear, because she thought that she was being sensitive to the questioner, that tact and sensitivity required that she not say the word "lesbian."

Completely embarrassed by now, I struggled to respond to the rest of the woman's question about work being done by lesbians and about lesbians on the Bible and history, referring her to the very limited historical work I knew about.[2] I also summarized an article I was contemplating, on paired women's names in the New Testament as indicating women's missionary partnerships. "But," I said, puzzled and worried, "I can't really tell you what you're asking. Even if I know someone is a lesbian and is out in some contexts, I can't tell you that she is a lesbian and has written such and such an article. That would be unethical on my part; it would endanger her."

"But that helps," my questioner replied; "it helps to have you admit that."

This experience has had a very unsettling effect on me; it did push me to write and publish the article on women partners.[3] And it has left me with a continuing and queasy sense of the operation of silence in my own work. Over and over I've discovered my reluctance to pursue many kinds of questions, both when they are put to me directly and when I know them to be an issue in the class, group, or audience. My silences are in fact like the evasion the panel chair used—they are inspired by anxiety about putting others on the spot, making their vulnerability visible, "outing" them. The conference planners had intended that the confrontation of theology and lesbian existence be addressed, but their intentions had been frustrated by a failure in communications with the one speaker who was expected to address this issue. It matters little whether the crucial information was unheard or unsaid. Such failures are inevitable in a society which requires that realities which are most central, most acutely important to people must be protected by silences that also deny them. No deliberate choice is necessary to silence such issues. The reflexes acquired by living with patriarchy are perfectly adequate to accomplish their goals without needing attention from the conscious mind.

This brief reflection will focus on three areas which require struggle to retrain hearing and speaking to decode the interactions of speech and silence in ancient and contemporary religious discourse: sexuality and biblical imagery, twentieth-century racism and ancient patterns of domination, the representation of Judaism in ancient and contemporary Christianity.

The first of these, sexual imagery, is an area in which feminist hearing ought to be, and often is, acute. But there are significant areas in which ancient and twentieth century silencing continue. One of these is the interface between sex workers' exploited lives and the biblical imagery of the prostitution in Christian discourse. While some feminist biblical scholars have analyzed the ways that this imagery endangers and degrades all women, its effect on the lives of sex workers is rarely noticed.[4] Prostitution is used both to name greed, ingratitude and exploitation and to displace the blame for these vices onto their victims. By charging sex workers with profiting inappropriately from their own bodies, the metaphorical use of prostitution conceals the reality of the millions of women sex workers who in fact do not profit from their alienated labor, whose status and lives differ little from those of the slaves and non-citizen women who performed sexual service in antiquity. This reality is increasingly named by feminists and feminist theologians of the southern countries, especially those of southeast Asia. In an important recent collection of "third-world" feminist theology, at least half the essays in a section on "Women's Pain and Oppression" describe its horrors, and at least one names the church's discourse as increasing the misery of women sex workers.[5] But none of the essays in the section on biblical interpretation connects their pain with the biblical texts that collaborate in the demonization of sex workers. This omission is to some degree the result of the section title: "The Bible as Source of Women's Empowerment." For these women (or at least for their "first world" editor), the biblical text is too powerful and too dangerous to be confronted; its power can only be invoked where it is beneficent, and offers an ally against society and/or the church. It is unsafe to speak too clearly of its role as an oppressor.[6]

Another type of sexual imagery from antique religion that has recently come into vogue is the image of the androgyne. References to androgynes and to male-females, the use of male and female imagery and names for divine beings and exhortations to or promises of an existence that is neither male nor female are widely read by scholars of early Christianity and gnosticism as religious hopes for transcendence of sexuality that promised wholeness of being to men or inclusion into the world of intellect or spirit for women.[7] Marie Delcourt, whose studies of the androgyne first aroused the interest of scholars of religion, made clear that ancient uses of the androgyne as an ideal are always purely ideal; a real human being born with defective or dual sexual organs was greeted as monstrous and disposed of with the violence and ritual that could be hoped to avert its ominous state.[8] I began to work on this imagery out of the suspicion with which feminists increasingly regarded this imagery.[9] But I never considered the plight of human beings whose bodies fail to meet the standards of sexual binary opposition, until one summer school participant very discreetly excused herself from the next day's sessions to accompany her eighteen-year-old niece, born with incomplete sexual definition, to corrective surgery. The percentage of intersexuals has been estimated to be as high as four percent of the population at birth.[10] For them, as for those who experience their sex and their gender at odds, transcending gender and sexuality is an experience of social and often surgical torture.[11] In the religious idealization of androgyny, as in the religious demonization of sex workers, the sleight of symbolism distracts the ear from acute human pain.

Racial difference is another context in which hearing and speaking across the centuries are distorted by silences and silencing. Here a complicated nexus of forces comes into play. The silences of antiquity differ from but collaborate with the silences of contemporary social realities. The color-based racism that afflicts western societies appears to have been unknown to antiquity; arguments that locate the emergence of this type of racism in the colonial periods are generally convincing.[12] Thus biblical texts, like other texts from the ancient world, rarely give information that would enable us to see them as speaking to or about race. Yet the structures of ancient slave-based societies, including Roman law on slavery, were reinstantiated in U.S. slavery and so have been formative in American racism. Not only the social arrangements but also the imagery of the New Testament texts derive from a slave-holding society. The African-American New Testament scholar Clarice Martin has delineated the way this reality is obscured by translations of *doulos* (slave) and related terms that accommodate the text to the hearing of the more privileged sectors of the Bible's twentieth-century audience.[13] When Paul uses this term of himself, it is translated "servant" (Phil 1:1, Phm 1:1).[14] Thus Paul's servitude to God is translated in terms that can make it a model for the mostly white, mostly male, mostly middle class translators. On the other hand, the household codes exhort "slaves" (*douloi*) to obey their masters; the (mostly white, mostly male, mostly middle class) translators do not expect these commands to be taken as a model, since they assume slavery (though not domestic service) has disappeared. In fact, a variety of official or virtual forms of slavery continue or have been invented in this last half of the twentieth century; they are largely organized along racial lines, and especially (but not exclusively) affect the lives of women domestic workers, sex workers, and "mail-order brides." For these women, the household codes in demanding submission of wives and obedience of slaves and sacralizing the master/lord make the Christian message a particularly deadly one.

Thus the biblical texts, relatively innocent on the issue of race, in the guise of decidedly compromised translations, produce a biblical silence on this issue that is exacerbated by a variety of hearing problems among white feminists that often leave women of color in a double bind. At some points white feminists have objected to the preference of African-American women interpreters for dwelling on the story of Hagar, asking why they didn't consider other biblical women. This failure to see attention to Hagar the African as an entry point from which to construct a new hermeneutical approach seems to proceed from a need to minimize the problems of race.[15] On the other hand, after local, semi-popular presentations by African-American feminist theologians, I have heard white feminist scholars object that the speakers weren't speaking so that "their people" could understand, perhaps that their talks were pitched at too high an intellectual level, or that they did not use the rhetorical and dialectical style associated with the black church. This reaction rather than trivializing particularity, absolutizes it, containing black women and the black congregation in a single identity. It is possible to look at the factors that these critics may have missed, like the way that complexity of multiple identities requires the most sophisticated and rigorous analytic tools and the need of African-American communities to see that their own spokespersons are in no way lacking in such tools.[16] But it seems more important to reflect upon white feminist hardness of hearing around particularity in intercultural feminist discourse.

Different issues arise around feminist attempts to deal with another particularity on which the Bible is far from silent. The New Testament is at almost every point concerned with representing Judaism, and collectively the representations of its texts absorb the Hebrew Bible into an "Old Testament" that can function in Christian communities to indict the Jews as other. Judith Plaskow has repeatedly described the ways that the first Christian feminist attempts to address the Bible extended and exploited the early Christian apologetic, attributing whatever was patriarchal and restrictive of women to Hebrew or Jewish culture. She points especially to the problems of attempts to depict Jesus as a feminist; it can only be claimed that Jesus was a feminist or was concerned with the liberation of women by means of contrasting him with a negative representation of the Judaism(s) of his time.[17] Christian women (esp. Roman Catholic women) who have acknowledged the problem of anti-Judaism often continue to foster it by presenting Jesus' "opposition to (or by) the religious authorities of his day." This euphemism is pointless; anyone who has forgotten who these authorities are need only turn to the text. Thus it repeats the gospels' negative characterization of the Jewish leaders while pretending to cloak their Jewish identity. Further, it encourages the assumption that the Pharisees and/or the high priest had the kind of power the popes have had, and used it in similar ways. It badly distorts the diverse Judaisms of the period before 70.

Instead of resorting to euphemism, feminist Christian interpreters need to explicitly address the anti-Judaism of early Christian texts, extending the same hermeneutical suspicion we use on depictions of women to depictions of the Jews, by other Christian interpreters and by the New Testament texts, especially the gospels. Above I used the word "characterization"; it is increasingly recognized by scholars that the Pharisees and scribes of the gospels are characters created to fulfill literary roles as opponents.[18] These roles function not only to enhance the characterization of Jesus, but also to minimize conflict with the Romans. Learning to look for the imprint of imperial politics should be a major endeavor of feminist interpretation.[19]

In reconstructing the participation of women in early Christianity, Christian feminists need to focus upon a larger attempt to construct a religious history of women in antiquity.[20] Such an attempt requires collaboration among Christian and Jewish feminist scholars. The Judaisms of antiquity must be presented not merely as that out of which Christianity grew, but as the living source of a living community, the source out of which our Jewish sisters speak. And Christian feminists must be ready to hear Jewish feminist interpreters not only on the Jewish texts, but also on Christian texts.[21]

Sexuality, race and representing Judaism are not the only issues in which we need to speak more clearly in order to hear each other and the texts and traditions of ancient Christianity. Class and disability are two areas which come to mind, and there are doubtless others on which I have as yet no awareness. Feminist theologians and interpreters must cultivate a practice of speaking out in order to hear each other more fully into speech, of using silences only to listen, never to deny. Perhaps Adrienne Rich's words can give us a key to such a practice: "To question everything. To remember what it has been forbidden even to mention."[22]

Notes

[1] See on this Sandra R. Joshel, "Listening to Silence," *Work, Identity and Legal Status at Rome: A Study of the Occupational Inscriptions* (Norman, Okla. and London: University of Oklahoma Press, 1992), 3-24.

[2] Bernadette Brooten, "Paul's Views on the Nature of Women and Female Homoeroticism," *Immaculate and Powerful: The Female in Sacred Image and Social Reality* (edited by Clarissa W. Atkinson, Constance H. Buchanan and

Margaret M. Miles; Harvard Women's Studies in Religion Series; Boston: Beacon, 1985), 61-87; E. Ann Matter, "My Sister, My Spouse: Woman-Identified Women in Medieval Christianity," *Journal of Feminist Studies in Religion* 2 (1986), 81-94. Judith Brown, "Lesbian Sexuality in Renaissance Italy: The Case of Sister Benedetta Carlini," *Signs: Journal of Women in Culture and Society* 9 (1984), 751-758; *Immodest Acts: the Life of a Lesbian Nun in Renaissance Italy* (New York: Oxford University, 1986).

³ "Women Partners in the New Testament," *Journal of Feminist Studies in Religion* 6 (1990), 65-86.

⁴ See e.g. Tina Pippin, *Death and Desire: The Rhetoric of Gender in the Apocalypse of John* (Literary Currents in Biblical Interpretation; Louisville, KY: Westminster/John Knox, 1992), esp. 57-68; Susan R. Garrett, "Revelation," *Women's Bible Commentary* (ed. Carol A. Newman and Sharon H. Ringe; Louisville KY: Westminster/ John Knox, 1992), 377-382, esp. 382.

⁵ *Feminist Theology from the Third World: A Reader* (ed. Ursula King; London: SPCK; Maryknoll, NY: Orbis, 1994). See Ranjani Rebera, "Challenging Patriarchy," 105-112, Marianne Katoppo, "The Church and Prostitution in Asia," 114-122, Yayori Matsui, "Violence against Women in Development, Militarism, and Culture," 124-133, and the Asian Women's Consultation on Justice, Peace and Integrity of Creation, "Letter to the Women of the World," 177-179.

⁶ The exception in the collection is Elsa Tamez' article, "Women's Rereading of the Bible," 190-200. On the problems with use of the Bible for Latinas, see Ada María Isasi-Díaz, "The Bible and Mujerista Theology," in *Lift Every Voice: Constructing Christian Theologies from the Underside* (ed. Susan Brooks Thistlethwaite and Mary Potter Engels; San Francisco: Harper San Francisco, 1990), 261-267, esp. 265-267; Ivone Gebara, "The Face of Transcendence as a Challenge to the Reading of the Bible in Latin America" in *Searching the Scriptures: A Feminist Introduction* (ed. Elisabeth Schüssler Fiorenza; New York: Crossroad, 1993), 172-186, esp. 174-177; in the same volume, see Kwok Pui-lan on the use of the Bible against both women and indigenous cultures; "Racism and Ethnocentrism in Feminist Biblical Interpretation," 101-116.

⁷ See e. g. Wayne A. Meeks, "The Image of the Androgyne: Some Uses of a Symbol in Earliest Christianity," *History of Religions* 13 (1974); Dennis Ronald MacDonald, *There Is No Male and Female: The Fate of a Dominical Saying in Paul and Gnosticism* (Philadelphia; Fortress Press, 1983); Deirdre J. Good, "Gender and Generation: Observations on Coptic Terminology with Particular Attention to Valentinian Texts," in *Images of the Feminine in Gnosticism* (ed. Karen L. King; Philadelphia: Fortress, 1988), 23-40.

⁸ See Delcourt, *Hermaphrodite: Myths and Rites of the Bisexual Figure in Classical Antiquity*; translated from the French by Jennifer Nicholson (London: Studio Books, 1961), 43-46, 60. Diodorus Siculus recounts but deplores the execution of hermaphrodites in Italy; he insists that they are not monsters, nor are they really both male and female—rather "nature sketches falsely through the parts of the body" (32.12.1). See also Livy, 31.11-12, 27.37.

[9] D'Angelo, "The Androgyne Revisited: Imagining the Body in Antiquity," (Society of Biblical Literature Annual Meeting 1989): D'Angelo, "No 'Male and Female': Gen. 1:27 in Gal. 3:28" (Society of Biblical Literature Annual Meeting 1986); D'Angelo, " 'Woman from Man': Paul and the Debate over the Creation of Eve" (Society of Biblical Literature Annual Meeting 1985); D'Angelo, "The Garden Once and Not Again: 1 Cor. 11:11-12 as an Interpretation of Gen. 1:26," in *Intrigue in the Garden: Studies in the History of Exegesis of Genesis 1-3* (ed. Gregory Robbins; New York and Toronto: Edwin Mellen, 1988), 1-42.

[10] See Anne Fausto-Sterling, "How Many Sexes Are There?" *The New York Times*, OP-ED, Friday, March 12, 1993.

[11] See Fausto-Sterling and Amy Bloom, "The Body Lies," *New Yorker* (July 18, 1994), 38-49.

[12] See also Barbara Geller Nathanson, "Toward a Multicultural Ecumenical History of Women in the First Century/ies C.E." in Schüssler Fiorenza, ed., *Searching the Scriptures*, 272-273. For the basic case, see Frank M. Snowden, Jr., *Before Color Prejudice: The Ancient View of Blacks* (Cambridge, MA and London: Harvard University Press, 1983). For the rise of racism, see Martin Bernal, *Black Athena: The Afroasiatic Roots of Classical Civilization* (New Brunswick, NJ: Rutgers University Press, 1987-1993).

[13] Clarice J. Martin, "Womanist Interpretation of the New Testament: The Quest for Holistic and Inclusive Translation and Interpretation," *Journal of Feminist Studies in Religion* 6 (1990), 41-62. See also Martin, "The Haustafeln (Household Codes) in African American Biblical Interpretation: 'Free Slaves' and 'Subordinate Women,' " in *Stony the Road We Trod: African American Biblical Interpretation* (ed. Cain Hope Felder. Minneapolis: Fortress, 1991), 206-231.

[14] The NRSV offers the translation "slave" in footnotes.

[15] "Racism and Ethnocentrism," 113-114.

[16] On the multiple identities of women of color see Kwok Pui-lan, "Racism and Ethnocentrism," 111-112.

[17] Judith Plaskow, "Anti-Judaism in Christian Feminist Interpretation," 117-129.

[18] On the question of the role of the Pharisees see the survey in E. P. Sanders, *Jesus and Judaism*, 291-292; for a study of the characterization of the Jewish leaders in the gospels that takes literary concerns fully into account, see Elizabeth Struthers Malbon, "The Jewish Leaders in the Gospel of Mark: A Literary Study of Marcan Characterization," *Journal of Biblical Literature* 108 (1989): 259-281; also D'Angelo, "Re-membering Jesus: Women, Prophecy and Resistance in the Memory of the Early Churches," *Horizons: Journal of the College Theology Society* 19 (Fall, 1992): 199-218.

[19] See D'Angelo, "Re-membering Jesus," 199-218; D'Angelo, "*Abba* and 'Father': Imperial Theology and the Traditions about Jesus," *Journal of Biblical Literature* 111:4 (1992), 611-630; D'Angelo "Theology in Mark and Q: Abba and 'Father' in Context," *Harvard Theological Review* 85 (1992): 149-174.

[20] See Geller Nathanson, "Toward a Multicultural Ecumenical History," 272-

273; for a model of such a history, see Ross Shepard Kraemer, *Her Share of the Blessings: Women's Religions Among Pagans, Jews and Christians in the Greco-Roman World* (New York and Oxford; Oxford University Press, 1992).

[21] In addition to the works by Ross Kraemer and Barbara Geller Nathanson cited above, see Kraemer, "The Conversion of Women to Ascetic Forms of Christianity," *Signs* 6 (1980-81): 298-307, Amy-Jill Levine, "Who's Catering the Q Affair? Feminist Observations on Q Paranesis," *Semeia* 50 (1990): 145-161; Levine, "Matthew," *The Women's Bible Commentary* (Louisville, KY: Westminster, 1992), 252-262; Adele Reinharz, "From Narrative to History: The Resurrection of Mary and Martha," in Amy-Jill Levine (ed.) *"Women Like This": New Perspectives on Jewish Women in the Greco-Roman World* (SBL Early Judaism and Its Literature 1; Atlanta, GA: Scholars Press, 1991), 161-185; in the same volume, Kraemer, "Women's Authorship of Jewish and Christian Literature in the Greco-Roman Period," 221-242.

[22] Adrienne Rich, *On Lies, Secrets and Silences: Selected Prose 1966-1978* (New York: W.W. Norton, 1979), 13.

Emergent Feminist Theology from Asia

Kwok Pui-lan

Asia is the home for over half of the world's population. Divided into seven major linguistic zones, Asian people have lived for centuries in a multi-racial, multi-cultural, and multi-religious world. From Japan to Papua, New Guinea, and from the Philippines to Inner Asia, people live in different socio-political realities and divergent cultural worlds. Asian mental constructs, approaches to reality, ways of life, and spirituality are in many ways radically different from people in the West.

For centuries, Asian people were under the heavy yoke of Spanish, Dutch, British, French, and Japanese colonial powers. The United States was also deeply involved in the politics of Asia since the colonization of the Philippines. Women, the oppressed among the oppressed and the poor among the poor, were systematically exploited and sexually abused during the military encroachment of Asia. They suffered from unspeakable crimes and atrocities.

Even though many Asian countries regained their independence after the Second World War, the situation of women has not been greatly improved. Today, three-quarters of the world's illiterate population live in Asia. In Pakistan and Nepal, 80 percent of the women are illiterate, and the percentage in some parts of India and Bangladesh is also as high as 70 percent. In the Asian cities of Seoul, Manila, Jakarta, Bangkok, Taipei and Hong Kong, many women and young girls are working as prostitutes in the bars, nightclubs, discos, and other entertainment industries. This international flesh trade had flourished under the protection of local police and the military, and with the blessing of the international powers in the region.[1] Before the closing of American military bases in the Philippines, many hospitality girls, prostitutes, and waitresses worked in the vicinity of the bases. According to a recent report by the United Nations, among the 400,000 prostitutes in Thailand, more than 60 percent, or 250,000, are HIV positive. Behind each of these figures is a human body mutilated, defiled, and transgressed.

Although economic development in some Asian countries creates new job opportunities for women, many women are exploited because of sexual discrimination in the workplace. In factories and multi-national corporations in Hong Kong, Korea, and Singapore, many unskilled female workers work for long hours without adequate compensation and job security. Workers in some Asian countries are not allowed to organize into unions or to strike. In other Asian countries, unemployment and poverty drive many women to seek employment in other countries. In Hong Kong and Singapore, a growing number of Filipino women work as domestic helpers. Other Asian women are working in the Middle East and in other countries. These migrant female workers often find their host culture as alien and unfriendly, and they are often exploited in the foreign lands.

The situation of women in Asia calls for responses from women's organizations, civic groups, and churches. In the Philippines, GABRIELA has worked among the prostitutes, and in Thailand, Korea, India, and Japan, women's groups are beginning to form networks to effect changes in government policies. They have also called for international cooperation to address the ugly human flesh trade behind sex tourism.

Listening to the cry of our sisters, Asian women theologians begin to reread their Bible and reexamine the Christian heritage in an attempt to discern the liberating message. Increasingly we have found the kind of western theology we have learned is inadequate and inappropriate to address our situation. Who is this God who is said to be immovable, unchanging, unaffected by human suffering? Is this an idol or God? Who is this mysterious Jesus, who is said to be both God and human, and who has ascended into heaven to be united with the Father God? What has this Jesus to do with our salvation? We concur with other feminist theologians that we must liberate God from the bondage of male language and imagination, which speaks only from the experience of the rich, the powerful, and the dominant in society.

Faced with the difficult task of finding a new language for theology, Asian women theologians know that they have to reconnect with their Asian roots and spirituality. As one of their poems indicates:

Asia . . .
We pause in silence
Before the awesome reality of Asia,
Her vastness, variety and complexity,
Her peoples, languages, cultures,
The richness of history
And the present poverty of her peoples.
We take Asia to our hearts,
See her and feel her within us,
Embrace her
In her wholeness and brokenness,
While her rivers and tears flow through us,
Her winds, her sighs, her spirits,
Her moans, her howls blow within us.[2]

To embark on this new journey, Asian women theologians try to find new sources, symbols, images, stories that articulate our experiences. We do not live in the Christian culture alone, but in an enchanting world of gods and goddesses with colorful religious rituals, and many alternative forms of spirituality. For a long time, we have seen other religions as superstitious and idolatrous, having nothing to do with Christian faith. But as we begin to search for an authentic Asian voice, we find that we cannot close our ears to what the majority of the Asians are saying. Our sisters and brothers of other faiths make up 97 percent of the Asian population. As Asians, we speak the same tongue, we face the same harsh Asian reality, and we share hope for peace and justice in our societies. We can only speak of our Christian identity in relation to, and not in spite of, the indigenous traditions of our motherland. We are happy to know that religious pluralism, which is a key Asian theological issue, has occupied the attention of many theologians in the West.

The statement issued by the first Asian women's consultation on interfaith dialogue in 1989 clearly says that "as a result of religious discrimination, women of all religions continue to be marginalized and discriminated against at the societal level. And societal prejudices in turn influence religion in a cyclic fashion."[3] And as women trying to transform the world religions for the sake of our salvation, we have an obligation to empower each other by sharing what lies beyond patriarchy in our own traditions.[4]

Speaking this religious language of multiplicity and dialogue, Asian women theologians raise significant questions for theology. First, the whole understanding of revelation in the Christian tradition needs to be reconsidered. From the standpoint of us as Asians, revelation cannot be something that is sealed off and capsuled in the Bible which was written some two thousand years ago, and the majority of the Asian people had not participated in its conception and interpretation. From the perspective of Asian women, we are painfully aware that the voices that came to dominate and be embedded in the Bible are for the most part male, elitist, and patriarchal. As I have said some time ago, Asian women must reclaim the power to look at the Bible with our own eyes and come up with our own interpretative principles. The critical principle lies not in the Bible, but "in the community of women and men who read the Bible and who through their dialogical imagination appropriate it for their own liberation."[5]

Living in a multi-racial and multi-cultural world, Asians are challenged to reject the notion that truth is available only to a particular chosen people. The Chinese have always called their country the Middle Kingdom as if all other peoples are surrounding them as the center. Americans have also believed they are the chosen people and the Kingdom of God is found in America. The Jewish people have for centuries believed that they are the particular chosen people of Yahweh and they are to be the light of the nations. Today we must seriously ask ourselves do people of other faiths have a right to live or not. With honesty and integrity we have to answer the question whether at any time in our history, women have really been included in the chosen people or not.

The liberation of truth from the monopoly of one Bible or one people challenges us to reexamine some of the basic theological foundations of Christianity. Should we speak of one God or many gods, monotheism or polytheism? In his classic book *The Responsible Self*, H. Richard Niebuhr has posited a radical monotheism to guarantee the unity of the self.[6] Feminist theorists have questioned this androcentric understanding of the "self" and have begun to speak of the multiple selves and multiple identities of women. Catherine Keller has said: "Philosophically and theologically, a radical monism or monotheism too easily tempts us away from a truly multiple integrity."[7] Many Asian female Christians have begun to search for a way of approaching monotheism from a more inclusive point of view. Faith in God must lead us to listen to and have dialogue with other spiritual sources and truths.

Asian women are beginning to reinterpret the doctrine of Christology. For Asian feminists, the maleness of Jesus is a problem only if one is assuming a Chalcedonian, substantive understanding of Christ. Western doctrine has turned what Virginia Fabella has called a "historical accident" into an ontological necessity. Asian feminist theologians find Jesus liberating not as a male, but as a person who led a particular way of life.[8] The presence of many gods and goddesses in Asian religions also makes it easier for us to relativize the significance of the gender of God. Jesus exemplifies a way of relating to God and to the world that is significant for Christians. But Jesus is not the final, unique, or exclusive disclosure of God because no single human being can reveal God to the fullest extent. God is more encompassing and cosmological than we have hitherto assumed. Some Asian theologians have contrasted the western ontological understanding of incarnation which is tied to a single unique man with an Asian epiphanic understanding of incarnation in which Christ is one revelatory moment. In our ecological crisis, we might need to broaden our theological imagination to speak of God's incarnated presence in the trees, the rivers, the birds, and the stones as well.

Salvation brought forth by Christ applies not only to human beings alone, but to the whole groaning and mourning creation. Sin must not simply be construed as wrongdoing that individual persons have done. Christians must collectively try to find a new language to speak about sin. The Augustinian understanding that original sin comes into the world as a result of human sexuality does not help us address our modern crisis for it despises the body, the material world, and fertility. Sin, just as salvation, must be reconceived in a more wholistic way. Sin is stopping or obstructing the work of the Holy Spirit. Sin is when we break the great chains of beings. Sin is an offense against God, against our fellow human beings, and against the whole creation. Sin is the systematic and structural evil which allows a tiny minority of the human family to use up the resources meant for the existence of all. Sin is patriarchy which enables the male to subjugate the other half of the human race. Sin is the power and principalities which work against the oppressed, marginalized and the indigenous people. Sin is a situation with no love and compassion when we close our eyes and ears to the cry of people, rivers, and trees. Sin is the brokenness that drives us to despair.

I believe that some of the traditional ways of speaking about God, sin, and salvation do not help to address the issues we face in the modern world. For people in the Third World, this old style of doing theology is morally bankrupt because it has been used to legitimate cultural imperialism and exploitation of our inhabited earth. We are on the threshold of making Christianity more relevant to women's experiences, to the ecological crisis, and to the struggles of poor and oppressed people of the world. Christians in Asia are just learning to speak of Christianity that is not offensive to our Buddhist, Hindu, and Confucian friends. We hope the voices of Asian women can contribute to the global feminist theological chorus. Together we may find new ways to speak about the divine so that we may all live and live abundantly.

Notes

[1] See Thanh-dam Truong, *Sex, Money and Morality: Prostitution and Tourism in South-East Asia* (London: Zed Books, 1990).

[2] Virginia Fabella, Peter K.H. Lee and David Kwang-sun Suh, eds., *Asian Christian Spirituality: Reclaiming Traditions* (Maryknoll, N.Y.: Orbis Books, 1992), 148.

[3] See Dulcie Abraham, Sun Ai Lee Park, and Yvonne Dahlin, eds., *Faith Renewed: A Report on the First Asian Women's Consultation on Interfaith Dialogue* (Hong Kong: Asian Women's Resource Center for Culture and Theology, n.d.), 121.

[4] See Paula M. Cooey, William R. Eakin, and Jay B. McDaniel, eds., *After Patriarchy: Feminist Transformations of the World Religions* (Maryknoll, N.Y.: Orbis Books, 1991).

[5] Kwok Pui-lan, "Discovering the Bible in the Non-Biblical World," *Semeia 47* (1989): 37.

[6] H. Richard Niebuhr, *The Responsible Self* (New York: Harper & Row, 1963).

[7] Catherine Keller, *From a Broken Web: Separation, Sexism, and Self* (Boston: Beacon Press, 1986), 181.

[8] Virginia Fabella, "A Common Methodology for Diverse Christologies?" in *With Passion and Compassion: Third World Women Doing Theology*, ed. Virginia Fabella and Mercy Amba Oduyoye (Maryknoll, N.Y.: Orbis Books, 1988), 108-17.

Hearing One Another into Speech: Latin American Women

María Pilar Aquino

My intervention in this panel seeks to present briefly some of the factors that intervene in the act of creating and shaping a feminist discourse from the standpoint of Latina/Latin American women. Similar to any other social and ecclesial context, feminist speech is not subscribed to by all women who belong to our cultural universe. Such speech is relevant to those women who acknowledge both the predatory logic inherent to present social structures and civilization, and the urgent necessity of a commitment to transform them toward the achievement of justice and full integrity for women and for all earth organisms. In our milieu, women interested in articulating a feminist speech are frequently engaged in larger grass-roots movements for justice, but the focus of intellectual and practical action is connected to social and ecclesial groups formed by impoverished and oppressed women seeking a better life for ourselves and liberation for all.

I want to start my intervention with the words of Jean-Paul Sartre in order to illustrate not so much what he has to say about Latina or Third World women, but rather what he is saying to his own people about the attitude of dominant colonizing peoples toward the non-European peoples and cultures. In the preface to Frantz Fanon's book *The Wretched of the Earth* Sartre states:

> Not so very long ago, the earth numbered two thousand million inhabitants: five hundred million men, and one thousand five hundred million natives. The former had the Word; the others had the use of it. Between the two there were hired kinglets, over-lords, and a bourgeoisie, sham from beginning to end, which

served as go-betweens. In the colonies the truth stood naked, but the citizens of the mother country preferred it with clothes on: the natives had to love them, something in the way mothers are loved. The European elite undertook to manufacture a native elite. They picked out promising adolescents; they branded them, as with a red-hot iron, with the principles of Western culture, they stuffed their mouths full with high-sounding phrases . . . After a short stay in the [metropolis] they were sent home, whitewashed. These walking lies had nothing left to say to their [people]; they only echoed . . . [But this] came to an end; the mouths opened themselves; the yellow and black voices still spoke of our humanism but only to reproach us with our inhumanity . . . In short, the Third World finds itself and speaks to itself through [its own] voice.[1]

In the same manner, not so very long ago, natives and women have undertaken as well the shaping of our own speech.

These words can be understood adequately only within the framework of power that social relations established between different social groups which often advocate opposite goals, interests, and needs. The present configuration of society and church shows that social relations are marked by a deep inequality in terms of the capacity to access the basic rights and resources to support human integrity for all. Collective exclusion, inhumanity, and premature death of the impoverished social sectors are the final consequence of today's model of society. In the same manner, asymmetrical social relations are expressed in the polarity of colonizers and colonized, center and periphery, oppressors and oppressed, dominators and dominated.

In this model of society, social relationships are articulated through the domination of a social elite over and against the larger population. Expressions of dominance may vary in shape, duration, and intensity, in such a way that it cannot be said that the major form of domination consists of economical, cultural, political, racial, or sexual oppression. Rather, in all cases, dominance is present when oppressed social sectors have been compelled to take as their own the vision, interests and historical goals of the dominant elite. The violent nature of present society stems from the fact that this society has been shaped in such a way that it frustrates systematically the needs and dreams of the impoverished social sectors and of planetary life itself.

To raise the question of women in this context will lead me necessarily to address briefly the social construction of reality which historically has been and is at present, asymmetrical. Rooted first in colonization, and later reformulated by the process of modernity in its dual expression of capitalism and historical socialism, contemporary society has been conceived as an order inherently Eurocentric and androcentric as well. Its functioning and its outcome can be better appreciated by the effects it has had on the lives of women, on non-white races, on the poor and oppressed, and on the earth.

In our perception of reality, social relations have become a useful reading key for understanding the significance, the purpose, and the finality of women's speech. No parcel of society can escape an examination of social relations based on culture, gender, class, or race. In fact, every sphere of society is marked by a multiplicity of relations that interact and co-determine one another. A critical approach to the social fabric in which we find ourselves gives us the possibility of attaining more clarity regarding common avenues for women's liberation from the platform of feminist theology as it is verbalized in our different contexts.

For many Latin American women, several factors must be taken into account in the elaboration of theological discourse. The first factor is the self-understanding of our theological agenda as women of the geo-political South. It has to do with the significance of our speech. We can envision an alternative social order as possible and plausible only if the reappropriation of our own power and self-esteem is affirmed and recognized. Given the sustained character of colonization, there cannot be a credible solution to our interests and needs if we continue to support and promote projects which are foreign to our own bodily condition and social reality. In our milieu, colonization has historically been carried out as concomitant to patriarchy, both of which have based their dominance over women on the control of our minds, our bodies, our labor and our dreams. In the past, the words were not ours, but an echo of the colonizers.

While these have covered up their own injustice and violence against women, quite often employing theological reasoning, we have chosen to use the power of speech in order to uncover reality in its cruder realism by exposing their oppressive works and words, and by naming anew the emancipatory components of our being. We do not seek to be heard by the colonizers since we do not speak for them. By selecting the women's movement and feminist sectors as our privileged interlocutors, we seek to reveal ourselves and to unveil our own subjectivity, which is nourished by our own sources of knowing and living. In the search to explain who we are, the colonizing cultures will perhaps discover who they are and what they have become, based on what they have done to others. Nonetheless, mere words cannot liberate us from oppression and injustice. Liberation will take place only through a conscious intervention in social movements that seek justice and integrity for all. A prerequisite of that justice and integrity for liberation, however, is the conscious appropriation of our own minds, bodies, labor and dreams.

From my standpoint as a Third World woman, five hundred years of colonization do not presuppose that we have a history built solely on exploitation, violence and cultural dependence. Our history has been shaped not only by the realities brought in by the European colonizers and their successors, that is, by what they have given to us. Our history is also shaped by what we have done with their works. They have given us chains and wounds, but solidarity, creativity, and laughter could only come from the deep humanism of our ancestral cultures. Our history is one of subversive action and imagination, of hope, of resistance, and of the shared conviction that liberation and justice are possible here on earth. This understanding of our own history is the key to the formulation of a self-determined theological discourse.

A second factor to take into account in our speech is the complexity of today's social phenomena and the diversity of social practices. As I have pointed out in other works, our theology is elaborated in a context which can be characterized as a "social milieu that has produced a systemic, articulated, and multifaceted oppression of women."[2] This is due to the fact that today's reality shows an efficient combination of three major social structures that operate in daily life producing and reproducing the present social system as a whole. By the reinforcement of one another, by their pervasive character in the shaping of social relations, and by the justification of these with hierarchical theories, a triad system has been formed articulating totalitarian capitalism, the patriarchal structure, and contemporary colonialism. Structurally activated by the class-based, the racial, and the sexual division of social labor, this system has secured the development, comfort and well-being of the Eurocentric and androcentric metropolitan North. Its correlation is the counter-development, discomfort and inhumanity to which women and Third World peoples are driven.

In this conflictive context, efforts for social change must be accepted in their diversity. There cannot be a single strategy against the multiple forms of oppression given the fact that we are not abstract subjects nor is our experience the same. Women must acknowledge that "dominant asymmetrical power, including patriarchy, is polycentric and it involves multiple power relations. Asymmetrical power carries within it a relational character that expresses itself in multiple forms. Consequently, [feminist movements and feminist theologies] are required to recognize and accept the inevitable diversity of struggles that oppose asymmetrical power."[3] This understanding of our critical response to present reality emphasizes the need for widening the analytical and epistemological scope of our theologizing.

The third aspect to take into account is related to the internal logic that presides in our speech. This logic is expressed in active principles regarded both as an adequate and necessary response to our needs and as a challenge. Due to the internal logic presiding in the civilization model of the North, a logic which is based essentially on exclusive accumulation, profit, centralization of power, antagonistic world markets, suppression of alterities, and depredation of the earth, this model of society cannot be universalized. By its logic of exclusion, this civilization cannot be democratic nor participatory for all. The level of consumerism and food waste, as lived in the First World, is simply non-viable for the majority of the world's population located in the South. Peace, true world development, justice and equality for all are increasingly unattainable. This civilization is antagonistic, as it opposes the North against the South, development against ecological equilibrium, science against culture, men against women, present against future, white against non-white races, competitiveness against solidarity, and so forth. This civilization cannot be the civilization of the future. It cannot be endorsed by any social group sensitive to basic human dignity, and much less by critical feminist liberation theology.

Therefore, vis-a-vis the internal death-giving logic of today's society, Latina/Latin American feminists propose an alternate one, a life-giving logic presided by the ethical and theological principles of justice, wholeness of life for all, the social and political recognition of each one's subjectivity, true autonomy and self-determination, integral development, effective participation and ecological equilibrium. These principles are the characteristic notes of our speech. In considering the diversity of our social location, we might stress or combine these principles in a variety of forms, but what remains as a common task is the advancement of the social, religious, and political recognition of women's full human integrity.

Notes

[1] Jean-Paul Sartre, "Preface," in Frantz Fanon, *The Wretched of the Earth* (New York: Grove Press, 1963), pp. 7, 8, 10. The brackets are mine.

[2] María Pilar Aquino, "The Collective 'Dis-Covery' of Our Own Power: Latina American Feminist Theology," Aliens in Jerusalem Symposium, Drew University, April 1-17, 1994, p. 12; *Our Cry for Life: Feminist Theology from Latin America*, (Maryknoll, N.Y.: Orbis Books, 1994), pp. 26-41.

[3] María Pilar Aquino, "The Collective 'Dis-Covery' of Our Own Power," p. 12.

From Hearing to Collaboration: Steps for the Privileged toward a Praxis of Solidarity

Anne E. Patrick

The present essay will argue a paradoxical point, namely that it is time for theologians to deepen our commitment to hearing one another into speech and it is also time to go beyond the "hearing one another into speech stage" and press the next questions: Speech about what? And where is the talk taking us? I shall proceed by stating two assumptions I bring to this discussion and then suggesting three steps toward a praxis of solidarity, which may be small ones, but I hope are steps in the right direction.

The first assumption is that all of us here are sufficiently privileged as educated North Americans to know that the call to conversion and solidarity is meant for us. If we are also tenured and white, the call is all the more urgent. But the response is not about getting it right at last, as if Pelagian efforts at justification by hand-wringing, or politically correct gestures of class disloyalty, will suffice for salvation. Indeed, part of Shawn Copeland's message in her address is that the challenges to our profession are as deep as the mystery of sin and grace itself. This entails that the struggle toward justice requires daily effort and daily forgiveness, and recommitment to the process in the morning.

A second assumption is that although it is indeed time to ask the questions—"Speech about what?" and "Where is the talk taking us?"— the effort to hear one another into speech itself remains both valuable and vulnerable. European-American theologians especially need to emulate the self-critical stance taken by philosopher Elisabeth V. Spelman in her book *Inessential Woman: Problems of Exclusion in*

Feminist Thought. In this 1988 study, Spelmen points out that white feminists have tended to employ the term "woman" generically in a manner that parallels the way the term "man" has functioned in the male philosophical tradition, obscuring the "heterogeneity of women" and blinding us to the significance that such factors as race, culture, class, and sexual orientation have in women's diverse experiences of oppression and liberation.[1] Lorraine Bethel had good reason to ask in 1979, "What Chou Mean *We*, White Girl?"[2] The tone of anger in Bethel's question suggests one reason why the effort to hear diverse women into speech is a vulnerable enterprise as well as a valuable one. It is difficult to sustain the conversation when we do not feel heard. We can probably all think of occasions when goals of promoting inclusiveness and respect for diversity have been painfully incomplete in their realization. Sometimes efforts at hearing each other into speech feel more like the Tower of Babel than Pentecost; these are the times to recommit to the struggle and to pray for the gifts of the Spirit.

So much for the assumptions. Now for three steps toward a praxis of solidarity. The first can be called *contextualizing the voices*, that is, hearing them in their complex relational settings. This involves something I term the "Rachel principle." Rachel is one of the original "mothers of the disappeared." Her voice comes wailing out of Matthew's gospel just before John's voice is heard crying for repentance because God's reign is near:

> "A cry was heard at Ramah,
>   sobbing and loud lamentation:
> Rachel bewailing her children;
>   no comfort for her, since they are no more."
>
>   (Matt. 2:18, NAB)

Rachel is everywoman, mourning every loss from violence and injustice. The Rachel principle suggests that if we hear that anguish into speech, the questions of action will get answered soon enough. Speech about what? About the violence and loss Rachel is suffering. And where should the talk be taking us? Wherever it requires for Rachel to know that there is hope for her future, which is what God assures Rachel in the prophecy that Matthew is calling to mind in his quotation:

In Ramah is heard the sound of moaning,
    of bitter weeping!
Rachel mourns her children,
    she refuses to be consoled because her children are
        no more.
    Thus says the LORD:
Cease your cries of mourning,
    wipe the tears from your eyes.
The sorrow you have known shall have its reward,
    says the LORD,
    they shall return from the enemy's land.
There is hope for your future, says the LORD.
                    (Jer. 31:15-17, NAB)

How to support this hope is something we must figure out together, Rachel and we, or better, Rachel in others and Rachel in us.

Something to notice here is that a scandal of particularity is associated with Rachel. She is one of four women who bore Jacob's children in the Genesis narrative, and because she is the one most favored by patriarchy, her losses are recalled by Jeremiah and lifted up by Matthew. This privilege does not invalidate the Rachel principle, but it does suggest that we will do well to remember that for every Rachel on our syllabus, there is a Leah and a Zilpah and a Bilhah, a less favored sister and a pair of female slaves. Being attuned to all these voices, then, is the first step toward a praxis of solidarity—hearing them not as a disembodied sound track, but insofar as possible, contextually, in a way that connects with the human richness and complex relatedness of the speakers. Collaborating on common projects is an excellent way to promote this contextual hearing.

Internalizing the voices of the victims of injustice is the second step toward a praxis of solidarity, which means hearing them regularly in one's own self-talk. This may in fact be the distinguishing characteristic of that elusive entity we call a "properly formed conscience"—one that hears the voices of those adversely affected by the systems we live by, as well as by what we choose to do and what we never get around to doing.[3]

Because the praxis of solidarity is so idealistic and so demanding, I would suggest as a third step something on the order of *harmonizing the voices.* This image is not meant to suggest a classical blend of "easy listening," but rather a mode of hearing that allows us to retain inner peace as much as possible. Perhaps a better way of expressing what I have in mind is this: to allow the challenging protests and demands to play over a ground bass, or even better, a ground alto, of God's healing and empowering and justice-making love for us all.

The virtue of humility is not given a chapter in William Bennett's current bestseller, *The Book of Virtues.*[4] But the combination of humility and trust in God's mercy is essential if we are to get past the Babel of alienating and empty rhetoric about solidarity and receive the Pentecost gifts we need for the praxis commended to us so eloquently by Shawn Copeland.

Notes

[1] Elisabeth V. Spelman, *Inessential Woman: Problems of Exclusion in Feminist Thought* (Boston: Beacon, 1988), p. ix. A new concern emerges when recognition and assertion of difference lead to diversification of women's theologies. The fact that "feminist" theology is now complemented by "womanist theology," "mujerista theology," and "minjung theology," to mention examples of women's theology from African-American, U.S. Latina, and Korean perspectives, is indeed a promising development. At the same time it must be noted that these "women's theologies of color" are at some risk of marginalization when anthologies and course syllabi are put together.

[2] Lorraine Bethel, "What Chou Mean *We*, White Girl?" *Conditions: Five* 11 (Autumn 1979), 86-92.

[3] H. Richard Niebuhr discusses the conversational character of conscience in "The Ego-Alter Dialectic and the Other," *The Journal of Philosophy* 42 (1945): 352-59. His conclusion offers a particularly useful set of distinctions: "The choice does not lie between the good conscience of a self which has kept all its laws and the bad conscience of the transgressor, but between the dull conscience which does not discern the greatness of the other and the loftiness of his [God's] demands, the agonized conscience of the awakened, and the consoled conscience of one who in the company of the Spirit seeks to fulfill the infinite demands of the infinite other" (359).

[4] William J. Bennett, *The Book of Virtues* (New York: Simon & Schuster, 1993).

Amnesia in the Catholic Sunday Lectionary: Women—Silenced from the Memories of Salvation History

Regina A. Boisclair

Introduction

The pericopes from the Bible that are introduced in Catholic public worship are predetermined and published in a lectionary.[1] A lectionary, by its very nature, excludes some ancient traditions as it includes others, recasts its selections into designated collections, and assigns each collection to a particular context in the church calendar. Thus, devising any lectionary, not only reproduces in large measure what James A. Sanders calls "the canonical process" that produced the Bible,[2] but also establishes a "canon within the canon." The contemporary Catholic lectionary for Sundays and Solemnities (hereafter: Sunday lectionary) is a "canon within the canon."

When selections from the Sunday lectionary are proclaimed during the liturgy, they become lections.[3] Each lection concludes with the phrase "Word (or Gospel) of the Lord," to which the assembly verbalizes its assent. The members of a worshipping assembly enter into a liturgical process that evokes *anamnesis*, i.e., remembrance, and by listening to and affirming the lections the Word becomes "real and present" in their minds and hearts. The liturgical process is designed by the rubrics to lead the assembly to internalize what is heard as a matter of faith: *lex supplicandi* communicates *lex credendi*.[4] The whole liturgy effects *anamnesis*, but a significant part of who and what an assembly remembers is established by what is *set into* and *heard from* the assigned lections. The Sunday lectionary has an overwhelming influence on determining what I call "the story in the heads and hearts of Christians."

Marjorie Proctor-Smith claims that when it comes to women, the Sunday lectionary suffers from amnesia.[5] The Bible sacralizes a patriarchal social structure, founded on an androcentric view of God and humanity, and is chiefly preoccupied with stories of men. However, it also includes female images for God and provides accounts of many women in the unfolding stories of Israel, Jesus, and the early Church. Were these female images and stories of women well represented in the Sunday lectionary, it could better balance the story in the heads and hearts of Christians. Instead, as Eileen Schuller recognizes: "the Sunday readings give the impression that the Bible is even more male-centered than one would find if one sat down and read it through as a whole."[6]

The first part of this study: 1) provides a brief history of the contemporary Catholic Sunday lectionary and its ecumenical influence; 2) describes the efforts and problems with respect to gender-inclusive language lectionaries; and 3) applies George Lindbeck's cultural linguistic model to explain why the silencing of the biblical witness of women in the lectionary is detrimental to Christians. The second part examines: 1) the First Testament readings; 2) the Second Testament lessons; and 3) the Gospel selections.[7] This second part: names many women who have been omitted, eliminated, or hidden in the Sunday lectionary; draws out the implications of three specific collections of lectionary readings; and identifies some of the premises of the androcentric hermeneutic that unconsciously influenced the compilers of the Sunday lectionary.[8]

The Catholic Sunday Lectionary

The Second Vatican Council called for a revision of the lectionary used in the Roman Rite since 1570. The new lectionary (hereafter: RL), promulgated in 1969,[9] was introduced in the United States and Canada on the First Sunday of Advent, 1970.[10] The *ordo* for Sundays and Solemnities had three major innovations: 1) it replaced an annual table of readings with a three year cycle;[11] 2) it provided for three biblical selections together with a psalm or canticle where previously a gospel pericope had been preceded by a brief segment from an epistle;[12] 3) it appointed regular readings from the First Testament that were rarely included in the 1570 *ordo*.[13] When the 1969 RL was slightly revised in 1981,[14] no substantive changes were made.[15] The 1981 edition (hereafter: RL2) has been used in Canada since the First Sunday of Advent, 1992;[16] it has not been introduced in the United States. Vatican II envisioned a new lectionary in which "the treasures of the Bible are . . . opened up more lavishly so that a richer share in God's Word may be provided for the faithful."[17] When it is compared to the 1570 *ordo*, it is beyond question that RL realized the intention of the Council.

As early as 1970, other American churches began to modify and use the new Catholic *ordo*.[18] The ecumenical influence of the RL was unexpected.[19] No one who devised the RL ever anticipated that it would be acclaimed as "Catholicism's greatest gift to Protestant preaching."[20] Today, the RL and the RL2 as well as its variant lectionaries, in the 1979 Episcopal *Book of Common Prayer* (hereafter: EL),[21] the 1980 *Lutheran Book of Worship* (hereafter: LL),[22] and the 1992 *Revised Common Lectionary* (hereafter: CL2),[23] issued by the Consultation on Common Texts, are widely used in North America and elsewhere. I find these lectionaries are sufficiently similar to call them "synoptic lectionaries." While this study is focused on the Catholic *ordo*, some secondary studies based on other synoptic lectionaries have been taken into consideration. Many observations made in this study apply as much to the EL and the LL as they do to the RL and the RL2.[24]

The RL was designed to assign the texts considered "of greatest importance" to Sundays and major feasts.[25] While Eileen Schuller insists that "there is no systematic plot to exclude women from the [Sunday] lectionary,"[26] Marjorie Proctor-Smith claims that an androcentric hermeneutic influenced both the selection and the way the collections of three selections and a psalm or canticle were put together.[27] The lections in Catholic Sunday lectionary disclose the male voice of "Mother Church" safeguarding the interest of "her" sons.

Gender Language

Lectionaries necessarily adopt an established version of the English Bible. In the early 1980's some feminist scholars recognized that, while awaiting forthcoming gender-inclusive translations of the Bible, immediate action needed to be taken to eliminate linguistic androcentrism from public proclamation. The National Council of Churches sponsored the preparation of *An Inclusive Language*

Lectionary based on the Revised Standard Version (hereafter: RSV) to provide gender-inclusive readings for the CL.[28] *The Lectionary for the Christian People*, devised by Gail Ramshaw and Gordon Lathrop, supplied gender-inclusive readings based on the RSV for the RL, EL, and LL.[29] Interim efforts were also made at the local level; but the practice of making *ad hoc* changes placed too much responsibility on individuals with little training to discern when and what changes would or would not be appropriate. For those churches that use a pulpit Bible, the publication of the New Revised Standard Version (hereafter: NRSV) resolves the problem for the moment.

Catholics publish full-text lectionaries that are designed to be used in liturgies. These lectionaries eliminate the difficulty readers experience in finding the proper selections in a Bible and then having to skip over verses not designated for proclamation. The Committee on Liturgy of the National Conference of Catholic Bishops (hereafter: NCCB) addressed the issue of gender-language while preparing an American text of the 1981 *ordo*.[30] The NCCB was also committed to using the New American Bible (hereafter: NAB) as its master text.[31] This meant that all the relevant pericopes in the NAB would need to be reviewed because the revised "inclusive-language" New Testament, introduced in 1986, was unsatisfactory.[32]

The NCCB recognized that "the concern for gender-inclusive language had reached the point that further changes in horizontal language, that is, language referring to persons, was imperative."[33] Members of the Catholic Biblical Association of America (hereafter: CBA) revised all the pericopes in the NAB that were appointed by the RL2 to insure that "the language . . . [would] facilitate the full, conscious and active participation of all members of the church, women and men, in worship."[34] Three specific principles guided their decisions: 1) Clauses in the third person masculine singular were put either into the plural or the second person "so as to be inclusive in meaning . . . when this does not affect the meaning of the clause." 2) The Greek *adelphoi* was translated as brothers and sisters "in a context that, in the judgement of scripture scholars, includes men and women." 3) "In those instances where the meaning of the text would not be altered, a word that is exclusive in meaning is replaced by an inclusive word or words when the context includes women as well as men."[35] These principles do not allow the alternating use of "she" and "he" (him and her) to convey inclusive meanings. These principles also insure that nothing that is said to or about males would be represented inclusively. The new lectionary was approved by the American Bishops in June, 1992. It awaits ratification from Rome. The 1981 *ordo* has been available for some time; the proposed U.S. text is not; it is not possible to assess this lectionary at the moment. However, it is now an open question if this lectionary will ever be issued.

On October 25, 1994 the Vatican Congregation of the Doctrine of the Faith rescinded the approval of the Congregation for Divine Worship for liturgical use of the NRSV.[36] These Europeans presume they can "authoritatively" define the use and meaning of English for Catholics in North America. The Vatican curia has chosen to cast down a gauntlet on inclusive language. In the process, it has insulted women, the ecumenical community, the North American bishops and biblical scholars, as well as the CBA, because the Vatican also rejected the inclusive-language Psalter that was introduced by the CBA into the NAB in 1993. North American Catholic biblical scholars plan to discuss this issue in Rome; it would be precipitous to speculate about the final outcome in the context of this study.

Although all these efforts are important, by the mid-1980's some feminist scholars realized that the Bible cannot be "rescued" with better translations or even feminist interpretations.[37] Other feminist scholars recognized that problems in the lectionaries can never be resolved by the present forms of gender-inclusive translations.[38] Feminist lectionaries are beginning to appear. However, these important alternative resources are neither designed nor intended to be substitutes for the existing Sunday lectionaries in the institutional churches.[39]

Silencing Women's Witness: A Systemic Problem

In the last decade some feminist scholars identified a more systemic problem in the RL and its variants. These lectionaries tend to omit passages that introduce women, eliminate women from approved shorter readings, hide women in long lections, and emphasize passages that reinforce patriarchal presuppositions.[40] The Sunday readings silence the very texts that could balance the Bible's androcentric and patriarchal perspectives. In her study of the EL, Jean Campbell observes:

The fullness of the compassionate, merciful and loving God, as well as the history of the women who have been faithful, have not been considered of value to be heard publicly in the gathering of the community of faith.[41]

The significance of the tendencies to marginalize or silence the female imagery and women witnesses from the Bible, while including passages that sacralize patriarchy, can be clarified by applying a cultural-linguistic understanding to how lectionaries and liturgy function. George A. Lindbeck develops a cultural linguistic model to explain the nature and function of doctrine, theology, and the Bible in the believing community.[42] He claims that the Bible shapes the experience of Christians by providing the paradigmatic stories from which the "language" of discursive and non-discursive symbols establish the world of Christian culture. Thus, for Lindbeck, the inner experiences of Christians are "derived from" and "identified by" the world that the biblical stories construct. Lindbeck calls this process "intertextuality" and claims that it is through "intertextuality" that Christians "make the biblical story their own."[43] As Lindbeck explains:

To become a Christian involves learning the story of Israel and of Jesus well enough to interpret and experience oneself and one's world in its terms. A religious system is above all, an external word, a *verbum externum*, that molds and shapes the self and its world, rather than an expression of a pre-existing self or of pre-conceptual experience.[44]

John Reumann recognizes "the lectionaries are the Bible for the vast majority of Christians in America."[45] For most Catholics, liturgy is the obvious way Lindbeck's "intertextuality" is realized. Members of the assembly participate in the process of celebrating liturgy, and that process leads them to interpret and experience themselves, others, and the world, according to the categories it establishes. Through this liturgical process, the assembly communicates, remembers, and reinforces Christian culture. The liturgical rubrics are designed to insure that the proclamations from the lectionary effect "intertextuality" that engenders *anamnesis*.

The influence of the Catholic Sunday lectionary, however, also extends beyond the limits of public worship: parochial Bible studies,[46] catechetical programs,[47] and spiritual guides[48] often follow lectionary selections. The Sunday lectionary is the only canon heard, read, preached, or studied by most churchgoing Catholics. When women and female images are silenced from this canon within the canon, the witness they provide in the Bible does not shape the inner experiences or the world of most Christians. When women and female images are marginalized in the lectionary, women are interpreted as marginal beings. When androcentric and patriarchal texts are emphasized, many Christian women internalize androcentric self-understandings and many Christians assume that patriarchy is a divinely designed social order.

First Testament Readings: Derivative, Disposable, Dangerous Women

In the Sunday *ordo*, First Testament readings correspond to the Gospel and/or to the Second Testament lesson in the same collection. Four readings from the First Testament include Eve,[49] one mentions Sarah,[50] two introduce the widow of Zarephath,[51] and another features the Shunammite woman.[52] Eight selections introduce only four women as participants in the story of Israel and these selections are appointed to only ten occasions over a period of three years![53] The RL remembers dozens of male heroes and holy men—but Hagar, Rebekah, Rachel, Leah, Tamar, Shiphrah, Puah, Moses' mother, Zipporah, Miriam, Rahab, Deborah, Jael, Naomi, Ruth, Hannah, Abigail, Bathsheba,[54] Hulda, Judith, and Esther are never mentioned. The RL2 introduces Hagar, in an additional reading about Sarah,[55] and provides a selection that includes Hannah.[56] However, both these new readings are optional; celebrants may choose to use neither. For the compilers of the RL, the women of ancient Israel were not among "the treasures of the Bible" Vatican II spoke about.[57]

The assembly hears the empowering female imagery associated with Lady Wisdom at least twice each year;[58] but other female images for God are heard only twice in three years—and both are introduced in the same year! Is 49:14-15, "Can a mother forget her infant,"[59] and Is 66:13, "as a mother comforts her child"[60]—are overwhelmed when images of God as King, Lord of Hosts, and Father are so prominent. The community never hears of God imaged as a mother eagle (Dt 32:11-12), or the endearing image of God teaching the toddler Ephraim to walk (Hos 11:3-4), to mention two other possibilities.

The selections from the First Testament cannot be looked at in isolation. These lessons correspond to the gospel readings with which they are collected. The collections clarify what is intentionally and unconsciously stressed in the selections appointed to one day. In addition, any selection can also reinforce the premises of other selections. Three selections from Genesis (2:18-24, 18:1-10a and 2:7-9, and 3:1-7) convey the idea that women are derivative, disposable, or dangerous. These premises are reinforced by the collections with which each of these readings is assigned. In addition, each reading lends support to premises that are introduced in the other two passages.

The story of the woman's derivative creation from Gn 2:18-24[61] begins by suggesting that the woman is a divine afterthought: "it is not good for the man to be alone." As it continues, the reading recounts that the man names creation and thereby sacralizes a male perspective of reality. The lection also allows the woman to appear as a creature whose only purpose is to be "useful" to the man.[62]

Although Phyllis Trible's rhetorical studies demonstrate that in Gn 2 only grammatical gender necessarily applies to the "earth-creature" (*ha-adam*) before Gn 2:23c, when the terms woman and man (*issa* and *is*) are first introduced,[63] it is also true that the ancient authors could never have conceived of the androgynous being Trible postulates.[64] Susan Brooks Thistlethwaite insists that "feminist interpretation must also recognize that the history of control of women's bodies is at stake in this text and must become part of its interpretation."[65] The RL introduces Gn 2:18-24 in public worship with Mk 10:2-16. In this gospel passage Jesus affirms the indissolubility of marriage. The harmful potential of this collection is illustrated in real history by an episode Thistlethwaite recounts:

A Maryland woman who was severely abused over many years told me that when she complained after some attacks that she had sustained injuries, her husband would retort that "your bones are my bones—just like it says in the Bible."[66]

The compilers of the RL certainly never intended for this collection to legitimize wife-battering. However, in another selection the RL illustrates that the compilers never thought that there was anything wrong with the idea that women's only purpose is to be productive for and reproductive of men. The only lection in the RL that introduces Sarah is Gn 18:1-10a.[67] Here, Sarah is instructed by Abraham to produce flour rolls to serve his male visitors at Mamre. Then, her future reproductive role as the mother of a son becomes the topic of the men's conversation. The lection ends before Sarah becomes a subject who overhears the prediction of her pregnancy, reflects on sexual pleasure, laughs, and denies that she did so. It eliminates the fact that Sarah spoke to God and that God responded to Sarah.[68] This passive Sarah "is certainly not the Sarah we find in Genesis."[69] The compilers dispossessed Sarah of herself by the way they disposed of her in this selection. Her brief appearance reinforces a number of standard misinterpretations of Gn 2. Gn 18:1-10a suggests that a) women were created to be useful to men, b) wives must be disposed to provide what suits their husbands, and c) short of divorcing them, husbands may dispose of their wives as objects rather than persons with whom they are partners and equals.

The account of Abraham and his visitors at Mamre is collected with the story of Mary and Martha from Lk 8:38-42. Since Abraham's hospitality is a typological foreshadowing of the sisters' hospitality, Sarah recedes even further. Leaving aside the relative merits of typology[70]—a longer account from Genesis that introduces Sarah as an active subject would provide even more symmetry. Sarah's laughter, and even her denial, serve as a type of Martha's misunderstanding of the meaning of serving Jesus. The compilers of the RL were fearful that people in the twentieth century could not listen to three long readings. Selections are often so short that one observer declares the compilers "chickenhearted."[71] In this instance, the selection was shortened because the compilers were blind to Sarah as a person. They should have noticed that a slightly longer reading would have strengthened the symmetry they wanted to suggest. Gn 18:1-15 would also allow the assembly to hear that God listens and speaks to women and perhaps even to conclude that Jesus praises Mary not for sitting in silence but for speaking as well as listening.

On the First Sunday in Lent in Year A, Gn 2:7-9; 3:1-7 is proclaimed. The passage recounts the story of the disobedience of the first couple. Traditional androcentric interpretations of Gn 3 assume that the woman was tempted because she was the inferior, weaker creature.[72] However, the woman has a discussion, considers the options, and decides before she acts. She makes a conscious decision;

Adam simply eats. She then acknowledges that she had been deceived and recognizes her culpability; Adam blames God ("the woman YOU gave me").[73]

During the festal season, all three readings in every collection generally correspond to each other. During Lent, the First Testament selections tend to correspond more closely to the Second Testament lessons than to the gospel pericopes.[74] However, on the First Sunday in Lent in Year A, Gn 2:7-9; 3:1-7 closely corresponds to both Rom 5:12-19 and Mt 4:1-11. In the pericope from Romans, Paul contrasts Adam's disobedience with the obedience of Christ. To provide gender symmetry Paul discards the woman from the story and disregards her as a moral agent. By overlooking Eve's dubious honor, Paul ignores the only one who made a conscious human act of disobedience. Only the man's act is important and only the man is credited with the moral culpability. In this combination of readings, the woman's only significance is her influence on Adam. The collection suggests that apart from their capacity to influence men, women's acts are irrelevant.

The idea that women are dangerous is reinforced by the gospel. Together, Gn 2:7-9; 3:1-7 and Mt 4:1-11 contrast gender. The woman, Eve, is deceived by the serpent, the man, Jesus, resists the devil; Jesus orders Satan to depart, Eve encouraged her husband to eat. In a collection with Rom 5:12-19 and Mt 4:1-11 the reading from Genesis can only convey the idea that women are dangerous to men. This premise is another aspect of the unconscious androcentric hermeneutic that the compilers introduced into the lectionary. The three readings from Genesis suggest that women are derivative of men, dangerous to men, and except as the mothers of sons, they are just as disposable by men, as the lectionary disposes of the other women in Genesis.

Second Testament Lessons: Forgotten Women

All but two early church women who were important enough to be named are forgotten by the RL and the RL2. Mary, the mother of Jesus, and Chloe are named in passing,[75] but Mary, the mother of John Mark, and Rhoda, Tabitha, Lydia, Prisca, the four prophet daughters of Philip, Phoebe, Mary of Rome, Junia, Tryphaena, Tryphosa, Persis, the mother of Rufus, Julia, the sister of Nereus, Euodia, Syntyche, Apphia, Nympha, Eunice, Lois, and Claudia are never mentioned. Early

Christian women are all but eliminated from the lectionary and the witness they could provide to contemporary congregations is unremembered and uncelebrated as "Word of the Lord."

In the RL and the RL2, three lections from Acts: 1) acknowledge women's presence in the earliest community;[76] 2) recognize that women as well as men were receptive to the early *kerygma*;[77] 3) portray women as objects of the church's ongoing ministry;[78] and 4) mention that some women opposed Paul's mission.[79] Thus, two lections from Acts remember that women were objects to be ministered to and in the one lesson in which women are subjects, they are opponents of and dangerous to the male missionaries.

From the Pauline letters, the RL and the RL2 recognize Jesus' Jewish mother each year on the Solemnity of Mary,[80] and once in Year C the assembly hears Gal 3:28, which declares that in Christ "there is neither male nor female."[81] None of the readings disclose that Paul worked with women or that he recognized that women had noteworthy roles in the early communities. Rom 16:1-19 could have been an especially interesting lection. This passage notes that Phoebe was a deacon, Junia was an apostle, names other significant women in the early community in Rome, and then recommends that Christians cease splintering into factions. Christians never hear this list of early women leaders. Thus, it is not surprising that many, including some who should know better, assume that feminists are "deceiving the hearts of the innocent" (Rom 16:18). It is the lectionary that deceives Catholic assemblies by forgetting the witness of early Christian women.

Admittedly, things could have been worse. Many of the most notorious Pauline passages that pertain to women are not found in the Sunday lectionary.[82] However, the infamous "household codes" were included. The RL and the RL2 introduce Eph 5:21-32 in Year B,[83] and the RL appoints Col 3:12-17 every year on the feast of the Holy Family that is celebrated on the Sunday after Christmas. In the RL2, Col 3:12-17 is assigned to the feast of the Holy Family in Year A and is designated as an option for Years B and C. These selections from Colossians and Ephesians omit the adjoining parenesis that admonishes slaves to obey their masters. The compilers insured that the Sunday lectionary would not suggest that slavery is an acceptable social institution but they provided readings that promote patriarchal marriage as a Christian ideal.

Since Vatican II North American Catholic women began to examine their marginalization by the church. They found the patriarchal ideals represented by the household codes offensive to their dignity as persons, as wives, and as Christians. Several years ago the American Catholic bishops recognized that it would be pastorally expedient to follow the lectionary's own principle to omit "biblical texts which contain serious literary, critical or exegetical problems,"[84] when they authorized eliminating the verses in question from these readings. The proposed new American RL2 also allows for these verses to be optional.[85] Still, an option to exclude is an option to include. An either/or option is not the clear stand. It will be interesting to see which option is printed as the first and second choice; first choices are usually used.[86]

In the Sunday lectionary, the readings from Acts and Paul barely whisper about women. It is interesting to juxtapose this fact with the following words from "The Role of Women in Evangelization of Peoples," a document issued in 1975 by the Vatican Congregation for the Evangelization of Peoples: "Women are capable of giving themselves without counting the cost . . . The church can never thank them enough. . . . Silence and contemplation, for which women are suited by nature, should find expression in liturgy and para-liturgy."[87]

Selfless giving and silence are strategies that women have perfected over the centuries to survive and to participate in the world from which they have been marginalized. These strategies can be powerful but they also have undesirable effects. Feminists have long recognized that the root sin of women as women is the negation of self and the dependence on others for self-affirmation.[88]

The Vatican document, briefly cited above, contains a long-winded stereotypical description of women's selfless qualities, celebrates and praises women's silence in purple prose, and thanks women as if they were not already part of the church. The Sunday lectionary emulates the silence the Vatican claims to be integral to women's nature. This silence discloses another premise of the androcentric hermeneutic set into the lectionary: the women from the early church are incidental. The compilers of the RL allowed this lectionary to forget the early Christian women because they could not conceive that women's presence or prominence in the early church was significant. This silencing betrays a predisposition to assume that women in the church today are incidental.

The Gospels: Women's Silenced Witness

The gospel readings appointed to Solemnities, such as Christmas, and some Sundays, such as the annual observance of the Baptism of the Lord on Sunday following Epiphany, feature passages that recount the particular event in the life of Jesus that is being celebrated. Sundays in the festal seasons are assigned gospel pericopes that lend themselves to the themes that are associated with each season. Other Sundays are provided with semi-continuous passages from the synoptic Gospel that is assigned to each year. The compilers tended to skip over the pericopes that were introduced in the seasons or on Solemnities,[89] and once they introduced a story from one Gospel, they often skipped the parallel accounts in the other Gospels. However, some stories that feature the male disciples in an especially favorable light appear in every variation. Thus, the lectionary includes all four accounts of the call of the first male disciples[90] and the four accounts of Peter's profession of faith.[91] A few other stories are included from two Gospels but, except for the accounts of the women who discover the empty tomb, none of the accounts that feature an encounter between Jesus and a woman is introduced more than once.[92] Thus, the stories of women that Jesus encountered in his ministry are heard only once every three years.

While the problems of gender-exclusive language and the household codes received considerable attention, the fact that several pericopes in the Gospels, which feature women, were not in the RL, was only recently introduced in a popular Catholic publication.[93] The RL2 does not add any relevant gospel pericopes to the RL. What follows identifies the women's stories and images from the Gospels that are (1) omitted, (2) eliminated in shorter readings, (3) hidden in long lections, and (4) considers how the Sunday lectionary marginalizes one especially significant gospel tradition.[94] In the process the women and female images included in the Sunday lectionary are acknowledged.

Omitted Women

Three important pericopes that feature women are never introduced in a gospel reading in the Sunday lectionary. Lk 13:10-17 provides an account of Jesus healing a woman that he identifies as a "daughter of Abraham" (13:16). The story of this woman who likely suffered from osteoporosis is not included in the Sunday *ordo*. John provides an account of Jesus' appearance to Mary Magdalene on Easter morning. This important story in Jn 20:11-18 about the first witness to the Resurrection is omitted from the Sunday lectionary. The Gospel for the Solemnity of the Assumption in Year B is from the canonical ending of Mark. However, the verses that describe Jesus' appearance to Mary Magdalene (Mk 16:9-11) are not provided in the reading.

Jesus' healing of Simon's mother-in-law and her response of serving illustrate the ideal of Christian discipleship. The story appears in Matthew, Mark, and Luke but only Mark's account (1:29-31) is introduced in the lectionary.[95] Jesus' healing of the Gentile Canaanite woman from Mt 15:21-28 is provided[96] but the parallel story from Mk 7:24-30 is not. This story is particularly interesting because it is the only occasion in which Jesus initially refused to heal and it is the only occasion where somebody's persistence and astute wit forced Jesus to change his mind. Although Mt 15:21-28 makes the same point, by excluding the story from Mark's account the lectionary minimizes the fact that women benefited by Jesus' ministry and avoids a second opportunity to portray a woman as an extraordinarily intelligent person.

The RL and the RL2 excludes most accounts in which Jesus' teachings make use of women or female images. In Mt 23:37 and Lk 13:34 Jesus images himself as mother hen; in Lk 13:20-21 Jesus uses an image of a woman kneading bread to illustrate the growth of the *basilea tou theou* (i.e., the reign of God); in Lk 15:8-10 Jesus images God as a woman seeking a lost coin; in Jn 16:21 Jesus likens the impending distress of his disciples to a woman in labor and then likens their future joy to a mother with her newborn. These analogies are never heard because none of these verses is incorporated in the Sunday readings. Jesus called attention to a poor widow who contributed two coins to the treasure and identified her as the paradigm for true devotion to God in Mk 12:41-44 and Lk 21:1-4, but only Mark's account is included in a reading.[97]

The pericopes that recount the stories of Mary, the mother of Jesus, are included in the *ordo*, especially during the seasons of Advent and Christmas. Mary also appears in the story of the Wedding at Cana on the Second Sunday of Year C. However, other passages that introduce Mary during the ministry of Jesus are all but ignored. Both passing references to Jesus as the "son of Mary" in Mt 13:55-56 and Mk 6:3 are omitted and the brief episode in which Mary and his siblings call to Jesus from outside the crowd is included only in its Markan form.[98] It is a happy coincidence that the pericope from Mark's Gospel was introduced because Mark provides two female images for Jesus' followers when Jesus claims that those who do God's will are his *mother*, brothers and *sisters* (Mk 3:35). However, the Sunday lectionary could have emphasized an important feature of Catholic Marian devotion had it included Mt 12:45-60 and Lk 8:19-21 where Jesus also identifies those who do the will of God as his mother.

In Year B the lectionary includes Mk 10:17-30. In this lection Jesus reinforces the commandment to honor both mother and father.[99] Jesus also cites this commandment in Mk 7:10-13, Mt 15:4-5, 19:18, and Lk 18:20. A reading that includes this teaching from Matthew in Year A and Luke in Year C should have been introduced. Care of the aging is one of the major moral dilemmas of this generation. Women tend to live longer than men and make up a large majority of the dependent elderly. It is unfortunate that Jesus' strong support of the obligation to care for the elderly is seldom heard in communities that have to grapple with new understandings of just what such care means.

There are a few other passing references in Jesus' teachings that allude to women: he refers to the Queen of the South in Mt 12:42 and Lk 11:31, to women in the eschatological travails in Mt 24:19, Mk 13:17, Lk 17:35, 21:23; to family disruption as a cost of discipleship that specifically identifies women family members in Mt 19:29, Lk 14:26, 18:29. None of these verses appears in any lection. Only Mk 10:29-30, which speaks of the disruption that discipleship will bring to families, is part of a gospel selection.[100] There is, however, a positive note. Mark's is the only gospel in which Jesus acknowledges that women may initiate divorce. The only gospel lection that includes Jesus' teaching regarding divorce is from Mk 10:2-16. This text provides an explicit affirmation of women's civil-right to divorce even as Jesus counsels both men and women not to exercise the right to do so. However, as was noted above, the collection in which this passage is introduced lends itself to the idea that women are derivative beings whose purpose is to be useful to men.

Eliminated or Hidden Women

Some approved shorter gospel readings must be noted. On the Third Sunday of Lent in Year A, the Gospel introduces the story of Jesus' encounter with the Samaritan woman that is unique to John's gospel.[101] Although the shorter reading eliminates Jn 4:29-30 in which this woman evangelizes her city, it also eliminates Jn 4:16-18 in which Samaria's theological syncretism is imaged by the woman's marriages.[102] The shorter selection concludes with Jn 4:39-42 and these verses acknowledge that the Samaritans first believed in Jesus because of this woman's testimony. Thus, the shorter reading actually provides a more positive picture of the very first evangelist in John's gospel. However, most shorter readings do not improve the presentation of women; they eliminate the women.

The Gospel appointed to the Fifth Sunday of Lent in Year A is the account of the raising of Lazarus after Jesus discussed the situation with Martha and then Mary.[103] In the shorter reading Mary is all but eliminated.[104] On the feast of the Holy Family in Year B, the gospel text is Lk 2:22-40. This reading includes an account of the woman prophet, Anna. After seeing the infant Jesus, she "gave thanks to God and talked about the child to all who looked forward to the deliverance of Jerusalem" (Lk 2:38). Anna functions as an evangelist. In the shorter reading, Anna is eliminated. Although the shorter reading provides celebrants with a respite after Christmas, it eradicates another woman's story from the memory of the assembly.

The account of Jesus healing Jairus' daughter and the woman with the hemorrhage is found in all the synoptics (Mt 9:18-26; Mk 5:21-43; Lk 8:40-56). This double story is only appointed as a lection in its Markan form.[105] It is unfortunate that the compilers did not choose to introduce each healing on separate Sundays every year to balance the many accounts of Jesus healing men. Instead the compilers provided a shorter reading that removes the story of the older woman, who had taken a great personal risk to seek healing. In assemblies that use the shorter reading, only the story of the young girl healed by Jesus is proclaimed and her healing represents a favor to a man.

Some women are hidden by the lectionary. On Palm Sunday the passion narrative from one of the synoptic Gospels is proclaimed. Matthew is introduced in Year A, Mark in Year B, and Luke in C. The approved shorter readings for Years A and B end with a statement by the centurion who identifies Jesus as the Son of God. As a result, the faithful women who stood and watched from a distance are removed from the memory of the community.[106] Mt 27:55-56 and Mk 15:40-41 also provide the only reference in their respective Gospels to the fact that women were part of Jesus' inner circle. Admittedly, when the longer reading is proclaimed, these women and the important information about them are hidden in the very long passion narrative. In Year C, the shorter reading continues through Lk 23:49. In that verse Luke includes Jesus' male friends with the women who witnessed the crucifixion. The compilers, no doubt, continued as far as Lk 23:49 because Luke's centurion only declares that Jesus was an innocent man (Lk 23:47) and this is an inadequate Christological statement and an inadequate conclusion to a liturgical reading. However, it is noteworthy that the only time the shorter passion narrative provided for Palm Sunday includes the memory that women did not abandon Jesus but witnessed the crucifixion is from the only synoptic account in which men are with them.

A Paradigmatic Tradition

In Mk 14:3-9 an anonymous woman in Bethany anoints Jesus' head. Her act is a symbolic Christological confession.[107] Matthew 26:6-13 reproduces Mark's story. In Lk 7:36-50 a sinful woman in Galilee washes Jesus' feet with her tears, wipes them with her hair, kisses them, and anoints them with ointment. Luke's story may be based on a different memory but the account in Luke has many affinities with Mark's story of the woman from Bethany.[108] In Jn 12:1-8, Mary of Bethany anoints Jesus' feet. This Johannine account touches on both Mark's and Luke's versions of the story. The story is situated in Bethany shortly before Jesus' death, as in Mark and Matthew. Although Mary is identified by name and is not considered a sinner, like the anonymous sinful woman in Luke, she washes and anoints Jesus' feet.

Mark's story of the anonymous woman from Bethany is included in the longer reading for Palm Sunday but it is omitted in the shorter reading. Thus, this woman's story is either hidden in a very long reading or eliminated altogether. This pericope, as well as its parallel account in Matthew could have been easily isolated and introduced on another Sunday. This woman's symbolic Christological gesture should have been given greater prominence. Jesus declared that this woman would be remembered "wherever the good news is proclaimed in the whole world" (Mk 14:9); the compilers show that they never considered that promises to a woman even made by Jesus should be taken very seriously and honored.

Proctor-Smith considers Mk 14:3-9 the paradigmatic illustration of the amnesia of the Sunday lectionary.[109] The lectionary's treatment of this whole tradition provides a fuller paradigm. John's account of Mary of Bethany's loving act is not introduced; neither is Matthew's account of the anonymous woman. Mark's account is eliminated or hidden. The lectionary features Luke's pericope of a sinful woman in both a longer and shorter reading.[110] The longer reading attaches the three verses that follow this woman's story (Lk 8:1-3). These verses note that many women were part of Jesus' inner circle and identifies Mary Magdalene, Joanna, and Susanna among them. However, the story of the woman whose tears wash Jesus' feet quickly grasps the imagination; the other women are either hidden by the longer reading or silenced from the shorter lection. This is all complicated by the fact that many "interpreters" assume that the sinful woman in Lk 7:36-50 was a prostitute and frequently conclude that she was Mary Magdalene.[111]

While all Christians are sinners and should model their lives on the repentant woman in Luke's Gospel, the Sunday lectionary balances the good and sinful features of men but eliminates or marginalizes the good features of women. By featuring this tradition from Luke, omitting the accounts from Matthew and John, and hiding or eliminating that of Mark, the lectionary discloses another premise of the androcentric hermeneutic of the compilers: women who are deficient from the male human norm are an appropriate image for human deficiencies.[112]

Conclusion

Amnesia is an illness of the mind. Although every one connected with a person who suffers from this disorder is affected, amnesia is not infectious. The amnesia in the lectionary is contagious. It infects the *anamnesis* of the liturgical process and afflicts many members of the assembly who, by means of intertextuality, internalize a systemic culture in which women are marginally important and even just marginally human. Proctor-Smith recognizes that this is not only detrimental to women, it is dangerous for the church:

Without . . . a firm grounding in the particularity of historical events, which when connected with God's faithfulness make liturgical celebration possible, Christianity runs the risk of drifting into gnosticism. But Christian liturgy also suffers when its memory of those particulars is faulty or incomplete. Then Christian liturgy may tend toward heresy, or self-deception. Thus the restoration of women's memory to liturgical anamnesis is of critical importance to the church as a whole, as well as to women whose memories and experiences have been distorted, misused or ignored."[113]

When Vatican II asked for a lectionary with "richer fare" it was comparing its vision to the 1570 Lectionary. The Pontifical Biblical Commission's (hereafter: PBC) recent document, "The Interpretation of the Bible in the Church," compares the Roman *ordo* to the Bible. This document notes that while Vatican II called for a lectionary with a more abundant, varied, and suitable representation of the Bible, the lectionary "in its present state, . . . only partially fulfills this goal."[114]

The PBC did not recognize that the absence of women in the lectionary is among its deficiencies. The PBC did acknowledge that feminist hermeneutics "brought many benefits . . . [that] unmask and correct certain commonly accepted interpretations which were tendentious and sought to justify the male domination of women."[115] This feminist study has demonstrated that the Sunday lectionary silences women's witness and female images. It has identified some androcentric premises that the compilers unconsciously disclosed when they determined their selections. The foundational principle for devising the RL was to provide readings that disclose the "mystery of Christ and salvation history,"[116] their selections disclose that they assumed that, apart from giving birth to sons, women are marginal to the mystery of Christ and the history of salvation.

The critique of the lectionary by the PBC may signal that a real revision of the lectionary is being considered. This is an important moment for feminist exegetes and theologians. Every relevant selection and collection must be subjected to feminist analysis because a future revision will only be as adequate as the efforts that are made to unmask the present problems. *Ad hoc* modifications will fail to address the systemic problem. A lectionary is by nature, a canon within the canon. It can be designed to provide a better gender-balance than the canon of the Bible.

Because women's witness from the Bible is silenced, the present Sunday lectionary teaches that, apart from their function as the mothers of sons, there is nothing significant enough about women's experience to celebrate as "Word of the Lord." This silence betrays a mindset that women are human only to the degree that they are like men. It tells women that they should be honored to identify with the stories and images of men and to make them their own ideal. It tells men that they have nothing to learn from the women in the Bible; it appears to be protecting them from identifying with these lesser humans. This silence also discloses another premise of the androcentric hermeneutic of the compilers of the lectionary: women's particular experiences as women are irrelevant to the lives of Christians. Thus, it is perfectly consistent to suppress and silence the images and stories of the women in the Bible and honor the admonition: "I permit no woman to teach or have authority over a man; she is to keep silent" (1 Tim 2:12). An androcentric hermeneutic that conceives of women as the most appropriate image for human deficiencies, marginalizes women as derivative, disposable beings, who, if not silent, silenced, and submissive are dangerous to men, has significant negative consequence for both the sons and daughters of an institution that claims for itself the image of "mother."

Notes

[1] A lectionary is (1) a table of readings (or *ordo*) that are appointed to specific occasions on the church calendar or (2) a book that contains the full-text of these readings in the sequence in which they will be introduced. Unless otherwise noted, the term "lectionary" refers to a table of readings and words "lectionary," "table of readings," and "*ordo*" are synonymous in this study.

[2] James A. Sanders, *Canon and Community: A Guide to Canonical Criticism* (Philadelphia: Fortress, 1984), 178.

[3] Fritz West, "From Scripture to Lection: Toward a Hermeneutic of the Roman Lectionary," *Proceedings of the North American Academy of Liturgy: Annual Meeting, St. Louis, Mo. 2-5 January*, 1990 (Valparaiso, IN: Valparaiso University, 1990), 120-121.

[4] The words and actions of liturgical rites are designed to enact and to convey what the church believes.

[5] Marjorie Proctor-Smith, "Liturgical Anamnesis and Women's Memory: 'Something Missing'," *Worship* 61 (1987): 406.

⁶ Eileen Schuller, "Women in the Lectionary," *National Liturgy Bulletin* (Canada) 27 (1994): 108.

⁷ A brief discussion of the inherent problems in the terms "Old" and "New Testament" and other designations for the two collections in the Christian Bible is found in James A. Sanders, "First Testament and Second," *Biblical Theology Bulletin* 17 (1987): 47-9.

⁸ Feminist exegetes, liturgical scholars, and theologians have been aware of problems in the Sunday lectionary for some time. However, few publications are devoted to how women are presented in the contemporary lectionaries; even fewer focus on the Catholic lectionary. Studies that are not cited elsewhere in this article include: Brigit Janetsky, "Ihre Namen sind im Buch des Lebens: Frauengeschichte und erneuertes Lektionar," in Teresa Berger and Albert Gerhards, eds., *Liturgie und Frauenfrage* (St. Ottilien: OES, 1990); Marjorie Proctor-Smith, "Lectionaries—Principles and Problems: Alternative Perspectives," *Studia Liturgica* 22 (1992): 84-99; Carol J. Schlueter, "The Lectionary: Toward a More Balanced Selection of Texts," *Consensus* 18 (1992): 65-75, and her "The Gender Balance of Texts from the Gospels. The Revised Common Lectionary and the Lutheran Book of Worship," *Currents in Theology and Mission* 20 (1993): 177-186; Eileen Schuller, "Some Criteria for the Choice of Scripture Texts in the Roman Lectionary," in Peter C. Finn and James M. Schellman, eds., *Shaping English Liturgy. Studies in Honor of Archbishop Dennis Hurley* (Washington DC: Pastoral Press, 1990), 385-404.

⁹ Missale Romanum ex Decreto Sacrosancti Œcumenici Concilii Vaticani II. Instauratum Auctoritate Pauli PP. VI Promulgatum, *Ordo Lectionum Missae*. Editio Typica (Vatican City: Typis Polyglottis Vaticanis, 1969).

¹⁰ Use of this lectionary became mandatory throughout the world on the First Sunday of Advent, 1971.

¹¹ The sigla A, B, and C are used to designate each year. Year C is assigned to the calendar years that are divisible by 3.

¹² Each year is assigned one of the synoptic gospels: A = Matthew, B = Mark, C = Luke. John's Gospel supplements all three years.

¹³ Annibale Bugnini, *The Reform of the Liturgy 1948-1975*, tr., Matthew J. O'Connell (Collegeville: Liturgical Press, 1990), 406-25.

¹⁴ Missale Romanum ex Decreto Sacrosancti Œcumenici Concilii Vaticani II. Instauratum Auctoritate Pauli PP. VI Promulgatum, *Ordo Lectionum Missae*. Editio Typica Altera (Vatican City: Libreria Editrice Vaticana, 1981).

¹⁵ The RL assigned different gospel selections for each year in the triennial cycle to feasts such as Holy Family, the Baptism of the Lord, Ascension, and Pentecost but it provided only one set of first and second readings for each of these feasts. The RL2 retains the readings assigned by the RL and assigns them to Year A, provides alternative sets of first and second readings for Years B and C, and indicates that the first and second readings assigned to year A may be used in Years B and C. Other changes are minimal. See Alan Detscher, "The Second Edition of the Lectionary for Mass," *Liturgy* 90 (1993): 4.

¹⁶ National Liturgical Office, *Lectionary: Sundays and Solemnities* (Ottawa:

Canadian Conference of Catholic Bishops, 1992). This full-text lectionary provides readings from the New Revised Standard Version, modified slightly.

[17] Vatican II, "*Sacrosanctum Concilium*," 51, in Austin P. Flannery, ed., *Documents of Vatican II* (Grand Rapids: Eerdmans, 1975), 17.

[18] John Reumann, "A History of Lectionaries: From the Synagogue at Nazareth to Post-Vatican II," *Interpretation* 31 (April, 1977): 129. For a list of the American lectionaries see Horace T. Allen, Jr., "Introduction," *Common Lectionary: The Lectionary Proposed by the Consultation on Common Texts* (New York: Church Hymnal Corporation, 1983), 8 and 24-5 notes 7-14.

[19] Eileen Schuller, "The Bible in the Lectionary," in Donald Senior, et al., eds., *The Catholic Study Bible* (New York and Oxford: Oxford University Press, 1990), 450.

[20] James White, *Christian Worship in Transition* (Nashville: Abingdon, 1976), 139.

[21] Protestant Episcopal Church in the United States of America, *The Book of Common Prayer and Administration of the Sacraments and Other Rites and Ceremonies of the Church* (New York: Seabury and Church Hymnal Corporation, 1979), 889-921.

[22] Inter-Lutheran Commission on Worship, *Lutheran Book of Worship*, Ministers' Desk Edition (Minneapolis: Augsburg and Philadelphia: Board of Publication, Lutheran Church in America, 1978), 121-170.

[23] Consultation on Common Texts, *The Revised Common Lectionary* (Nashville: Abingdon, 1992). *The Common Lectionary* (hereafter: CL) was designed as a consensus lectionary. It was patterned on the RL and its variants. CL provided a table of semi-continuous First Testament selections for most of the Sundays after Pentecost. The CL was adopted by many Anglican and Protestant churches throughout the world. It was replaced by the CL2 in 1992. The CL2: a) expands the table of semi-continuous First Testament readings for Sundays after Pentecost; b) provides an alternative table of First Testament readings that correspond to the gospel selections following the pattern of the RL, EL, and LL; c) adds or adjusts pericopes to call greater attention to the women in the Bible; d) attempts to avoid readings that lend themselves to anti-Judaic interpretations (see "The Story of the Common Lectionary," in Consultation on Common Texts, Revised Common Lectionary, 75-9). The CL2 was approved for use as an alternative lectionary by the 1994 General Convention of the Episcopal Church. It will be adopted by the Evangelical Lutheran Church of America on the First Sunday of Advent, 1995.

[24] Although the selections in the CL2 introduced many more women into its selections, many problems found in the RL and its earlier variants were not resolved by the CL2. An analysis of the issues pertaining to women in the CL2 is a separate exercise. A preliminary study, "Women in the Roman and Common Lectionaries: Interpretations of Women from the Bible," was presented by the author at the annual meeting of the Society of Biblical Literature, Chicago, 1994.

[25] "Introduction," I:2, *Lectionary for Mass* (New York: Catholic Book Publishing Co., 1970), 9.

[26] Schuller, "Women in the Lectionary," 112.

[27] Marjorie Proctor-Smith, *In Her Own Rite: Constructing Feminist Liturgical Tradition* (Nashville: Abingdon, 1990), 125-6.

[28] National Council of the Churches of Christ in the U.S.A. Division of Education and Ministry, *An Inclusive Language Lectionary* (Atlanta: John Knox, 1983-1985, Rev. ed. 1986-1988).

[29] Gail Ramshaw and Gordon Lathrop, comps., *Lectionary for the Christian People* (New York: Pueblo, 1986).

[30] See Detscher, "The Second Edition," 4-7.

[31] Although the NCCB has authorized the use of other versions of the Bible in Catholic liturgies, the copyright of the NAB is held by the Confraternity of Christian Doctrine, Washington, DC. There are financial incentives for promoting the NAB as royalties are paid for its use in ambo lectionaries, personal missals, and disposable missalettes.

[32] For an assessment of the 1986 revision see Herbert G. Grether, "Translations and the Gender Gap," *Theology Today* 47 (1990): 302.

[33] Detscher, "The Second Edition," 5.

[34] Ibid., 6.

[35] Ibid., 7.

[36] At present, the Canadian Bishops remain committed to the NRSV.

[37] See Letty Russell, *Feminist Interpretation of the Bible*, ed., Letty Russell (Philadelphia: Westminster, 1985).

[38] God-language is the very heart of the Bible and liturgy, and God-language continue to perpetuate and reinforce an androcentric ideology in public worship. If there is a growing consensus between feminists and the institutional churches that when speaking about humans it is essential to use inclusive terms, the institutional churches have shown little inclination to make more than modest adjustments to the prominence of male-specific terms for God and male images of God in liturgy. This issue is discussed in Proctor-Smith, *In Her Own Rite*, 85-115; Mary Collins, "Naming God in Public Prayer," *Worship* 59 (1985): 301; Gail Ramshaw-Schmidt, *Christ in Sacred Speech: The Meaning of Liturgical Language* (Philadelphia: Fortress, 1986), 54-6. (See also Elisabeth A. Johnson, *She Who Is: The Mystery of God in Feminist Theological Discourse* [New York: Crossroad, 1992]).

[39] Miriam Therese Winter, *A Feminist Lectionary and Psalter*, 3 vols. (New York: Crossroads, 1990-92); Barbara Bowe, et al., comps. and eds., *Silent Voices and Sacred Lives. Women's Readings for the Liturgical Year* (New York and Mahwah: Paulist Press, 1992).

[40] Marjorie Proctor-Smith, "Images of Women in the Lectionary," in Elisabeth Schüssler Fiorenza and Mary Collins, eds., *Women Invisible in Church and Theology* (Edinburg: T & T Clark, 1985), 53-60.

[41] Jean Campbell, "The Feminine as Omitted, Optional, or Alternative Story: A Feminist Review of the Episcopal Eucharistic Lectionary," *Proceedings of the North American Academy of Liturgy* (1990), 66.

[42] George A. Lindbeck, *The Nature of Doctrine: Religion and Theology in a Postliberal Age* (Philadelphia: Westminster, 1984).

[43] Ibid., 118.

[44] Ibid., 34.

[45] Reumann, "History of Lectionaries," 129.

[46] E.g., Philip McBrien, *How to Teach with the Lectionary* (Mystic, CT: Twenty-Third Publications, 1992).

[47] E.g., *Seasons of Faith* (New York: Brown-Roa, 1991); *Lectionary Teaching Resources* (Denver: Living the Good News, Inc., 1976-1995); *Opening the Word* (New York: Sadlier, 1991).

[48] E.g., David Philippart, ed., *At Home with the Word* (Chicago: Liturgical Training Publications, 1993).

[49] (1) Gn 2:18-24 is appointed to the 27th Sunday in Year B (hereafter the symbol "=" will be used in place of the words "is appointed to the" when noting the occasion of each assignment); (2) Gn 2:7-8, 3:1-7 = 1st Sunday in Lent A; (3) Gn 3:9-15 = 10th Sunday in Year B; Gn 3:9-15, 20 = Immaculate Conception. Note: Three Sundays that fall between the 6th and 12th Sundays of the Year are dropped each year to accommodate the date of Easter and the American observance of Corpus Christi on the Sunday that follows Trinity Sunday. Thus, in Year B the readings for 10th Sunday are not used when this Sunday is suppressed to accommodate the date of Easter.

[50] Gn 18:1-10a = 16th Sunday in Year C. Sarah is also mentioned in Heb 11:1-2, 8-19 = 19th Sunday in Year C.

[51] 1 Kgs 17:10-16 = 32nd Sunday in Year B; 1 Kgs 17:17-24 = 10th Sunday in Year C.

[52] 2 Kgs 4:8-11, 15-16a = 13th Sunday in Year A.

[53] The RL and RL2 authorize using the readings assigned to Lent in Year A every year. This practice is recommended by the Rite of Christian Initiation for Adults.

[54] Bathsheba is obliquely referred to as the "wife of Uriah" in 2 Sam 12:7-13 = 11th Sunday in Year C. In addition, Tamar, Rahab, Ruth and the wife of Uriah are introduced in Mt 1:1-25 that is included in the gospel on Vigil of Christmas.

[55] Gn 16:1-6, 21:1-3 = Holy Family B.

[56] 1 Sm 1:20-22, 24-28 = Holy Family C.

[57] The only specific reading from the First Testament that must be read at the Easter Vigil is the account of the crossing of the sea from Ex 14:15-15:1. Although the 1981 *ordo* did not change this selection, the new Canadian lectionary inserts Ex 15:20 before 15:1a. Thus, the lesson used in Canada introduces Miriam the prophet who led women with tambourines in a dance to celebrate the deliverance at the sea. It is possible that this verse was also added to the U.S. edition. It is only one verse, but it is a commendable adjustment.

[58] Wis 6:12-16 = 32nd Sunday in Year A; Prov 9:1-6 = 20th Sunday in Year B; Wis 7:7-11 = 28 in Year B; Prov 8:22-31 = Trinity Sunday in Year C; Sir 24:1-4, 8-12 = 2nd Sunday after Christmas ABC; Bar 3:9-15, 32-4:4 = Easter Vigil ABC.

[59] 8th Sunday in Year C. The 8th Sunday of Year may be dropped to adjust for

the date of Easter. See note 49 above.

[60] Is 66:10-14c = 14th Sunday in Year C.

[61] 27th Sunday in Year B. Gn 1:26-30 and 5:1b-2 speak of a two-gender simultaneous creation in which both female and male are endowed with the image and/or the likeness of God. Gn 5:1b-2 is not in a selection, but Gn 1:1-2:2 is appointed to the annual Easter Vigil. By appointing Gn 1:1-2:2a to the Easter Vigil, the lectionary provides a lesson that affirms the equality of all humanity at its most solemn liturgy. Although this lesson may be dropped from the Vigil readings, the majestic creation hymn that opens Genesis is generally read.

[62] Phyllis Trible calls attention to the fact that the term *ezer* (NRSV = helper; NAB = partner) is most often used to describe God's relationship to Israel in *God and the Rhetoric of Sexuality* (Philadelphia: Fortress, 1978), 90.

[63] Trible, *God and the Rhetoric of Sexuality*, 72-143.

[64] David Joblin, "The Myth and Its Limits in Genesis 2:4b-3:24," in *The Sense of Biblical Narrative: Structural Analysis in the Hebrew Bible* (Sheffield, England: JSOT Press, 1986), 17-43. See also Pamela J. Milne, "Eve and Adam: Is a Feminist Reading Possible," *Bible Review* 4 (1988): 12-21, 39.

[65] Susan Brooks Thistlethwaite, "Every Two Minutes: Battered Women and Feminist Interpretation," in Judith Plaskow and Carol P. Christ, eds., *Weaving the Visions: New Patterns in Feminist Spirituality* (San Francisco: Harper & Row, 1989), 311.

[66] Ibid., 311.

[67] 16th Sunday in Year C.

[68] Susan Judith, "Genesis," in Carol A. Newsom and Sharon H. Ringe, eds., *Women's Bible Commentary* (London: SPCK and Louisville, KY: Westminster, John Knox, 1992), 18.

[69] Marie Louise Uhr, "The Portrayal of Women in the Lectionary," *St Marks Review* 135 (1988): 23.

[70] Typology is a complex issue that often lends support to Christian anti-Judaism. See Gail Ramshaw, "The First Testament in Christian Lectionaries," *Worship* 64 (1990): 494-510.

[71] Eugene O'Sullivan, "Some Criticisms of the Lectionary," in Patrick Rogers, ed., *Sowing the Word; Biblical-Liturgical Essays* (Dublin: Dominican Publications, 1983), 31.

[72] Ann McGrew Bennett, *From Woman-Pain to Woman-Vision: Writings in Feminist Theology*, ed., Mary E. Hunt (Minneapolis: Fortress, 1989), 81-2.

[73] Trible, *God and the Rhetoric of Sexuality*, 40.

[74] Reginald H. Fuller, "The Three-Year Eucharistic Lectionary," *Occasional Papers. Standing Liturgical Commission* 1 (November, 1982): 2.

[75] Acts 1:12-14 = 7 Easter A; 1 Cor 1:10-13, 17 = 3rd Sunday in Year A.

[76] Acts 1:14 = 7th Sunday in Easter A.

[77] Acts 5:14 = 2nd Sunday in Easter C.

[78] Acts 6:1 = 5th Sunday in Easter A.

[79] Acts 13:50 = 4th Sunday in Easter C.

[80] Gal 4:4-7 = Mary Mother of God (January 1).

[81] Gal 3:26-29 = 12th Sunday in Year C. When the American observance of Corpus Christi falls on the 12th Sunday of the Year in Year C, this reading will not be introduced. See note 50 above.

[82] I.e., 1 Cor 11:2-15, which decrees women are to be veiled; 1 Cor 14:34-35, which demands women's silence in the church; 1 Thes 4:4, which advises men to take "a wife" to insure their own holiness (note: "wife" is a translation of *skeuos* that literally means "a vessel"); 2 Tim 3:6-7, which describes women as unstable and incapable of making a rational decision; 1 Tim 2:9-15, which denies women the right to teach and makes women's salvation dependent on childbearing "provided she lives a sensible life in constant faith and holiness" (1 Tim 2:15).

[83] 21st Sunday in Year B.

[84] "Introduction," VI:7:c, *The Lectionary for Mass*, 10.

[85] Detscher, "The Second Edition," 5.

[86] The RL2 provides alternative second readings for Years B and C but the reading from Col 3 remains an option. It will be interesting to see if parishes use the reading for Year A every year or introduce the alternative selections in Years B and C.

[87] *Origins* 5 (1975): 702-6.

[88] Valerie Saiving, "The Human Situation: A Feminine View," in Carol P. Christ and Judith Plaskow, eds., *Womanspirit Rising: A Feminist Reader in Religion* (San Francisco: Harper & Row, 1979), 37; Wanda Deifelt, "Of Gardens and Theology: Women of Faith Respond," in Musimbi R.A. Kanyoro and Wendy S. Robins, eds., *The Power We Celebrate: Women's Stories of Faith and Power* (Geneva: WCC Publications, 1992), 11.

[89] "Structure and Order of Readings from Mass," 66, 93, 95, 97, 99, 100, 105, 108, *Lectionary for Sundays and Solemnities*, xxii-xxx.

[90] Mt 4:12-23 = 3rd Sunday in Year A; Mk 1:14-20 = 3rd Sunday in Year B; Lk 5:1-11 = 5th Sunday in Year C; Jn 1:35-42 = 2nd Sunday in Year B.

[91] Mt 16:13-20 = 21st Sunday in Year A and the Feast of Sts. Peter and Paul (The Feast of Sts. Peter and Paul has precedence over the Sunday cycle whenever June 29th falls on a Sunday); Mk 8:27-35 = 24th Sunday in Year B; Lk 9:18-24 = 12th Sunday in Year C; Jn 6:60-69 = 21st Sunday in Year B.

[92] For a list of the gospel parallels introduced in the RL2 see Normand Bonneau, "The Synoptic Gospels in the Sunday Lectionary: Ordinary Time," *Questions Liturgiques. Studies in Liturgy* 74 (1994): 154-69.

[93] Ruth Fox, "Strange Omission of Key Women in Lectionary," *National Catholic Reporter* 30 (May 13, 1994): 13-4.

[94] For a list of the gospel readings in the RL2 that introduce stories about women see Schuller, "Women in the Lectionary," 110-2.

[95] Mk 1:29-39 = 5th Sunday in Year B.

[96] 20th Sunday in Year A.

[97] Mk 12:38-44 = 32nd Sunday in Year B.

[98] Mk 3:31-35 = 10th Sunday in Year B.

[99] 28th Sunday in Year B.

[100] Mk 10:17-30 = 28th Sunday in Year B.

[101] Jn 4:5-42.

[102] Jn 4:4-5, 19-26, 39-42.

[103] Jn 11:1-45.

[104] Jn 11:3-7, 17, 20-27, 33-45.

[105] 13th Sunday in Year B.

[106] The passion narrative from John is introduced on Good Friday. This narrative mentions that Mary the mother of Jesus, Mary the wife of Clopas, and Mary Magdalene stood at the foot of the cross. It also reports Jesus' discussion about his mother with the disciple he loved (Jn 19:25b-27).

[107] Elisabeth Schüssler Fiorenza, *In Memory of Her: A Feminist Theological Reconstruction of Christian Origins* (New York: Crossroads, 1983), xiii-xiv.

[108] Ibid., 128-30.

[109] Proctor-Smith, "Liturgical Anamnesis," 405-6.

[110] Lk 7:36-8:3 = 11th Sunday in Year C.

[111] Jane Schaber, "How Mary Magdalene Became a Whore," *Bible Review* 8 (1992): 30-37, 51-52.

[112] In Year C Lk 7:36-50 (11th Sunday) and Jn 8:1-18 (5th Sunday of Lent) use women to image human sinfulness. Jn 8:1-18 is the story of Jesus' encounter with a woman caught in adultery. Although the men who wish to stone the woman come to recognize that they too are sinful, the woman's sin is specifically associated with gender, the sins of the men are not. Together the two readings can lend themselves to the suggestion that women, as women, are especially inclined to sinfulness.

[113] Proctor-Smith, "Liturgical Anamnesis," 406-7.

[114] Pontifical Biblical Commission, "The Interpretation of the Bible in the Church," IV:C:1, *Origins* 23 (January 6, 1994) 1, 499-524.

[115] Pontifical Biblical Commission, "The Interpretation of the Bible in the Church," I:E:2, 524.

[116] Bugnini, *The Reform of the Liturgy*, 410.

Historical Perspectives on Women Religious: Implications for Creating a Feminist Theology of Religious Life

Susan Marie Maloney

Feminist theology seeks to give voice to women's experience in the past as well as in the present. Its task is not only to unmask the oppressive nature of patriarchal theology but also to construct a critical theology of liberation for women and the entire Christian community. Feminist liberation theology "articulates as its core-problem how androcentric language, theoretical frameworks, and theological scholarship function to sustain and perpetuate patriarchal structures in society and the Church."[1] Therefore feminist theologians must examine carefully and critically the sources of theoretical frameworks and theological scholarship. One such source in need of critical examination is the history commonly used in the construction of theologies of religious life.

Philip Sheldrake summarizes the problem. He writes:

> . . . history-making has tended to record what men do, or at least what a theory of history created in a male dominated world, finds significant. In terms of mainstream spirituality, women have been conceived as generally marginal to its creation. Alongside other marginalized groups, their absence distorts our historical mentality and causes conceptual errors . . . They are effectively excluded from the formation of theory which determines not only what history is but what spirituality is . . . Exclusion from the account of history not only reinforces [their] subordination but, more damagingly, may create a sense of being *essentially* insignificant.[2]

Until recently, the history of women religious was either ignored or fused with the recorded achievements of male religious orders. For example, the experience of women religious has generally been absent from histories of the U.S. Catholic Church.[3] This neglect, a fault in itself, has negative consequences for the construction of a feminist theory of religious life for women. For any theologian the complex relationship of history and theological interpretation is problematic. It is still more complicated for the feminist seeking to write a theology of religious life. Male dominated history, its interpretation and its use in the construction of an historical paradigm to describe the development of religious life[4] have kept the experience of women from its rightful place in the construction of a theology of religious life for women.

To understand the import of such an assertion it will be necessary: 1) to examine the dominant historical paradigm used in theories of religious life, 2) to explore historical scholarship on the lives of women religious written from the perspective of women-centered history, and 3) to argue that the appropriation of "the new feminist religious history"[5] by theologians is imperative in order to construct a theology of religious life for women which accurately reflects their life experiences.

As a white middle-class U.S. Catholic woman my social location influences the theological enterprise I undertake. I am acutely aware that this essay does not address the cultural and ethnic concerns involved in the appropriation of historical scholarship for the construction of a theology of religious life for women of the United States. This is another project which must be addressed in a future article. In this article, however, my thesis is that the construction of a contemporary feminist theology of religious life for women of the United States is dependent on a history centered on the lives of women religious which accurately represents their past lives, commitments and achievements.'

The Hostie-Cada Traditional Model

For the last twenty years, scholars of religious life have relied on the theoretical model of the history of Western religious orders as constructed by the French historian Raymond Hostie. Hostie's paradigm spans the history of religious life from the early third and fourth centuries to the contemporary period.[6]

Familiar to many, this model of religious life divides the history of religious life into five eras: the flight into the desert, the age of the monastics, the mendicant era, the age of the apostolic orders, and the age of the teaching congregations. According to this traditional perspective, each of these eras represents a "natural" evolutionary stage in the development of religious life. The flight into the desert was a response to the growing institutionalization of the Church during the first centuries of Christianity. The rise of monasticism was a reaction to the chaos and instability of Western culture beset by invasion and war. The mendicant orders were formed in answer to the materialism of the thirteenth century and the widespread deprivation among the poor. The apostolic orders were founded to counter the critique of the Protestant Reformation. The growth in teaching congregations during the eighteenth and nineteenth centuries, especially in the United States, met the growing social needs of health care and education, particularly for the immigrant Catholic population.[7]

An interdisciplinary team of scholars headed by Lawrence Cada used Hostie's model and popularized it by creating a sociological life cycle for religious congregations which applied the earlier author's work.[8] Later, other scholars from the disciplines of theology,[9] sociology,[10] anthropology[11] as well as popular writers on religious life adopted both the Hostie historical model and Cada's sociological cycle to explain the social/scientific perspective on religious life.[12] Even prominent contemporary works, such as the Nygren and Ukeritis study, entitled *The Future of Religious Orders in the United States: Transformation and Commitment*, and the study commissioned by the Leadership Conference of Women Religious (LCWR), and edited by Anne Munley, *Threads for the Loom*, rely on Hostie's historical model appropriated by Cada and Padberg.[13] A few examples will demonstrate how the model and its treatment of women are inadequate for use in the construction of a theology of religious life for contemporary women.

Treatment of Women in the Hostie-Cada Model

The traditional Hostie model as popularized by Lawrence Cada and his colleagues does not ignore or neglect the lives of women. Rather the eras of the model, determined on the basis of the development of male religious life, create a periodization which makes invisible some of the obvious achievements of women religious. One brief example illustrates this point. In Cada's study, Brigit of Kildare is cited as the foundress of a double monastery (women and men) in fifth-century (480) Ireland. However, because her life falls within the Hostie periodization for the age of the desert (the eremetical era), Brigit's name and achievement receive no recognition in the development of religious life. Despite the clear evidence that Brigit headed a double monastery approximately fifty years prior to Benedict, Cada and associates fail to confront the question of whether or not Brigit rather than Benedict is the initiator of monastic religious life.[14]

Cada and his co-authors do admit the limitations of adhering strictly to an historical model that underrepresents the lives of women religious. They write: "a still more gaping lacuna is the sketchy analysis of the way that women's religious lives differed from or followed the same pattern as that of men."[15]

Despite this admission of neglect by the authors, they persist in the use of the Hostie model, thus implying such neglect to be inconsequential. However, that consistent neglect leads not only to an inaccuracy in recording the past lives of women religious but also perpetuates a notion that women religious are not the initiators and shapers of their own religious lives. It further perpetuates the notion that the experience of women religious is similar to that of male religious simply because they aspire to the same ideals. Its repeated use by authors who accept it uncritically or modify it slightly[16] has distorted women's experience in the general accounts of the development and theology of religious life.

Implications of the Hostie-Cada Model

A synopsis of the Hostie-Cada paradigm reveals: 1) that its repeated use by authors in a variety of disciplines grants it an historical status which is unwarranted; 2) that the evident differences in the lives of women religious get collapsed into a pre-determined cycle of change based on the lives of men thus making the achievements of women religious invisible;[17] 3) that where disputes between women and male church authorities occur they are either dismissed, or viewed as personality conflicts, not as historical events which would significantly challenge the five-era paradigm of change. Conversely, when women religious bend to the demands of the hierarchy, this coerced response is idealized as obedience to a holy rule rather than an instance of repression of women's ideas or practices.[18]

The Hostie-Cada model with its five-era periodic paradigm of change supports a unitary understanding of the development of religious life—that is, it supports the understanding that the lives of women religious will develop and change along the same lines as those of men. It also serves to perpetuate a single theory of religious life. In the past, theological theories of religious life were written primarily by men for both men and women. The model easily complemented these theologies. Women religious need a history of their own which neither denies their repression nor discounts their achievements. Historical scholarship centered on the lives of women religious gives the feminist theologian the concrete foundation on which to build an authentic theology of religious life for women.

Women's History and the History of Women Religious

Current historical studies which focus on the lives of women religious offer an alternative to the periodic sequence of the Hostie-Cada paradigm and the subordinate role it assigns to women. This section will look at women-centered historical studies which deal with women in the early Christian era, women in monasticism, women in the counter-reformation. It will then give special attention to the history of women religious in the U.S. Through their work these scholars document a past which makes the motivations and achievements of women religious the subject of history and not simply complementary events of male dominated projects.

Religious Women in the Early Christian Era

When Jo Ann McNamara,[19] a historian of early Christianity, began her study of ascetic women, she assumed that the traditional beginning of religious life was the flight of St. Antony to the desert.[20] However, in reading Athanasius' life of Antony, she was startled by a brief sentence. Prior to his venturing into the desert Antony was obliged to make arrangements for his orphaned sister. McNamara quotes from Athanasius: "He solved the problem by placing her in a house of consecrated women."[21]

From McNamara's work in the period of early Christianity six points may be summarized. First, the virginal life of women was fully sanctioned by patristic writers only *after* women had made it a practical reality. Second, women chose to have a celibate life, contrary to popular opinion that it was foisted upon them. Third, in actuality the early Christian Fathers reacted to the activities of women, they did not initiate them.[22] Fourth, independent women who chose a new form of life disturbed the social order by remaining unmarried. Fifth, in addition to their sexual independence from men these women carried out ministerial functions like preaching and teaching. Their actions came under sharp critical attacks by the hierarchy, though, eventually the widespread practice of these functions by Christian women in large numbers forced the social and ecclesial order to accept them. Sixth, in time, the clergy of the early Church acted to define and give recognition to "true virgins" thus establishing conditions for such recognition.[23]

McNamara's research documents the ability of women in early Christianity to claim their own religious lives, contrary to social norms. Her study details not only the struggle of women to be religiously autonomous but also details the gradual success of the clergy in defining these independent women along a continuum of virtuous womanhood. McNamara argues that communities of consecrated women existed before the fathers of the church found a place for them in the larger institutional structure of the church.[24] The women of these communities sought to balance a claim to define their own religious lives and at the same time to participate in the ministries of the Church. The tension between the need for approval from the clergy and resistance to undue control by them was settled, for a time.[25]

Thus, we can see that McNamara's research not only provides an alternative to the dominant Hostie-Cada historical model of religious life for women during the age of the desert but also casts a new light on the origins of religious life for women, particularly in the early period of Christianity. In addition, it places the tensions between present day women religious and the Church hierarchy relative to autonomy in an historical context which values women's experience. It also provides insight into the relationship between male control over women and the institutionalization which accompanies it. The recurring reality of male institutionalization of the lives of women religious reappears again as a theme in the age of monasticism.

Women in Monasticism

Writing on the rule of monastic enclosure, Jane Tibbetts Schulenburg suggests that the mandate for cloister was applied differently to women than to men.[26] Initially, enclosure was expected and required for both monks and nuns. This fostered an atmosphere of worship and prayer in the monastery. It also put nuns on an equal footing with the monks; their similar practices of prayer, fasting and worship made them appear as equal before God.

Schulenburg's findings show that twelfth-century reforms reversed this equality of monks and nuns.[27] The "reforms" established a uniform and rigid policy of claustration for all nuns but not for monks. Over time this difference of treatment with its disparity of gendered ideals contributed to the decline of women's monasticism. According to Schulenburg the policy of strict enclosure lessened the autonomy of nuns' communities, reinforced the basic assumption that nuns could not control their own lives, aided the financial decline of women's monastic communities, and legislated increased dependence of nuns on bishops.[28]

Schulenburg concludes that underlying these reforms were the fears of the clergy; she writes: "At its root this restrictive policy seems to have been based on the clerical reformers' fear of female sexuality and their pervasive distrust of women. It seems to reflect the underlying misogynism which one finds especially during periods of reform."[29] Similar to the research of McNamara, Schulenburg's work gives contemporary women religious an insight into the historical and institutional manifestation of misogynism in the Church. The author uncovers the misogynist ideology underlying the monastic cloister. On the one hand, nuns are revered as spiritually superior to other women, while on the other hand, enclosure is the material expression of male control and protection of women. Undoubtedly monastic life had some advantages for women. However, Schulenburg's research reveals that the traditional understanding of women in monasticism is more complex than the Hostie-Cada model indicates. In the Hostie-Cada model the interpretation of the cloister for women is one of limitation and protection. In Schulenburg's interpretation of the cloister, she sees the significance of the issue of male control over female religious.

Women Religious in the Counter-Reformation Period

An alternative interpretation to the Hostie-Cada model in the counter-reformation period is the work of historian Elizabeth Rapley. In her groundbreaking study of women dévotées in seventeenth-century France,[30] Rapley frames the rise of women's religious orders within a social and ecclesial context of great turmoil. She argues that most historians of seventeenth-century France chronicle an unfavorable description of women's communities because of an aggressive anti-feminism and irresistible trend toward patriarchy which generally characterizes this period. Women's religious communities are perceived in these studies as female subsidiaries of male orders, passive to clerical and secular authorities. When their activities are recorded they frequently are subjects of church prohibitions or exclusion.[31]

Rapley's research provides an historical examination which counters this traditional thesis. She describes a religious movement of dévotées as deeply religious women who invaded the life of the church through the establishment of apostolates not under Church authority. This phenomenon, which preceded the existence of convents and official Church recognition, resulted in a "rush" into religious life. Driven by religious motivation and piety to serve and teach the faithful, these women threatened Church authority.

Rapley argues that despite the resistance of male Church authorities these women, fortified by their religious motivation and the recognition of their charitable works, overcame Church hostility and gained public support. They were creators of their own religious lives, and did not simply live according to the creation of others. Nor did these women simply fulfill a social need of providing health care and teaching during the seventeenth century. Their religious piety and energy fueled their apostolates and services, not vice versa. However, without a compromise they could not be considered nuns by the hierarchy. In order to follow their own consciences they renounced the title and appearances of religious life but followed many of its practices.

Unlike the Hostie-Cada model, Rapley's work documents a new phase of female religious life. "The *'filles séculières'* as they were called—knew full well that they were nuns in all but name."[32] She asserts that the contribution female congregations made in the seventeenth century to France is incalculable. "For three centuries they acted as the Church's teachers, nurses, and social workers, and the parish clergy's strong right arm."[33] But this promotion and recognition in hindsight was not without cost.

Rapley's findings provide a story of seventeenth-century French women religious which makes *them* the subject of historical research not their works, nor their relationship with their male mentors. Unlike the Hostie-Cada model, her research locates for the feminist theologian the historical stress points which accompany the theological tensions between the male clergy and women during the Counter Reformation. More importantly, Rapley's work reveals a distinctive portrait of religious women:

> Religious women registered an advance during a period that for most other women was characterized by retreat. Against a general background of feminine weakness, the feminine religious life became a nucleus of real, though always discreet, strength. The "great Catholic females of the Counter-Reformation" enjoyed opportunities for organizational activity far beyond anything that Protestant women were allowed. Their power and influence were transferred to the collectives which formed around them: their religious communities.[34]

Like Rapley's work, Ruth Liebowitz's study[35] of Angela Merici (b. 1474), Mary Ward (b. 1610) and Louise de Marillac (b. 1630) presents their endeavors, struggles and achievements as the subject of history rather than as adjunct events to male projects. Her research chronicles the controversy and intense opposition to their efforts from the hierarchy and the larger society of Catholic Europe.

These three great women developed apostolates of service and work in the world. According to Liebowitz they shared a similar vision: to establish a community of unmarried religious women in order to respond to critical social needs. They each initially rejected the constraints of the cloister and the vows. Angela in Italy, Mary in England, and Louise in France, each proposed a radical alternative to the conventual monasticism of her day. Their communities, called congregations, not orders, chose to live in small groups, forego the religious habit and work singly or with others in the public sphere. They were devoted to female education and charitable works for the poor.[36] Each wished to remain in a lay (non-canonical) status with a structured organization which coordinated its members under the leadership of women.

In spite of the championship of their new way of life by some Church authorities (especially for their charitable works), each woman—Angela, Mary and Louise—experienced trials, obstacles and hostility. In the end, according to Liebowitz, each of these women submitted to certain compromises in order to have her aims and goals partially achieved.[37]

Angela Merici was never a "true" religious, she never took vows. Her followers, the Ursulines, however, eventually were forced to compromise and to wear a habit, to live in a community and to take vows. Mary Ward's institute was suppressed by papal decree in 1629. She was imprisoned at one point as a heretic. It was not until the nineteenth century that Mary Ward's religious descendants would receive papal approval of their order. Louise de Marillac, and her followers, the Daughters of Charity, did receive Church approval. However, in order to achieve it, their compromises, among others, included wearing a habit, conformity to a regular schedule, and submission to the order of Vincent de Paul and his Mission Fathers. Under the influence of Vincent, they acquiesced to the obligation of simple vows renewed on an annual basis.[38]

Liebowitz's research, like Rapley's, shows that during the Counter-Reformation era, new forms of the commitment of religious life for women gained acceptance—at a great price. All three of the groups[39] failed to attain their original goal: apostolic work and autonomous religious lives designed and organized by women with the approval of Church authority. Liebowitz leads us to look at the deeper issues underlying these failures, compromises and partial victories. None of the three women ever questioned the basic assumptions about religious life. Their resistance was to the oppressive male-constructed norms which institutionalized their endeavors and commitment, not to the spiritual ideals of poverty and virginity.[40]

Furthermore, in the work of Rapley and Liebowitz the religious ideals of these great women, as developed through the interplay of ecclesial and social forces, are given the central position. Unlike those studies based on the Hostie-Cada model, studies like Rapley's and Liebowitz's radically change the focus of the history of the lives of women religious. In the Hostie-Cada model women are assigned subordinate roles and their achievements credited to their male mentors.[41] By contrast, in the women-centered analyses of Rapley and Liebowitz such women autonomously exhibit tenacity and courage in the face of hierarchical and patriarchal obstruction. These analyses also shed light on the struggles women undergo simply because they are women. Finally, these studies introduce us to the complexity of the cultural context in which women strove to attain religious self-determination. Similarly, historians of U.S. women religious seek to retrieve historical accounts which place women not only at the center of historical research but within a specific cultural context.

The Americanization of Religious Life for Women

The Americanization of religious life occurred over a period of several centuries.[42] The nineteenth century in the U.S. saw rapid growth in the number of women religious. Over 220 congregations were established in the U.S. between 1830 and 1900 alone. These figures include congregations of both European and American origin. During this time, great demands from the new democratic culture required rapid adaptation, of the life-style of women religious. These two factors, the rapid growth in numbers of women religious and the need for their cultural adaptation create a monumental task for the women-centered historian in weaving a coherent theory about the lives of women religious in the United States.

For these reasons this section has a limited focus. First, it will summarize the difficulties in the documentation of women-centered history of U.S. women religious. Second, it will demonstrate, through the work of Mary Ewens, the significant difference of a women-centered history, not only for the construction of a theology of religious life but also in the identification of the role U.S. women religious played in the development of American society.

Historical research about women religious in the United States for the nineteenth and twentieth centuries has been problematic for scholars of women's history. The lives of U.S. women religious until recently received scant attention from Church and secular historians.[43]

The work of historian Margaret Susan Thompson details many reasons for this historical neglect of the lives of U.S. women religious. She writes: "Sisters, like all women—and because they are women—have largely been ignored by both the Church and secular historians, nearly all of whom have been male."[44] Thompson suggests that the patriarchal and hierarchical organization of the Church lends itself to the omission of women from its records. When histories were written of women religious many were inspirational tracts, hagiographies rather than analytical studies. These historical works concentrated on the individual lives of women religious that were mainly hortatory biographies of women foundresses.[45]

In addition, Thompson cites the customs and attitudes of women religious in the past which contributed to this neglect. Each congregation kept its own archives;[46] secular historians had little or no access to this rich source of material. Also the ideal of the virtue of humility fostered a lack of self-esteem on the part of the women which hindered the preservation of records of their significant achievements for posterity. Unfortunately, this lack of historical evidence occurred despite the fact that women religious for the past 150 years outnumbered the clergy and men religious in the U.S. Church.[47]

Regardless of their attachment to institutional Church structures, the tendency to separate the history of women religious from the history of the achievement of the larger Church has one notable exception in the Catholic educational system. This exception is understandable since women religious held a monopoly on staffing Catholic schools in the U.S.A.[48]

Only within recent years have critical historical studies explored the lives of women religious, their adaptation to an egalitarian and democratic society and the changes this created in their lives. Much credit must be given to the Conference on the History of Women Religious, which seeks to make the past lives of women religious central to historical research. Through studies supported by this Conference evidence is slowly emerging chronicling how women religious adjusted their monastic lives of dedication to U.S. culture.

One such women-centered history is Mary Ewens' study of the nun in nineteenth-century America.[49] According to Ewens, U.S. sisters were generally regarded with suspicion and hostility in the nineteenth-century, largely because of the Protestant concept of a nun. This distorted image was primarily promoted in the anti-Catholic books prevalent in nineteenth-century European and American literature.[50] Ewens' study gives evidence of the falseness of this image. Her work demonstrates the active participation of sisters in the pioneering life of the growing nation.

One of the turning points in a change of attitude toward the U.S. nun, Ewens argues, was the sisters' response during the Civil War. Nuns volunteered to aid and nurse the soldiers. They were visible on the battle fields comforting the wounded and consoling the dying. This highly dangerous service gained them public respect for their Christian commitment and concern. It also lessened the prejudice and hostility towards the Catholic Church. In addition it provided widespread contact with nuns which dispelled negative public opinion about them. The attitudinal change was so dramatic after the war that nuns were given public recognition and acclaim by President Grant for their efforts.[51]

Women-centered studies, such as that of Ewens, are valuable and necessary but insufficient for the feminist theologian. Women-centered histories that describe the lives and events of women religious provide an alternative to the Hostie-Cada model of religious life. These descriptions of women's achievements, struggles and commitments give women religious their rightful place in history. However, for the theologian these essential works of women-centered histories need to be complemented by a feminist perspective which acts as a corrective to the interpretation of the recorded past.

New Feminist Religious History—Source for a Feminist Theology of Religious Life for Women

Feminist religious history takes women-centered history one step further. In her essay, "Women, Feminism, and the New Religious History: Catholic Sisters as a Case Study,"[52] Margaret Susan Thompson explains how a feminist historical perspective offers a further alternative to the Hostie-Cada model and provides a new portrait of women religious and their past.

One of the few historical works to examine the lives of women religious across congregational lines[53] Thompson's study shows that despite pietistic historiographies and spiritual writings, contention and disharmony characterize the lives and relationships of women religious. She writes:

the most pervasive pattern I encountered within women's religious orders was that of conflict. Disputes among sisters were frequent and usually centered on one or more of three sources of tension: class, ethnic antagonisms and the increasingly disparate visions of European superiors and women from their communities who were missioned in the U.S.[54]

However, she later acknowledges this internal discord among the sisters is less significant than the friction and confrontations between men and women. She states: "Gender-defined confrontations between women and men . . . occurred without exception in every one of the approximately 175 communities on which I have done research."[55]

Thompson's work documents that the struggle and tension between Church prelates and sisters was rooted in four factors: 1) generic clericalism, 2) patriarchy which delimits the role of women, 3) notions of authority within the Catholic hierarchy and 4) ambiguous treatment of women's congregations by Church authorities.[56] Without a feminist historical perspective, the story of one woman or one community's struggle is perceived only as an individual event. However, a feminist historical perspective, like that of Thompson, rightly identifies such an individual event as having social and religious implications for all women.

U.S. historians who employ the "new feminist religious history" offer a critique and analysis of the patriarchal power male clerics have wielded against women religious throughout the past. Feminist analysis takes into account the maintenance of patriarchal practices which have repressed women's initiatives and insights. The emerging women-centered histories of U.S. women religious with a feminist perspective, like those of Thompson,[57] give the feminist theologian new ground on which to construct a contemporary feminist theology of religious life. They not only provide new accounts of women's experience in the past but also give evidence of lives of virtue rooted in the actual practice and work of women religious. Feminist histories put into the forefront of their analysis the struggle of women religious. Conflict and tension to maintain their own autonomy and initiative in practicing their religious commitment is central to these studies. None of these contentions, with an analysis from a women's perspective, can emerge using an historical model based on the lives of male religious.

Conclusion

Women's history suggests that the experiences of women religious in the past were not only different from those of men but provided a source of a new identity as religious to women. The historical research indicates that when women sought to define their own religious lives, male Church authorities generally did not give approval unless women conformed to pre-conceived models. Such a model of religious life is exemplified in the traditional historical model of Hostie-Cada.

The paradigm of Hostie-Cada not only is based on male religious orders but also defines the boundaries of authentic religious life so as to include for study only those forms (or institutes or groups) which were institutionalized and approved by the hierarchical Church. The boundaries of the Hostie-Cada model eliminate the history of struggle and conflict that occurred for women religious as they carved out their own valid commitment within the Catholic tradition. Women who are ignored in the Hostie-Cada model, or not approved, or non-canonical, simply do not count as "true" religious. This history of the "losers" or the misfits in relationship to the evolution of the lives of women religious is critical. It is the story of the "misfits," or autonomous religious women, that may hold great insight for the future of contemporary religious life.

More important, the retrieval of the lost history of women religious, separate from men religious, gives women religious of the past a moral as well as historical identity. This moral identity is critical to the development of a feminist theology of religious life for women. Since women religious of the past were deprived of developing theological theories based on their own lives, the only means by which feminist theologians can gain some insight into theological and moral theory of their past is through the accounts of moral practices of women religious.

Hence, the studies of women religious by feminist historians carry a greater weight than initially thought. They function 1) to critique an historical system of patriarchy, 2) to connect hierarchical governance with male power over women, and 3) to retrieve a lost history of conflict between women religious and Church authorities. In addition, a feminist historical perspective establishes for the theologian that the tensions of the past between women religious and clerics are not simply descriptive. Rather they reveal the universal struggle between clerical men and women religious: the contest for control and theological interpretation of the lives of women.

Finally, the emerging history of women religious gives the feminist theologian historical evidence in understanding the experience of women religious as a valid theological ground unto itself. A women-centered history of women religious remains largely unexamined in the theological discourse of religious life and in particular in understanding new forms of religious life and public commitment. When feminist theologians begin to construct a theology of religious life from women's experience, the heritage they claim, in whatever culture, is a newly recovered past which breaks the dominant position of the Hostie-Cada model. But it is much more. Women-centered historical studies with a feminist perspective uncover for the feminist scholar a rich theological source of pre-institutionalized commitment based in the practice and work of women religious.

Notes

[1] Elisabeth Schüssler Fiorenza and Mary Collins, eds., *Women Invisible in Church and Theology, Concilium* 182 (Edinburgh: T & T Clark Ltd., 1985), p. 4.

[2] Philip Sheldrake, *Spirituality and History* (New York: Crossroad, 1992), p. 97.

[3] See Lora Ann Quiñonez and Mary Daniel Turner, *The Transformation of American Catholic Sisters* (Philadelphia: Temple University Press, 1992), viii. Margaret Susan Thompson, "Discovering Foremothers: Sisters, Society and the American Catholic Experience," in *The American Catholic Religious Life*, ed. Joseph White (New York: Garland Publishing, Inc., 1988), pp. 273-290.

[4] Sheldrake, *Spirituality and History*, pp. 107-132.

[5] Margaret Susan Thompson, "Women, Feminism and the New Religious History: Catholic Sisters as a Case Study," in *Belief and Behavior: Essays in the New Religious History*, ed. Philip VanderMeer and Robert P. Swierenga (New Brunswick, NJ: Rutgers University Press, 1991), pp. 136-63.

[6] Raymond Hostie, *La Vie et Mort des Ordres Religieux* (Paris: Desclée De Brouwer, 1972).

[7] Lawrence Cada, R. Fitz, G. Foley, T. Giardino and C. Lichtenberg, *Shaping the Coming Age of Religious Life* (New York: Seabury Press, 1979), pp. 11-50.

[8] Cada, *Shaping the Coming Age of Religious Life*, pp. 14; 51-76. In addition to Hostie's work as a source for data on the history of religious life, Cada lists the 1907 and 1967 versions of *The Catholic Encyclopedia*, the *Annuario Pontificio* and other Catholic compilations. Salesian priest Lorenzoni gives the following reflection on the *Annuario Pontificio*. "Its [*Annuario Pontificio*] outstanding feature, which distinguishes it from any other directory in the world (except perhaps the Ayatollah's organization in Iran), is the almost total absence of females in its pages. The alphabetical list at the end of the directory is consequently 99.99 percent male." Larry Lorenzoni, "The Annuario Pontificio and Women in the Church" *Sisters Today* 59:3 (November, 1987): p. 156.

[9] Thomas Regan, "New Needs . . . New Paradigms: The Changing Character of Religious Life" in *Review for Religious* 49:2 (March/April, 1990): pp. 220-225. John W. Padberg, "The Past as Prologue" in *Religious Life at the Crossroads*, ed. David Fleming (New York: Paulist Press, 1985), pp. 5-8. See also Marcello Azevedo, *Vocation for Mission: The Challenge of Religious Life Today* (New York: Paulist Press, 1988), p. 38.

[10] Patricia Wittberg, *Creating a Future for Religious Life: A Sociological Perspective* (New York: Paulist Press, 1991), p. 25.

[11] Gerald Arbuckle, *Out of Chaos: Refounding Religious Congregations* (New Jersey: Paulist Press, 1988), p. 70. See also Diarmuid O'Murchu, *Religious Life: Prophetic Vision* (Notre Dame: Ave Maria Press, 1991), p. 64.

[12] Mary Jo Leddy, *Reweaving Religious Life: Beyond the Liberal Model* (Mystic, CT: Twenty-Third Publications, 1990), p. 152. See endnote No. 5, p. 179.

[13] David J. Nygren and Miriam D. Ukeritis, *The Future of Religious Orders in the United States: Transformation and Commitment* (Westport, CT.: Praeger Publishers, 1993), xx. Anne Munley, *Threads for the Loom* (Silver Spring: Leadership Conference of Women Religious, 1992), p. 2.

[14] Cada, *Shaping the Coming Age of Religious Life*, pp. 19-20.

[15] Ibid., p. 44.

[16] Schneiders uses this historical schema but modifies it slightly by her statement: "In fact, the first religious were the virgins and widows of the first centuries of the Christian era." She does not suggest that this evidence alters the stages in the traditional historical perspective. Sandra Schneiders, *New Wineskins: Reimagining Religious Life Today* (New York: Paulist Press, 1986), p. 48. Similarly, Lozano acknowledges the historical evidence of virgins and widows in the early Christian era. He, however, treats this evidence in an excursus to explain the notion of consecration of virgins (read women). John Lozano, *Discipleship: Towards an Understanding of Religious Life* (Chicago: Claret Center for Resources in Spirituality, 1980), pp. 284-285.

[17] In justifying his use of Hostie's model, O'Murchu states, "The theoretical framework was initially outlined by French Jesuit Raymond Hostie. His theory makes many generalizations, is based on a number of unproven assumptions, and is modeled exclusively on male orders and congregations. Nonetheless, it carries a ring of truth and makes sense of historical developments that otherwise remain disconcerting and baffling." O'Murchu, *Religious Life: Prophetic Vision*, p. 64. For a discussion of the assumptions underlying the traditional model see Philip Sheldrake, "Revising Historical Perspectives" *The Way* 65 (Summer, 1989): pp. 66-67.

[18] Hostie, *La Vie et Mort des Ordres Religieux*, p. 6. See also Wittberg, *Creating a Future for Religious Life*, p. 29.

[19] Jo Ann McNamara, *A New Song: Celibate Women in the First Three Christian Centuries* (New York: Haworth Press, 1983), p. 1.

[20] See Elisabeth Schüssler Fiorenza, *In Memory of Her: A Feminist Theological Reconstruction of Christian Origins* (New York: Crossroad Publishing Co., 1985);

Rosemary Radford Ruether, ed. *Religion and Sexism: Images of Woman in the Jewish and Christian Traditions* (New York: Simon and Schuster, 1974); Jean LaPorte, *The Role of Women in Early Christianity* (New York: The Edwin Mellen Press, 1982).

[21] McNamara, *A New Song*, p. 1. See also Elisabeth Schüssler Fiorenza, "Word, Spirit and Power: Women in Early Christian Communities" in *Women of Spirit: Female Leadership in the Jewish and Christian Traditions*, eds. Rosemary Ruether and Eleanor McLaughlin (New York: Simon and Schuster, 1979), pp. 29-70.

[22] McNamara, *A New Song*, pp. 1-5.

[23] Ibid., pp. 67-76.

[24] Ibid., pp. 115-125.

[25] Ibid., pp. 120-124.

[26] Jane Tibbetts Schulenburg, "Strict Active Enclosure and Its Effects on the Female Monastic Experience (ca. 500-1000)" in *Distant Echoes*, ed. John Nichols and Lillian Thomas (Kalamazoo, MI: Cistercian Publications, 1984), pp. 51-85.

[27] Ibid., pp. 78-79.

[28] Ibid., pp. 77-85.

[29] Ibid., p. 79.

[30] Elizabeth Rapley, *The Dévotées: Women and Church in Seventeenth Century France* (Montreal: McGill-Queen's University Press, 1990).

[31] Ibid., pp. 3-5, 7.

[32] Ibid., p. 7.

[33] Ibid., p. 8.

[34] Ibid., p. 5.

[35] Ruth Liebowitz, "Virgins in the Service of Christ: The Dispute over an Active Apostolate for Women during the Counter-Reformation," in *Women of Spirit* , pp. 131-152.

[36] Ibid., p. 133.

[37] Lynn Jarrell provides an in-depth study of the legal and canonical implications of the struggle by Catholic women to attain apostolic autonomy and yet be recognized by Church authorities. See Lynn Jarrell, "The Development of Legal Structures for Women Religious between 1500 and 1900: A Study of Selected Institutes of Religious Life for Women," *U.S. Catholic Historian* 10 (1989): pp. 1-2, 25-32.

[38] Liebowitz, "Virgins in the Service of Christ," pp. 144-145.

[39] Liebowitz mentions other communities of women who suffered the same or similar fates: Jeanne de Chantal and the Visitation Sisters of France and Lodovica Torelli De Guastalla who founded the female Barnabites of Italy. Because of the restrictions of cloister, Guastalla left her community and founded a school for girls under the auspices of the civil authorities. Liebowitz, "Virgins in the Service of Christ," pp. 142-144.

[40] Ibid., pp. 130-132.

[41] For example, "The initiatives, however revolutionary, of Angela Merici and her subsequent avatars illustrate how strong and tenacious the traditional formulas

are in the evolution of religious life. As soon as the foundation expands, it is made to conform to the expectations and the imperatives of the prevailing mind set. But let us be fair. Certainly their protectors and promoters, Charles Borromeo especially, imposed it on them. But it is not less true that the members who came aspired to this model and worked toward it with all their energy. *One would even say that such a spectacular expansion could not have been realized without this reversal of perspective.*" Hostie, *La Vie et Mort des Ordres Religieux*, p. 43, [sic] quoted in Wittberg, *Creating a Future for Religious Life*, p. 29. Underlining by Wittberg.

[42] The Ursulines were the first sisters to arrive in American territory in New Orleans (1727). See Karen Kennelly, "Historical Perspectives on the Experience of Religious Life in the American Church," in *Religious Life in the U.S. Church: The New Dialogue*, ed. Robert J. Daly et al. (New York: Paulist Press, 1984), p. 81.

[43] Marie Augusta Neal writes, "almost all of the literature written prior to the Second Vatican Council was done by men ..." See her preface in Elizabeth Kolmer, *Religious Women in the United States: A Survey of Influential Literature from 1950 to 1983* (Wilmington, DE: Michael Glazier, Inc., 1984), p. 13. See Karen Kennelly, "Women as Church in a New Land" in *U.S. Catholic Historian*, 8:4 (Fall, 1989), p. 65. For samples of work which neglect women religious see Jay Dolan, *The American Catholic Experience* (New York: Doubleday, 1985) and James Hennesey, *American Catholics* (New York: Oxford University Press, 1981).

[44] Thompson, "Discovering Foremothers, p. 284.

[45] Ibid., pp. 284-85.

[46] For a list of holdings of over 500 archives of congregations of women religious, see E. Thomas, *Guide to the Archives of Congregations of Women Religious* (Washington, D.C.: The Smithsonian Institution, 1983).

[47] Kolmer, "Catholic Women Religious and Women's History: A Survey of the Literature," in *The American Catholic Religious Life*, p. 128.

[48] See Patricia Bauch, "Legacy of the 'Sisters' Schools,'" *Momentum* (September, 1990), pp. 23-27.

[49] Mary Ewens, *The Role of the Nun in Nineteenth Century America* (New York: Arno Press, 1978), p. 2. Also see Margaret Susan Thompson, "Philemon's Dilemma: Nuns and the Black Community in Nineteenth-Century America: Some Findings" in *The American Catholic Religious Life*, pp. 81-86.

[50] Ewens writes, "The anti-Catholic books which flooded England during the controversy over the Catholic Emancipation Bill of 1829 were distributed by American publishers in the 1830's. Among them were Scipio de Ricci's *Female Convents: Secrets of Nunneries Disclosed* and S. Sherwood's *The Nun . . .* They began to issue in book form tales of 'escaped nuns' that had hitherto been repeated only in newspapers or on the lecture platform ... [It reached] its zenith with Maria Monk's *Awful Disclosures*; these books were tremendously popular." Ibid., pp. 161-162. In each chapter of her work Ewens has specific examples of this anti-Catholic literature with its distorted image of the nun. See pp. 29-30, 75-84, 161-196, 243-251, 297-325. Ewens argues that at the close of the nineteenth century the literature gradually began to portray the nun less as a personification of Catholi-

cism and its evils and to reflect more positive attitudes towards her (p. 299).

[51] Ewens, *The Role of the Nun in Nineteenth Century America*, p. 221.

[52] Margàret Susan Thompson, "Women, Feminism, and the New Religious History," pp. 138-153.

[53] Even with this turn toward a more women-centered perspective, few historical studies have attempted to explain religious life for women across congregational lines. An exception to this trend occurs in the works of Mary Ewens, Barbara Misner, Margaret Susan Thompson and the Canadian historian Marta Danylewycz. In addition each sheds new light on the treatment of women religious as women and not simply as religious. Ewens, *The Role of the Nun*, p. 2. See also Barbara Misner, *Highly Respectable and Accomplished Ladies* (New York: Garland Publishing, Inc., 1988). See Margaret Susan Thompson's forthcoming work *Yoke of Grace: American Nuns and Social Change, 1808-1917*. For a cross-congregational study in a Canadian context see Marta Danylewycz, *Taking the Veil: An Alternative to Marriage, Motherhood and Spinsterhood in Quebec, 1840-1920* (Toronto: McClelland and Stewart, 1987).

[54] Thompson, "Women, Feminism and New Religious History," p. 142.

[55] Ibid., p. 142.

[56] Ibid., p. 143.

[57] See Margaret Susan Thompson, "Cultural Conundrum: Sisters, Ethnicity, and the Adaptation of American Catholicism," in *Mid-America: An Historical Review* (74:3) October, 1992, pp. 205-230.

Korean Women Theologians:
An Observer's Appreciation

Mary T. Rattigan

I offer this presentation on Korean women theologians as an outside observer who has followed their published works for the past few years. My interest in exploring these feminist theologians was first sparked by the concerted efforts we were making at the college to incorporate a multicultural perspective into the religious studies curriculum, especially the introductory course. I felt that reading Asian theologians would be a way of educating myself to look at religious issues through the eyes of the non-Western world.

I was drawn to examine the writings of Korean women, in particular, because of my current teaching situation in northern New Jersey. This is an area with a sizeable Korean population. My students from Korea are both traditional-age college students and wives of corporate executives who are studying to obtain a degree. These women have allowed me to become acquainted with the significant place the church holds in the life of Korean women. Their Christian identity piqued my curiosity about the extent of feminist theological activity in South Korea.

As I proceeded with my research, conversations with these students proved to be very helpful. It gave me a chance to verify my own understanding of many of the authors' ideas, especially their analysis of cultural mores. In this essay I wish to share my research, believing that the theological expressions of these feminists deserve to be made accessible to a wider audience. The publication of an observer's view provides yet another forum through which the voices of Korean women can be heard.

Some women theologians have sought to articulate the God-experiences of Korean women through the use of biblical images; others have moved to naming this experience by using the symbols and metaphors of traditional folk culture, especially Shamanism. In articulating a liberation theology, women attempt to uncover "her-story" in Korean history by focusing on specific aspects of women's pain—the pain known as *han*. In particular, they attend to the "gender specificity" of women's suffering arising from economic, cultural and religious sources. Writing from the perspective of the sufferings of the common masses of women, the *minjung*, feminist theology works for the liberation of women from various forms of oppression and the healing of their deepest pains. *Han* is a Korean word that signifies the pain of resentment, bitterness and broken heartedness which results from injustice. The release of pain (*han-pu-ri*) by means of the shamanistic ritual is used as a model to describe the liberating power of feminist theology.[1] This theology, with its methodology and resources, hopes to untangle Korean women's *han* and liberate them from bondage: "Its transforming power heals women to wholeness and enables them to celebrate their lives in fullness with other oppressed people in their communities."[2] A norm, then, for judging the effectiveness of feminist theology is to ask whether or not it keeps women from accumulating their *han* and staying in their *han*-ridden women's places.

The Korean Association of Women Theologians (KAWT) was organized in 1980 by Protestant Christian women of South Korea who recognized sexism in the church and society through their experiences in the 1970s. With the founding of the Asian feminist journal, *In God's Image* by Sun Ai Lee Park in 1982, the writings of Korean women on theology and ministry began to appear. This journal, now published by the Asian Women's Resource Centre for Culture and Theology in Seoul, presented works which began to reflect KAWT's adoption of the liberation method of EATWOT (The Ecumenical Association of Third World Theologians). Deeply touched by the stories of poor women at their convocation, KAWT's seminary-trained, middle-class women determined to create a theology directly connected with the life struggles of the poor. Some have since joined the struggles of women not only in their theologizing but also on the picketline. By the late 1980s, women theologians began looking at the myths, folktales and rituals of shamanism as a resource for theologizing. A committee of KAWT, for example, researched folk culture on a visit to Cheju Island for the specific purpose of developing a concept of the goddess for theology.

The most recent trend to emerge in feminist theology is an attempt to create a new Christian identity. The basic thrust of these "second-generation liberation theologians" is to integrate, synthesize and interconnect elements of non-Christian religions with the Christian tradition so that being Christian will embody a fuller expression of the Korean religious reality. Chung Hyun Kyung, a theology professor at Ewha Women's University in Seoul, reflects and typifies this new mood when she says, "I discovered my bowel is a shamanistic bowel, my heart is a Buddhist heart and my head is a Christian head."[3] This essay, then, will survey the published works of more than a decade, tracing these theological endeavors along the lines of KAWT's history of development. What follows is intended to be more than a review of the literature inasmuch as I have tried to respond to the authors with my own questions and observations throughout the essay.

Feminist theologians contend that Korean Christian women suffer under a double oppression: the church's hierarchal structure and prevailing social patterns. Both of these are supported by patriarchal ideology embedded in Christian theology and Confucian culture. For some time now women theologians who seek empowerment for liberation in the Bible have wrestled with the concept of God as a male ruler who wills male supremacy. To counteract this view, they have reclaimed the feminine images of God and interpreted creation "in the image of God" as the basis for the full dignity of women and for the formation of a community of equals. Using the feminist hermeneutic, they have centered on Jesus' treatment of women and his inclusive table community so as to enable the process of liberating women from their subservient mindsets and their subordinate positions in the church.

Most recently, Sook Ja Chung, a theologian and primary minister of Women Church in Seoul, offers a vision of "women's discipleship for partnership" through an interpretation of Luke 10:38-43. In examining the interactions of Martha and Mary with Jesus in this story, she finds a paradigm for partnership which would enable women to see themselves as disciples in a new way. The framework for this paradigm is provided by Letty Russell's definition of partnership as "a new focus of relationship in which there is continuing commitment and common struggle in interaction with a wider community context."[4] Sook addresses the situation found in male pastor-centered churches in which the interpretation of the Martha and Mary story often serves to limit women church workers to service in their local churches. The censure of Martha's "busyness" by Jesus, in particular, is understood as pertaining to women's involvement outside the church, thus keeping women as only pastor's servants. At the same time, the preferred role of Mary is often seen as nurturing a personal relationship with Jesus through prayer and Bible study. Since the "best part" is attributed to Mary in the gospel account, Sook considers the nature of her discipleship for the purpose of liberating church women for action in the community. She applies the characteristics of the Mary who anointed Jesus beforehand for his burial (Jn 12:1-8) to this Lucan story in order to describe the kind of woman Mary is. Mary's relationship with Jesus is seen to be one of mutuality; she both gives and receives. She helps Jesus by listening to his agony in making his decision to accept crucifixion. In the action of sharing his pain, she was able to see Jesus as a weak, suffering being, a symbol of all suffering and oppressed people (Is 53). Sook's point is that Mary received a new understanding of how women are to practice discipleship. Korean church women, like Mary, need to see their discipleship in a new dimension. They are called to form a partnership based on solidarity and mutuality with suffering and oppressed members of society, especially suffering women. It is in this relationship with poor and marginalized women that church women will be empowered in their own struggle for liberation.

A second source of oppression for Korean Christian women is the patriarchal social system in Korea based on Confucian ideology. Sun Ai Lee Park reflects on this cultural reality so as to sensitize women to the strong androcentrism which runs through the Confucian system. To the extent that women are energized to reject the dehumanizing aspects of this religio-cultural interpretation, they will begin to gain control over their own lives. Although it came to Korea during the fourth century C.E., it was not until the Chosun Dynasty (1392-1510), particularly after the sixteenth century, that Confucianism's social values became the norm. The Yi ruling house adopted a Confucian system grounded in patriarchal dualism and hierarchy, a system formed in opposition to Taoism's more egalitarian balance of the yin-yang dualism. This neo-Confucianism calls for the human order to be modeled on the cosmic order: "the relationship between heaven and earth is the most primal and most creative one in the universe. But their relationship is not in equality; it is hierarchal. The Heaven is superior and the Earth inferior."[5]

In this cosmology women's role is prescribed as *yin* and is identified with the earth as representing all things lowly and inferior. As the earth is characterized as yielding, receptive, and persevering, so women are made to be equally lowly and subservient in the hierarchy of the human community. On the other hand, the *yang* element allows men to be identified with fulfilling such heavenly tasks as initiating and ruling. The Korean saying, *nam-jon-yo'-bi*, "male high female low," expresses the Confucian pattern of harmony for the human community.

The ethical norms enforced by this social pattern require that women be subjected to three obediences: as a child a woman should obey her father, as a married woman her husband, and as a widow her son. Although marriage is the focal point of a woman's life, she is expected to remain an outsider. A married woman, for example, retains her maiden name and is not registered in the family tree of her husband's household. While many of these taboos are breaking down today, cultural values are slow to disappear. The Confucian influence upon family dynamics, i.e., that sons are favored much more than daughters, is still in evidence. Sun Ai Lee Park recounts the story of the recent suicides of four sisters who signed their note "the useless girls" to illustrate the fact that women are still capable of being brainwashed in such a way as to undervalue the worth of their lives. This indoctrination, direct or indirect, from traditional Confucian family upbringing or society at large, can even provoke women to voluntarily submit to violence or to inflict violence on themselves.[6]

While critical of the effects of Confucianism on Korean culture, Sun Ai Lee Park represents a current trend among women theologians to search for any positive insights that can be recovered from Asian philosophical-religious perspectives. She finds that the ideology of *jen* holds some potential provided it can be applied to everybody, particularly inclusive of women. *Jen* is the Confucian principle translated as benevolence, love and humaneness. It is the primary virtue that makes us human. When this quality is present and operative, people act with respect and courtesy toward each other, with reciprocity. The implications of this view, Park notes, is that human beings are to be in relationship and that *jen* is love for all and all things with discrimination or partiality.[7] Such a wholistic, non-individualistic, inclusive outlook for human relationships would need to be cultivated in order to combat the oppressive dimensions of the Confucian system.

Some Korean feminists have developed their theology in relation to current political and social movements. Reflection on the theological meaning of urgent issues is referred to as *hyun jang* theology.[8] The current reunification movement among the people of South Korea is taken up by Sun Ai Lee Park to discern the theological meaning of women's power as a force for the peaceful unity of a divided nation. She views the division of the land and people of Korea after World War II as a typical case of the powerless who suffer a tragic destiny imposed on them by the ideological and military conflict of the superpowers. This division then became a rationale for the expansion of militarism and brought on the Korean War of 1950-53, with the blood of six million being spilt on the land. Since Korea was pushed into being the local contractor in the superpowers' ideological warfare, Park contends that "the Korean War was the event that has turned the country into a sacrificial lamb that carries the sins of the world."[9]

Because of the salvific role which this biblical symbol bears, a solution for the Korean peninsula can be regarded as a light to all Third World countries in the way that the suffering lamb of Isaiah (Is 53) is called to be the lamb of redemption who redeems the sins of the world (Is 53). Among the multi-faceted consequences of the division of Korea, Park singles out the suffering that has resulted for many *minjung* women. This suffering is caused by the pain of separation of family members, a separation which also means the destruction and annihilation of women's life-long work and dedication to family. At the same time, Park observes, women are the ones who carry out the role of peace and harmony-makers in the homes, in the workplace and in the churches. Thus she claims that Korean women are "the most suffering of the suffering lambs, carrying out the role of immanent and potential redemption for all."[10]

While Park may too readily transform the suffering of women into a symbol of God's redemptive activity, this biblical theme can serve to evoke a sense of hope in Christian women as they join other groups in political action to achieve national unity. She believes that women already exercise the skills of making peace in the family but that now these experiences of sharing and sustaining life need to be extended into local, national and international communities. As women become equipped with political skills and backed by the constituency of the women's movement, Park sees that they will be able to bring peace to the divided and heavily militarized Korean peninsula.

Also working within the context of the reunification movement, biblical scholar and activist Lee Oo Chung offers a feminist theology of peace. Believing that true peace for Korea can only come through unification, she turns to Ephesians 2:11-22 to delineate the kind of reconciliation that will effect unity and peace. She understands "reconciliation with God" as a return to the original status of creation, that is, before the division into that of Jew and Gentile. Thus the creation of "one person in Christ" refers to the making of a new human community through the recovery of relationships among human beings. The dividing wall set up by enmity is broken down, and the divided community is made one through reconciliation with each other. Dr. Lee next offers a feminist interpretation of the expression, "All things become one under Christ," drawn from Ephesians 1:10. She employs the Greek philosphical concept of "the ideal perfection" for an understanding of the word "one." This concept signifies a perfection beyond plurality in oneness; it is a harmony or peace that is lost when a unit is divided. Lee notes that this notion of oneness bears comparison with other systems of thought: "In Oriental philosophy also, heaven and earth, yin and yang, become a harmonious one, where there is perfection, well-being, fullness . . . This is a situation similar to what the Bible describes as 'shalom.' "[11] The peace Lee envisions for the Korean peninsula means that no part would be sacrificed or alienated to achieve unity. It is a unity with variety: the different parts complement each other and cooperate with each other, so as to achieve a more perfect and harmonious world. For Lee, then, reconciliation and peace will happen when each side sees itself as complementing the other and regarding the other as an indispensable partner in the process of unification.

Dr. Lee believes that women hold out great promise as agents of reconciliation and reunification. From her reading of the gospel story of the woman who anoints Jesus beforehand for burial (Mk 14:6-9) she sees that this nameless woman, unlike the twelve disciples, understands what Jesus said about his suffering and destiny and reaches out to him by pouring perfume on his head. This story leads Lee to conjecture that perhaps women are blessed with the ability to grasp the reality of suffering because they share more of the pains of suffering.[12] Having endured discrimination and oppression, are they not the ones who can see injustices, and have understanding and love for those who suffer? As it so happens, South Korean women have already become a force for the creation of a new national community as they reach out to learn about the hopes and dreams of their sisters and brothers in the North. Moreover, church women in South and North Korea are now working together toward the "Year of Jubilee" declared by the Korean National Council of Churches. The year of jubilee, 1995, marks the fiftieth year of the division of the Korean peninsula. The spirit of jubilee found in Leviticus 25 engenders the hope that everything which is broken and lost will be restored to its original state. In envisaging a transformed world of peace, therefore, feminist theology can inspire church women to continue on the road toward national unification. Lee's view of unity and peace does not, in my opinion, adequately take into account the price that often has to be paid for reconciliation to occur. Those engaged in conflict resolution, for instance, remind us that solutions often demand more suffering, not less, as each party engages in some form of relinquishment of what is most valued. The reality of loss becomes a part of transformed existence, not eliminated from it.

Korean women's liberation theology is "*minjung* theology" developed from a feminist perspective. The term *minjung* translates "grassroot people" or "common folk," but it is used to designate those who are the victims of social injustice.

Minjung theology arose out of a sense of solidarity with the people's movements in South Korea as they struggled for justice under the political dictatorship and economic exploitation of the 1970s. Feminist theologians name poor women's status as "the *minjung* of the *minjung*," and have developed their theology in the context of poor women's experiences of oppression in industrial, rural and urban areas. A social analysis of the situation of poor wage-earning women, for example, reveals that they are victims of the national development program. As Young Sook Park explains:

> For the last 20 years or so, the economic policy of the successive dictatorial governments, concentrating primarily on rapid economic growth in close relationship with foreign economics, was carried out by means of the exploitation of the female labor force based on the sexual division of labor and on discriminatory wage payment.[13]

Soon-Hwa Sun reflects on the economic exploitation of women by telling the stories of women who were active in the women's worker movement. Women organized other women in the factories to start labor unions as a means of securing justice for themselves. The struggles of working women to change an oppressive situation, according to Sun, "present liberating principles for feminist theologians, and suggest an alternative concept of power: solidarity and self-dignity."[14] As these women combined their strengths to survive and in an act of resistance were able to take control of their lives, so too feminist theology exercises its power by rejecting the ideology of sexism which teaches that women are powerless and dispensable.

Chung Hyun Kyung depicts both the method and meaning of women's liberation theology in terms of the concept of *han*. She follows the lead of Young Hak Hyun who speaks of *han* as "a feeling of acute pain or sorrow in one's guts and bowels making the whole body writhe and wriggle, and an obstinate urge to take revenge and to right the wrong."[15] Chung thinks of *han* as the Korean people's "collective consciousness," and agrees with other *minjung* theologians that *han* as it exists in groups, whether an oppressed group within Korean society or in the race itself, will be expressed either as corporate despair or as the collective will to revolt.[16] Thus she examines the shaministic ritual *kut* for its liberative power in enabling women to survive their situations and for its potential for mobilizing women to participate in movements for change. This latter function of *kut* she sees being borne out today in young people's nationalistic movements. When the shamanistic ritual is performed in the midst of the people's demonstrations it functions as a seed of revolution. That is to say, the ritual is used both as a basis of community organization and a celebration of hope derived from a refusal to bow down to forces of oppression.[17]

Chung compares the release of women's pain (*han-pu-ri*) through the performance of *kut* by Korean shamans to the ability of feminist theology to assuage women's pain and empower them to action. In *kut* the shaman deals with *han*-ridden wandering ghosts of people who died in the world unjustly or who died without releasing the sense of impassibility in their lives. Chung outlines the three steps in shamanist *han-pu-ri*, showing it to be similar in method to Korean women's liberation theology.

The first step is speaking and hearing. The shaman gives the *han-ridden* persons or ghosts the chance to break their silence. The shaman enables the persons or ghosts to let their *han* out publicly. The shaman makes the community hear the *han-ridden* stories. The second step is naming. The shaman enables the *han-ridden* persons or ghosts (or their communities) to name the source of their oppression. The third step is changing the unjust situation by action so that *han-ridden* persons or ghosts can have peace.[18]

In the *kut* ritual the shaman is the central figure in a community of women. She invites them to participate in the spirits' work of righting the wrong. Through singing, dancing and weeping together, women are able to assuage their own pain and find strength to go on with their lives. As a goal of feminist theology, *han-pu-ri* is best illustrated by looking at the current situation of the "comfort women's movement." The dead Korean women who were forced to be official prostitutes for Japanese soldiers during World War II are considered to be wandering spirits or *han*-ridden ghosts who seek an opportunity to tell the truth. The stories of the poor, rural women who were recruited by force supposedly as "army labor forces," need to be heard so that the community can deal with this injustice. Today much is being done to hear the stories of the 135,000 Korean women victims, some of whom died of venereal diseases, others abandoned in foreign lands or killed when Japanese soldiers retreated from their battle lines. Many of the women who survived were prevented from returning home because of shame and a Korean morality that would not accept them back. It was church groups, Korean Church Women United and the Japan Women's Christian Temperance, that first arranged for the survivors to tell their stories so that the general public of both Korea and Japan could be made aware of the long-suppressed history of the so-called "comfort women." For the Japanese government to publicly acknowledge this atrocity would be a first step in healing the pain of the survivors and allow them to regain their sense of self-dignity. Seeking justice for both the living and the dead has led to the creation of feminist grassroots coalition politics: the comfort women's movement in Korea and Japan. As Alice Yun Chai reports: "For the first time in the history of Korea-Japan relations, Korean and Japanese women have engaged in formally organized coalition activities with the common goal of recovering and correcting Japan's official accounts of its colonial history."[19]

Further developments in this women's issue involve a recent conference in Seoul when the two Koreas came together over the Japanese war crimes against the World War II sex slaves.[20] Its purpose was to demand recompense for these women from the Japanese government. While the forum was not official, this contact between North and South Korea could be important for political reasons because it could help break the current deadlock in bilateral relations.

Women theologians see Korean indigenous religion, especially shamanism, as a resource for reconceiving Christian symbols. They claim, for example, that the image of Jesus Christ as "the priest of *han*" is one that makes sense for many *minjung* women. As the Korean shaman has been a healer, comforter, and counselor for these women, so too they can relate to Jesus Christ as the one who healed and comforted women in his ministry. Moreover, women shamans have acted as "big sisters" to many deprived women, helping them to cope with life's tribulations. Consequently, women take Jesus as a big sister just as they take the shaman as the big sister of their community.[21] Feminist theologians have refrained from developing further correlations between the shaman and Jesus other than the supportive role of each. Perhaps they recognize the limited potential this image holds for Christian thought. To this observer's mind, to draw any direct comparisons between the shaman's own possession and her methods and the gospel portrait of Jesus' healings, especially the exorcisms, would only result in a case of reductionism.

In addition to the role of the shaman, women also find a resource for theologizing in Korean folk culture, with its collection of songs and stories embodying the myths and legends of the indigenous people. Choi Man Ja uses the research on the goddess image which has been culled from the traditional culture still existent on Cheju Island[22] to interpret the meaning of the suffering servant image of Jesus. This christological image is the prevailing one in Korean women's theological expressions, and the image to which women relate most easily. Choi admits that traditional folklore presents mixed images of the goddess (positive and negative) as a consequence of the patriarchal view being imposed on the earlier mother goddess figure, but feels that these images can still provide valuable insights for Christian theology. In the legends the goddesses are presented, on the one hand, as autonomous, capable and strong. On the other hand, the female deities attain their divinity through self-sacrifice, patient endurance, and suffering. Choi recounts the myth of the female god of the earth, the god of cereals, to illustrate the manner in which female deities receive divine power from a higher god as a result of suffering:

> Ja-chung-bi was the daughter of Kim-jin-kuk and Jo-jin-kuk. She wanted to be the wife of Mun-do-ryung, the son of the god of heaven. However, his parents refused to allow her to become his wife. She eagerly appealed to them. Finally, the heaven god required that Ja-chung-bi take a hard test. She was asked to stand on the blade of a sword surrounded by flaming fire. Ja-chung-bi endured all of the suffering which was given by the heaven god, and eventually she became the wife of Mun-do-ryung. However, knaves killed Mun-do-ryung and captured Ja-chung-bi. She was able to defeat them and bring her husband back to life with the flower of rebirth from the western world. At last, Ja-chung-bi received the seeds of five grains from the heaven god. She was given power to control the fertility of grains and cattle, and power over wind and thunder. She became a goddess who loved people.[23]

This image of the goddess is that of a suffering savior whose bravery, strength and wisdom are represented in actions of caring, nurturing and healing—actions involving self-sacrifice and suffering so that others might live. Choi claims that the characteristics and works of the goddess can offer liberating insights for an interpretation of the suffering servant image found in Mark's gospel. That is to say, the double dimensions of strong/active and sacrificing/suffering posited by the goddess image permit us to view Jesus in a more powerful and life-giving way than does the image of submission and obedience portrayed by the Isaian servant (Is 53). Thus, in Mark's gospel Jesus' life, and especially his death, are seen to have transferred the paradigm of life from a ruling model to that of a suffering and serving life. Jesus' suffering, moreover, is seen in terms of exposing patriarchal evil, thus allowing the term "to suffer" take on a new dimension of meaning: "Jesus endures the yoke of the cross against the evil powers of this patriarchal world. This obedience is different from simple submission to the worldly authority and men."[24]

Understanding Jesus' self-sacrificing and suffering as a consequence of his choice for the new creation has practical implications for women. It empowers them with the wisdom to differentiate between the suf-

fering imposed by an oppressor and the suffering that is the consequence of one's choices for self-sacrificing love or taking a stand for
justice and human dignity. As Jesus' suffering for others was life-
giving, so too women's suffering can likewise be regarded as a source
of empowerment for themselves and for others whose experience is
defined by oppression. The problem, Choi contends, is how women
who are in the situation of suffering under and obeying oppressive
power can come to understand a new more liberative sense of being
suffering and obedient servants. The reality is that they need release
from the bondage of their lives of suffering and sacrifice, starting with
the domestic oppression. She points out that the term "to be servant"
can take on a new dimension of meaning in Mark's gospel when in-
fused with the values that the Korean goddess demonstrates. Feminist
theology is thus led to say that Mark puts the issue of "serving" in
direct contrast to the prevailing social structure. In his teaching on
discipleship (Mk 10:42-45) Jesus is talking to those for whom serving
others was connected with menial work, the work done by male slaves
or by women as they cared for the home and the upbringing of children. The redefining of the meaning of serving others can lead women
to re-estimate actions like sacrificing and suffering and seeing them as
positive values for the new humanity. This re-estimation of values
associated with women's work of comforting, nursing, providing and
caring for others could also generate the development of a new cognitive system for society. These alternate values would then become a
principle of humanity that men and women have to attain together.
Feminist values, then, form the basis of a vision of new humanity
which is best described along the lines of Jung's understanding of
anima-animus or the Asian principles of yin-yang harmony.[25]

Choi's position, I feel, is indicative of the strong desire of most
Korean women theologians to keep the suffering servant image of
Jesus as the major symbol of liberation theology. Interestingly, it is a
model that does not require any major change in women's values. It
assumes that women's current service roles of caring and nurturing
need but continue, and that changing women's role might only result
in reversing the present hierarchal form of oppression. This symbol of
Jesus does, however, fit the temper of the Asian form of liberation
theology which is different from other third world countries. The creative nature of Jesus' suffering functions as a basis for constructing a
vision of a new world order, one that reflects the Asian philosophical

view of harmony, in which complementarity is a basic principle and mode of operation. However, the idea of complementary roles to achieve the interrelatedness of a harmonious community always runs the risk of perpetuating stereotypical feminine roles for women rather than promoting roles that would ensure the development of a community of equals.

Lee Oo Chung shows how the perspective of Korean folk culture can transform the traditional Christian understanding of the incarnation. Sensing the difficulty that the doctrine "God becomes man" poses for the ordinary masses of people, she thinks the notion of "a man becomes a god" would be easier to understand. Since many Korean gods, especially female deities, ascend to the position of goddess through suffering and self-sacrifice, Lee proposes a similar idea for Jesus: Jesus Christ as Messiah can be better understood in the image of the historical Jesus who has loved his neighbors more than himself and for this great love went through surmountable suffering and sacrifice to become the Messiah, the Savior of humankind.[26]

This christology "from below" has implications for the liberation of Korean Christian women who need to get out of "imposed" service roles in church and society. The model of Jesus who attained messiahship or divinity can generate the elevation of women's self-consciousness "as high as in the realm of the divine." Since many Korean women relate to Jesus in terms of imitation of his life, this image allows them to experience the mystery of the incarnation and Emmanuel (God-with-us) by becoming like Jesus.

Because Jesus was male, some theologians believe there is a limit to how much he can be transformed to meet the needs of women. Chung Hyun Kyung, for example, claims that "Asian women's spirituality and theology must move away from christo-centrism toward life-centrism."[27] The heavy christocentrism of the past prevents women's theology from being transformed by the religious wisdom of the poor of Asia, the majority of whom are non-Christian. Chung herself has begun to articulate some features of a new spirituality and theology that is emerging from women's attempts to create alternate symbols and structures for empowerment and healing. The new generation of Korean women theologians, of which Chung is the leading exponent, emphasizes God as the life-giving spirit they can encounter within themselves and in everything that fosters life. Focusing on divine immanence allows for an image of God that is all-embracing: God as spirit who is present everywhere.

Chung finds that the Holy Spirit is the best symbol for addressing our present environmental crisis. The Spirit speaks her compassion and wisdom for life by calling for a change of vision that would empower human beings for the work of renewing the whole creation. The Holy Spirit is a wisdom figure, teaching us how to live in harmony with the earth for the sustainability of all life. The change of vision requires that we move from anthropocentric thinking so characterisic of Western creation theology which puts humans at the center of the world with power to control and dominate creation. Adopting a wholistic vision would also entail discarding the habit of dualistic thinking that causes nature to be objectified as "other," thus separating it from human life. For Chung the work of the Spirit involves the creation of a cosmic community characterized by interrelatedness and harmony. She finds that *ki*, which means breath or wind of life in Asian philosophy, provides a frame of reference for understanding the Spirit in Christian theology. "*Ki* thrives in the harmonious interconnection between sky, earth and people. When there is any division or separation, *Ki* cannot flow and this leads to the destruction and illness of all living beings."[28]

For a cosmic soteriology that would be in tune with women's popular religiosity, Chung turns to the image of *Kwan In*, a Buddhist bodhisattva, for an image of the Holy Spirit. *Kwan In* is an enlightened being who is venerated as the goddess of compassion and wisdom by East Asian women's popular religiosity. She can go into Nirvana any time she desires, but refuses to go by herself. Her compassion for all suffering living beings makes her stay in this world, enabling other living beings to achieve enlightenment. As Chung recounts the myth of the goddess, her compassionate wisdom heals all forms of life and empowers them to swim to the shore of Nirvana. She waits and waits until the whole universe—people, trees, birds, mountains, air, water—become enlightened. They can then go to Nirvana together where they will live collectively in eternal wisdom and compassion.[29]

Chung suggests that this goddess figure might also be a feminine image of Christ who is the firstborn among us, one who goes before and brings others with her. Using the Buddhist world view, Chung proposes a reconception of the Christ image found in Colossians 1:15-28 which would parallel a restructuring of the Christ symbol done by

Western feminist theologians. They see, for example, that biblical wisdom categories can support a concept of cosmic import with which to articulate the meaning of Christ and ourselves. When the saving activity of Jesus is interpreted by means of personified female Wisdom (Wis 7:12) or the master craftswoman (Prov 8:30), a new way of thinking emerges: "As the embodiment of Sophia who is fashioner of all that exists, Jesus' redeeming care extends to the flourishing of all creatures and the whole earth itself."[30] With this christological symbol, the Christian community can find its mandate to be in solidarity with the earth and at the forefront of ecological care.

Moving from a christocentric to a life-centristic approach to theology and spirituality has an extended meaning for Chung. Not only does women's life context become the primary text in their ongoing search for God but also the Bible and church tradition rank as just one among the many religious resources from which Korean women will draw insight and inspiration. In effect the use of non-Christian sources constitutes a movement away from the doctrinal purity of Christian theology to a syncretic Christianity. Chung draws on personal experiences, those of her birth mother and her adoptive mother, to give us a possible model for a syncretic Christian identity. Both of these women "mixed and matched" elements of Buddhism and Confucianism with being Christian: their center of spirituality was life itself. It was not dominated by any religious personalities such as Jesus, Buddha or Confucius. They selected (mostly unconsciously) the life-giving aspects of each religion and rejected the death-giving ones.[31]

Dr. Chung has emerged as the leading figure in the move to create a feminist theology which is multi-religious. It is a theology which selectively chooses the life-giving dimensions of Korea's multiple religious traditions so as to weave these strands into a new pattern of being Christian. This new wave in theology uses resources which are common to all the women of Asia. It can be regarded as a step taken to forge religious solidarity among women—Korean women themselves and ultimately all Asian women. The re-imaging of Jesus/Spirit in the role of a Buddhist goddess is but one example of how Korean feminist theology can cross the boundaries that separate Asian women of different religious persuasions. Promoting religious solidarity is, I feel, a worthy goal for Korean feminists to pursue. Such solidarity would go beyond the acceptance of religious pluralism to become a force for mobilizing Asian women toward common projects and actions.

I think Korean women theologians deserve our attention and appreciation for several reasons. First, from a teaching perspective I can identify with the way these theologians have addressed a genuine concern to translate doctrinal language and the symbols of Christian theology for a contemporary audience. They have directed their efforts, for example, to showing how the salvation of Christ can be perceived in a more meaningful way. While Jesus' suffering is at the core of Korean women's theology and spirituality, his suffering has been placed in a creative context by using the Asian world-view. In contrast to traditional thinking about salvation which focuses on the fall and atonement, this Eastern creation theology presents salvation as opening us up to the greater possibilities of life. Thus, Jesus' salvific suffering generates a more liberating spirituality, one that inspires women with hope for the future. Another reason for attending to Korean women's theology is that it represents a "new voice" being raised for both feminist theology and the whole theological enterprise. Informed as it is by Eastern philosophical and religious concepts, Korean women's theology has resulted in a perspective different from that of Western feminist thought. Eastern values of interrelatedness, community and harmonious wholeness are central to Korean feminist thinking. Because of these core values, freedom for empowerment is perceived not so much in terms of personal benefits accruing to an individual as much as it is to bring about the common good in whatever sphere—family, church, society or nation. This new voice of Korean feminist thought helps to make us more conscious of the role of Asian theology for the future. If the prediction of some contemporary thinkers is correct, then Asian theology is presenting Christian theology with a new methodology, a methodology that is ushering in a new theological era in which Eastern categories and symbols will play a leading role. Korean women's theology can indeed be recognized for the contribution it has already made towards the emerging role of Asian theology.

Notes

[1] Chung Hyun Kyung, "Han-pu-ri: Doing Theology from Korean Women's Perspective," *The Ecumenical Review*, vol. 40/1, 1987, pp. 27-36.

[2] Chung Hyun Kyung, *Struggle to Be the Sun Again: Introducing Asian Women's Theology* (Maryknoll, N.Y.: Orbis Books, 1990), p. 109.

[3] R.S. Sugirtharajah, ed., *Frontiers in Asian Theology: Emerging Trends*

(Maryknoll, N.Y.: Orbis Books, 1994), p. 5.

[4] Sook Ja Chung, "Women's Discipleship for Partnership: Lk 10:38-42," *In God's Image*, vol. 12/1, 1993, p. 20. See L. Russell, *The Future of Partnership,* (Philadelphia: Westminster Press, 1979), p. 18.

[5] Sun Ai Lee Park, "Confucianism and Women," *In God's Image*, June 1989, p. 27.

[6] Sun Ai Lee Park, "Confucianism and Violence Against Women," *In God's Image*, vol. 13/3, 1994, p. 42.

[7] Ibid., p. 38.

[8] Chung, *Struggle to Be the Sun Again*, p. 107.

[9] Sun Ai Lee Park, "Peace, Unification and Women: A Theological Reflection" in *We Dare to Dream: Doing Theology as Asian Women*, V. Fabella and S. Park, eds. (Maryknoll, N.Y.: Orbis Books, 1990), p. 76.

[10] Ibid., p. 77.

[11] Lee Oo Chung, "Peace, Unification and Women: A Bible Study," in *We Dare to Dream*, p. 68.

[12] Lee Oo Chung, "One Woman's Confession of Faith," in *New Eyes For Reading: Biblical and Theological Reflections by Women from the Third World*, J. Pobee and B. Potter, eds. (Oak Park, Ill: Meyer Stone Books, 1986), pp. 18-20.

[13] Young Sook Park, "Justice, Peace and the Integrity of Creation—Justice and Peace (Life) Movement and Korean Women," *In God's Image*, vol. 10/1, 1991, p. 43.

[14] Soon-Hwa Sun, "Women, Work and Theology in Korea," *Journal of Feminist Studies in Religion*, vol. 3/2, 1987, p. 132.

[15] Young Hak Hyun , "Minjung Theology and the Religion of Han," *East Asian Journal of Theology*, vol. 3/2, 1985, p. 354.

[16] Andrew Sung Park, *The Wounded Heart of God: The Asian Concept of Han and the Christian Doctrine of Sin* (Nashville: Abingdon Press, 1993), p. 31.

[17] Chung Hyun Kyung, "Opium or the Seed For Revolution? Shamanism: Women Centered Popular Religiosity in Korea," *Concilium*, May 1988, p. 101.

[18] Chung, "Han-pu-ri," p. 35.

[19] Alice Yun Chai, "Asian-Pacific Feminist Coalition Politics: The Chongshidae/ Jugunianfu ("Comfort Women") Movement," *Korean Studies*, vol. 17, 1993, p. 84.

[20] *The Bergen Record* (Hackensack, NJ) February 25, 1995 carried a report on the Seoul conference planned for February 27-March 1, 1995.

[21] Chung Hyun Kyung, "Who Is Jesus for Asian Women?" in *Asian Faces of Jesus*, R. S. Sugirtharajah, ed. (Maryknoll, N.Y.: Orbis Books, 1993) p. 236.

[22] Korean Association of Women Theologians, "Feminist Lighting on Goddess Image Imposed in Korean Folks Beliefs," *In God's Image*, September 1990, pp. 48-52.

[23] Choi Man Ja, "The Liberating Function of Feminine Images of God in Traditional Korean Religion," *Ching Feng*, vol. 35/1, 1992, p. 31.

[24] Ibid., p. 39.

[25] Ibid., p. 41.

[26] Chung, "Who Is Jesus for Asian Women?", p. 231.

[27] Chung, *Struggle to Be the Sun Again*, p. 114.

[28] Chung Hyun Kyung, "Come, Holy Spirit, Renew the Whole Creation," *In God's Image*, vol. 11/3, 1992, p. 69.

[29] Ibid., p. 29.

[30] Elizabeth Johnson, "Wisdom Was Made Flesh and Pitched Her Tent Among Us" in *Reconstructing the Christ Symbol: Essays in Feminist Christology*, Maryanne Stevens ed. (Mahwah, N.J.: Paulist Press, 1993), p. 113.

[31] Chung Hyun Kyung, "Following Naked Dancing and Long Dreaming" in *Inheriting Our Mothers' Garden: Feminist Theology in a Third World Perspective*. L. Russell, et al., eds. (Philadelphia: Westminster Press, 1988), p. 67.

Part III

CHANGING THE TERMS

The Dialogue between Women's Studies and Religious Studies

Mary Ann Hinsdale

Context

My observations and questions about the place of religious studies in women's studies have been shaped by several articles which have appeared over the last fifteen years in general feminist discussions concerning the impact of feminist research and pedagogy in the academy, as well as my own personal experience as a theologian teaching in the interdisciplinary field of women's studies. Let me briefly illustrate this context: In 1981 Rosemary Radford Ruether contributed an article entitled "The Feminist Critique in Religious Studies" to an interdisciplinary exploration called *A Feminist Perspective in the Academy: The Difference It Makes.*[1] Six years later Carol Christ wrote "Toward a Paradigm Shift in the Academy and in Religious Studies" which appeared in a collection edited by the Women's Studies Program of Indiana University, *The Impact of Feminist Research in the Academy.*[2] In 1993, Judith Plaskow's article "We Are Also Your Sisters: The Development of Women's Studies in Religion" appeared in the *Women's Studies Quarterly.*[3] This article reviews the last twenty-five years of feminist scholarship in religious studies. While I won't chronicle that development here, Plaskow observes an important feature of women's studies in religion that distinguishes it from women's studies in general. She claims that feminists in religious studies have maintained connections with grassroots women more effectively, since they are more often involved in real communities of accountability and testing than are their colleagues in women's studies whose relationships with non-academic women have become more attenuated, as the field has become more professionalized and debates and theory in some disciplines have become more abstract. Plaskow's assessment of the relationship between women's studies and religious studies is that:

> Women's studies in religion has been a bit of a stepsister within women's studies. The suspicion on the part of many intellectuals in our secular culture that anyone interested in religion must be a reactionary has served to marginalize and delegitimize feminist work in religion. While feminists can study and make use of other patriarchal ideologies, such as psychoanalytical theory, without automatically being seen as in collusion with them, the same trust—and interest—has not been extended to feminist work in religion.[4]

In addition to articles such as these, however, I am also reflecting on my own experience as a white, Celtic-Anglo North American, Catholic, lay, celibate, feminist, female working in the discipline of theology at the same time that I participate in the interdisciplinary field of women's studies at my school: a New England, Catholic, liberal arts college sponsored by the Jesuits, where 95 percent of the students are Roman Catholic. My experience confirms Plaskow's observations. I agree with her that the suspicion of religion and its neglect as a worthwhile and constructive enterprise in the field of women's studies are unfortunate for at least three reasons: 1) Plaskow argues that religion plays a key role in the dynamics of women's oppression (something that virtually no one in women's studies would deny) as well as women's liberation (a much more problematic assertion), and that the dynamic of oppression and liberation cannot be neglected (as the women's spirituality movements, the recovery of the goddess, etc. have shown); 2) women's studies in religion is a well-established and vital field; and 3) to a greater extent than is the case with many other areas of women's studies, feminists in religion maintain strong links to women outside the academy. I would add a fourth reason to Plaskow's trio: namely, that neglecting religion in the field of women's studies is unfortunate because of what feminist perspectives in religious studies have contributed to the politics of activist and marginalized scholarship, as well as the innovations in pedagogy which have been developed in undergraduate religious studies classrooms.

Observations and Assertions

While I agree with Plaskow that women's studies needs to know what has been going on in feminist studies of religion, religious studies and theology need to keep abreast of developments in women's studies—a well-nigh impossible task as anyone who subscribes to *The Women's Review of Books* or *Belles Lettres* knows. Here, however, alongside the impressive work being done in women's history and by feminist sociologists, anthropologists, psychologists, literary critics, political scientists and others, I would make a special plea to all of us who—to borrow a phrase from Anne Carr—see feminist perspectives as "transforming grace."[5] I urge those interested in transforming their biblical, ethical or theological teaching and research to become conversant with feminist theory and the debates which go on among the various cultural contexts which make up feminism: be they white Eurocentric, Latina, womanist, Asian, lesbian, differently-abled, etc. The works of Sandra Harding,[6] Evelyn Fox Keller,[7] Alison Jaggar[8] and Rosemarie Tong[9] need to be on our bookshelves and read as well as cited in our scholarship. And while we may not necessarily include feminist theoretical readings in our syllabi, our teaching must be self-conscious regarding the theoretical frameworks from which we approach whatever religious or theological questions we are pursuing. In my experience over the last three years of teaching an Introduction to Women's Studies course, the students' least favorite part is feminist theory. Rosemarie Tong reminds us of the words of contemporary philosopher Andrea Nye: "Contemporary feminist theory . . . is a tangled and forbidding web." Tong agrees that:

> Theory has had a bad reputation among many feminists—especially among those who have rebelled against arcane and abstract pedantry. And indeed, theory is likely to strike the poor woman struggling for adequate health benefits, or the abused woman fleeing from her enraged spouse, as a luxury for which she has neither the time, the energy, nor the patience. But even though theory can be and often is separated from that concrete reality we call "life" it should not be divorced from that which is, after all, its logical extension. For what is theory if not that which enables us to make sense of our existential situation—an expla-

nation of why things are the way they are and a blueprint for improving them?[10]

According to Tong, one of the most reassuring features of feminist thought is that they who *think* the theory are among the us that must *live* that theory. For this reason, it is important to celebrate how far feminist theory has come, as well as to lament the mistakes that have been made along the way. It is important to admit that feminist theology shares with feminism in general the unacknowledged social location[11] of relatively privileged, white, middle class, professional women and that such theologies, just as feminist theory, in Tong's assessment, are found wanting "to the degree that they have failed to incorporate the perspectives of women who ordinarily do not do theory: poor women, illiterate women, minority women, and so on."[12]

In doing some work on the interconnections among theology, spirituality and ecofeminism a few years back,[13] I became aware of how little conscious reference is made to the feminist frameworks out of which feminist theologians are operating. For example, Rosemarie Tong discusses no fewer than seven varieties of feminism in her book, *Feminist Thought: A Comprehensive Introduction*: liberal, Marxist, radical, psychoanalytic, socialist, existentialist and postmodern. Alison Jaggar prefers a simpler framework and discusses four: liberal, Marxist, radical and socialist. Feminist theologians also have recognized that there is pluralism within feminism and have become familiar with the designations of "reformist" and "radical," a distinction introduced originally by Sheila Collins and made popular by Carol Christ and Judith Plaskow in their collection *Womanspirit Rising*.[14] However, in the introduction to their collection of essays on new patterns in feminist spirituality, *Weaving the Visions*, Christ and Plaskow acknowledge the limitations of such categorization and announce that they will no longer use such terms. Nevertheless, they still perceive differences among feminist scholars in religion, for example in the distinction between feminist theologians and *thea*logians (goddess feminists). They admit: "The question of whether to struggle in relation to Judaism or Christianity or to focus on alternative resources for women's spirituality both divides us ideologically and institutionally and remains a deeply-felt personal issue. . . ."[15]

Unfortunately, neither Tong nor Jaggar discusses religious feminism in their books. In fact, Jaggar explicitly rejects its inclusion in her taxonomy, explaining that while such a conception may have historical significance (she also consciously omits existentialist feminism as exemplified by Simone de Beauvoir), she personally finds both existential and religious feminism "implausible." She says: "They are outside the mainstream of contemporary feminist theorizing, and they have little direct connection with socialist feminism, the version of feminist theory that I consider the most plausible."[16]

It is beyond the scope of this presentation to discuss Jaggar's refusal to take religious feminism seriously,[17] but it is ironic that she fails to mention that many of the radical versions of feminism she discusses qualify as "religious," though the religion espoused is certainly not that of the patriarchal traditions. At the same time, one must also pose a challenge to feminist theology and *thea*logy and ask how aware are they of the different conceptions of human nature, epistemology and political theory that feminist philosophers such as Tong and Jaggar delineate as being characteristic of particular brands of feminism? Although some progress has been made, especially because of the epistemological and anthropological standpoints which ecofeminists and womanist, mujerista/Latina, and other global feminist theologies have brought to the conversation, much more remains to be accomplished.[18]

The political issues which exist in religious studies and women's studies are similar. First, especially for women, but also for men, it is "dangerous" to engage teaching and research influenced by perspectives that have been marginalized by the academy. Both feminist theologians and women's studies professors have devoted a great deal of energy to the deconstruction of what Carol Christ calls "the ethos of objectivity." The difficulty with engaging in deconstruction in one's discipline has not only to do with distorted theories of subjectivity, reason and emotion which are rooted in the patriarchal structure of our thought and language, but such deconstruction is also economically and politically dangerous. As Christ says, "the first and easiest way to discredit our work is to call it personal or political, therefore not objective, therefore not scholarly, therefore no tenure."[19]

Secondly, the arguments and debates about mainstreaming also occur in both women's studies and religious studies. Should feminist perspectives be integrated into all subjects in the religious studies curriculum or should we have a curricular niche for such approaches?

Thirdly, a liability common to both women's studies and feminist studies in religion concerns how those who adopt feminist perspectives and feminist pedagogy are evaluated. Use of discussion techniques rather than the traditional lecture method leads to evaluations of courses as "not rigorous." Or, the kind of scholarship produced is too interdisciplinary, collaborative or activist, therefore, not "academic." Interdisciplinary scholarship is touted in the literature of higher education and even funded by granting agencies, but it is still problematic for tenure committees.

Finally, with regard to pedagogy, in religious studies, the recognition of the experiential and contextual bases of theology brought about by the various theologies of liberation and the incorporation of insights of developmental psychology on religious education (especially in the area of faith-development) have changed the classroom significantly. The use of journals, the valuing of the first person in written assignments, and dialogical, interactive methods of teaching have long since transformed the pedagogy of undergraduate religious studies. The notion that courses can and should have as a goal the transformation of consciousness (or, to use a religious term, the facilitation of conversion—be it intellectual, moral or religious) is not perhaps as problematic as it is in women's studies. I am thinking here of the debate unleashed by Karen Lehrman's investigation of introductory women's studies courses in an article last fall in *Mother Jones*, which critiqued the promotion of activism in the classroom:

> Discussions run from the personal to the political and back again, with mere pit stops at the academic.
>
> Women's studies is a misnomer. Most of the courses are designed not merely to study women, but also to improve the lives of women, both the individual students (the vast majority of whom are females) and women in general. Since professors believe that women have been effectively silenced in history, they often consider pedagogy that "nurtures voice" just as, if not more, important than the curriculum.
>
> Women's studies profs tend to be overtly warm, encouraging, maternal. You want to tell these women your problems and many students do. To foster a "safe environment" where women feel comfortable about talking, many teachers try to divest the classroom of power relations. They abandon their role as experts,

lecturing very little and sometimes allowing decisions to be made.[20]

Sound familiar? Here is where I believe the pedagogy of religious studies and theology, especially in Catholic colleges, can join forces with women's studies in the larger academic arena. Both are about a transformation of the way learning is accomplished as well as about a transformation of the learner. But as we all know, whether we are in women's studies or religious studies, it is difficult to reconstruct the discourse of one's own discipline and collaborate in articulating a different paradigm of academic scholarship and pedagogy when one is marginalized, not taken seriously, or in constant danger of being "thrown out." We need to develop strategies which will enable the constructive and reconstructive approaches of both disciplines to survive. Wouldn't it be great if we could engage in this task together? So, what do you think?

Notes

[1] Rosemary Radford Ruether, "The Feminist Critique in Religious Studies," in *A Feminist Perspective in the Academy: The Difference It Makes*, ed. Elizabeth Langland and Walter Gove (Chicago: University of Chicago Press, 1981), 52-66.

[2] Carol Christ, "Toward a Paradigm Shift in the Academy and in Religious Studies," in *The Impact of Feminist Research in the Academy*, ed. Christie Farnham (Bloomington: Indiana University Press, 1987), 53-76.

[3] Judith Plaskow, "We are Also Your Sisters: The Development of Women's Studies in Religion," *Women's Studies Quarterly* 21 (1993): 9-21.

[4] Ibid., 9.

[5] Anne Carr, *Transforming Grace: Christian Tradition and Women's Experience* (San Francisco: Harper and Row, 1988).

[6] Harding is a leading feminist theorist who has written on feminist epistemology. Her writings include: "Reinventing Ourselves as Other: More New Agents of History and Knowledge," in *American Feminist Thought at Century's End: A Reader*, ed. Linda Kaufman (Cambridge, MA: Blackwell, 1993), 140-164; *The Science Question in Feminism* (Ithaca: Cornell University Press, 1986); *Whose Science? Whose Knowledge? Thinking from Women's Lives* (Ithaca: Cornell University Press, 1991).

[7] Keller is a philosopher of science whose book *Reflections on Gender and Science* (New Haven: Yale University Press, 1985) has become a classic in feminist theory.

[8] Jaggar is a socialist feminist who has written widely on feminist epistemology. Her book (co-edited with Paula Rothenberg) *Feminist Frameworks: Alternative*

Theoretical Accounts of the Relations between Women and Men, 3rd ed. (New York: McGraw Hill, 1993) is a standard text in introductory women's studies courses. See also her *Feminist Politics and Human Nature* (Totowa, N.J.: Rowman and Littlefield, 1988) and (co-edited with Susan Bordo) *Gender/Body/Knowledge: Feminist Reconstruction of Being and Knowing* (New Brunswick: Rutgers University Press, 1989). Her most recent book is an edited collection, *Living with Contradictions: Controversies in Feminist Social Ethics* (Boulder: Westview Press, 1994).

[9] Tong's book *Feminist Thought: A Comprehensive Introduction* (Boulder: Westview Press, 1989) is another standard text in introductory women's studies courses. A feminist philosopher, Tong's most recent book is *Feminine and Feminist Ethics* (Belmont, CA: Wadsworth Publishing Co., 1993).

[10] Rosemarie Tong, "Feminine and Feminist Thinking," *Anima* 18 (1991): 31.

[11] "Totalization" and "essentialism" have been the labels given to the creation of a false universal female by many white, middle class, academic feminists. For further background on the challenges of "social location" for feminist theology, see Ann O'Hara Graff, "The Struggle to Name Women's Experience: Assessment and Implications for Theological Construction," *Horizons* 20 (1993): 215-33; Susan B. Thistlethwaite and Toinette M. Eugene, "A Survey of Contemporary Global Feminist, Womanist, and Mujerista Theologies," *Critical Review of Books in Religion* (Atlanta: Scholars Press, 1991), 21-44; "Affirming Cross Cultural Diversity: A Missiological Issue in Feminist Perspective," *International Review of Mission* 81 (1992): 253-58.

[12] Tong, "Feminist Thinking," 31.

[13] This was the subject of the concluding plenary that I gave at the College Theology Society Teaching Workshop in 1990 in New Orleans. A portion of this talk has been published as "Ecology, Feminism, and Theology," *Word and World* 11 (1991): 156-64.

[14] See Carol P. Christ and Judith Plaskow, eds., *Womanspirit Rising* (San Francisco: Harper and Row, 1979), 1-16.

[15] Judith Plaskow and Carol P. Christ, eds., *Weaving the Visions: New Patterns in Feminist Spirituality* (San Francisco: Harper and Row, 1989), 7-8.

[16] Jaggar, *Feminist Politics and Human Nature*, 10.

[17] Particularly in regard to the issue Alison Jaggar is discussing—feminist politics and human nature—the omission of religious feminism as a category is regrettable, in my opinion. Judith Plaskow and Elisabeth Schüssler Fiorenza explain that the reason for the establishment of the *Journal of Feminist Studies in Religion* is due, in part, because the mainstream women's studies journals "have tended to be suspicious of material dealing with religion, as if any concern with religion were by definition patriarchal and reactionary." This is unfortunate, since feminist scholarship in religion has developed into a significant, lively and diverse field which not only questions patriarchal texts, but is also involved in the recovery of women's history and the creative envisioning of new possibilities. See "Editors' Introduction" in *Journal of Feminist Studies in Religion* 1 (1985): 3.

[18] A call for a greater consciousness regarding "difference" without sacrifice of "commonality" was the subject of Lisa Sowle Cahill's presidential address to the Catholic Theological Society of America in 1993. See "Feminist Ethics and the Challenge of Cultures," *CTSA Proceedings* 48 (1993): 65-83.

[19] Carol Christ, "Toward a Paradigm Shift in the Academy and Religious Studies," 56.

[20] "Off Course: College Women's Studies Programs," *Mother Jones* 18 (5, 1993): 45 (10).

Toward a Methodology for Doing Theology across the Boundaries of Difference: Feminist Theory Meets Feminist Theology[1]

Linda A. Moody

Introduction

In the introduction to her work on feminist theory, *Feminist Thought: A Comprehensive Introduction*, Rosemarie Tong holds out the hope that women of varying and diverse backgrounds can meet the challenge of developing community. She offers a model for cross-cultural conversation which deserves to be considered by women doing theology: "It is a major challenge to contemporary feminism to reconcile the pressures for diversity and difference with those for integration and commonality. We need a home in which everyone has a room of her own, but one in which the walls are thin enough to permit a conversation, a community of friends in virtue, and partners in action."[2]

Feminist theory clearly has something to say to feminist and liberation theologians. We need to develop a methodology for doing theology across the boundaries of our difference if we are to meet the challenge raised by Tong. Already such conversations have begun under the rubric of "appropriation and reciprocity."[3] Women doing theology[4] must develop an ethic which insists on mutuality and respects difference if we are to engage in the shared, multi-cultural theological reflection which could lead us toward the construction of the home suggested by Tong.

This essay will suggest strategies for engaging in theological reflection across the boundaries of difference. It will name various obstacles to such a process and will suggest appropriate means for overcoming those obstacles. The thought of feminist theorists such as Elizabeth Spelman, bell hooks, Patricia Hills Collins, and Elizabeth Potter will be helpful in naming those obstacles. The reflections of theologians Ada María Isasi-Díaz, Elsa Tamez, and others will be useful in suggesting methods for overcoming those obstacles. This essay will suggest that future constructive theological efforts among women of very differing cultural backgrounds may be assisted by the notion of covenant. To this end, the idea of the Covenanting God will be explored in the context of the story of Ruth and Naomi. It is my hope that in developing strategies for doing cross-cultural theologizing, we can begin to lay the foundation for the home which Tong envisions, one in which each of us has our own room and yet where conversation can begin.

Obstacles to Theologizing across the Boundaries of Difference

To begin this discussion of obstacles that inhibit multi-cultural dialogue among women doing theology, five major issues will be addressed. The first is the problem of false unity or the masking of real difference which separates women of different cultural backgrounds. The second obstacle inhibiting real discussion stems from the dualistic split between mind and emotion which labels anger as irrational and unproductive. A third problem involves singularity of world view. This may take the extreme form of xenophobia, or fear of that which is "foreign," or it may simply result from lack of information and education about the theological resources of others whose backgrounds are different from ours. Ada María Isasi-Díaz is helpful at this point in her advocacy of "multi-world views." A fourth problem is the fear of saying anything at all. The problem of racism has become so complex that there is always the "temptation to silence," a problem which will be discussed in relation to Elizabeth Potter's ethics of knowledge. One final problem is that there are virtually no theological models for engaging in truly liberating cross-cultural dialogues about God. To address this problem the biblical story of Ruth and Naomi will be examined as a possible model for contemporary cross-cultural dialogue among women sharing a vision for a future free of oppression based on race, class, gender, sexual orientation, and other forms of marginalization.

In looking at some of the dynamics involved in these tensions among women doing theology, and in particular, in reference to racial tensions, Elizabeth Spelman's concept of the "inessential woman" may be helpful. Spelman's notion of the "inessential woman" is intended to demonstrate the importance of seeing difference among women. Her effort is intended to critique those who posit an "essential woman" who functions generically to mask real differences among diverse groups of women.

In trying to explain how the concept of a generic "woman" functions to mask differences, Spelman makes an analogy with the way that the generic use of the word "man" has functioned in Western language, obscuring the heterogeneity of men and women and cutting off "examination of the significance of such heterogeneity for feminist theory and political activity."[5] Similarly, argues Spelman, dominant Western feminist thought has largely ignored real differences due to race and class and has posited the experience of white, middle class women as normative for all women. She pointedly argues her case against the "essential woman" in the following statement:

> Don't misunderstand me: I've never met a generic woman I didn't like. But I wouldn't want my brother or my sister to marry one. And I certainly wouldn't want to be one: generic women don't eat rice and beans, collard greens, samosa, challah, hot dogs, or Wonder Bread; even in Cambridge, Massachusetts, I've never seen one eating a croissant. And while it is true that generic women don't have bad breath, that is hardly any consolation, I should think, for having no breath at all.[6]

In her work, Spelman insists that in order for women to work together across the boundaries of difference, attention must be given to the unique fabric of each woman's life and to the racial, ethnic, class, sexual orientation, and language backdrop of each one's particular situation.

A second obstacle to women in the theological arena being able to hear each other revolves around the taboos associated with emotion and anger in scholarship. For those white women whose Christian training under patriarchy has taught them to silence their own anger and to fear others', it may be difficult to understand the anger of some women. Audre Lorde addresses the need for anger to be expressed when she writes, "If I speak to you in anger, at least I have spoken to you: I have not put a gun to your head and shot you down in the street. . . ."[7]

The need for white women to hear the angry concerns of women of color has been apparent for some time. It very well may be, in fact, that as women engage in more cross cultural theologizing, and as more marginalized women voice their concerns, anger will be an emotion which women theologians may need to examine more closely, as Alison Jaggar has done.

In looking more closely at the emotional, often angry exchanges between women of color and white women, Alison Jaggar's concept of "outlaw emotion" may be helpful. Jaggar reminds us that feminist theorists "have pointed out that the western tradition has not seen everyone as equally emotional. Instead, reason has been associated with members of dominant political, social, and cultural groups and emotion with members of subordinate groups."[8] If Jaggar is correct, then it may well be that women of color are perceived by white women to be angry and emotional while white women fail to recognize the emotional content of their own disguising, de-spirited discourse. Therefore, it may be that lesbian women, disabled women, or women of color are not *more* emotional or *more* angry than straight, white, able-bodied women, but rather that they are simply perceived in that manner by some.

While in white society, many women have been conditioned to view displays of anger as negative or even "unChristian," there very well may be an instructive aspect to anger. In discussing what she describes as "outlaw emotions," Jaggar refers to those emotions which "are distinguished by their incompatibility with the dominant perceptions and values . . ."[9] They are generally the emotions of oppressed persons "who pay a disproportionately high price for maintaining the status quo."[10] These emotions, because they are based in an understanding of oppression which is not experienced by dominant groups, may provide the basis for a subculture which challenges dominant patterns and becomes "politically because epistemically subversive."[11] Here Jaggar refers to the notion of the "epistemic privilege of the oppressed," which she describes as follows: "the perspective on reality available from the standpoint of the oppressed . . . is a perspective that offers a less partial and distorted and therefore more reliable view."[12]

According to Jaggar's view, one could understand the emotional encounters between white women and women of color doing theology together as a sign of healthy movement. As emotions inform our understanding of systemic, institutionalized racism, our perceptions can be reformulated and actions generated based on new understandings. This alternative epistemological model proposed by Jaggar replaces the dualistic split in traditional philosophical categories between emotion and reason with an understanding that our emotions inform our perceptions and ethical actions, which then cause us to re-think our theoretical perspectives. By applying Jaggar's epistemological model to a new model for doing theology across the lines of cultural difference, we may begin to address the issues of personal and institutional racism, along with other forms of oppression, which have limited the theological enterprise of women to date.

A third obstacle facing women doing theology is the tendency toward a singular world view. If we are lucky, we may know and understand our own situation and the theology which has developed out of its context, and we may be able to deconstruct the oppressive features of its heritage and develop constructive, liberating theologies. However, we are much less likely to speak another's language or understand the linguistic shorthand, culture, and theology which develops out of another's own particular situation. To confront this obstacle, Ada María Isasi-Díaz has proposed a new "multi-world view" which will lead to a new world order based on critical conscientization and liberation. In a speech given to the National Association of Women in Education, Isasi-Díaz claimed that the goal of this critical conscientization is liberation, which she described as "the act of achievement by persons of full development of their potential."[13] This liberation involves persons who conduct themselves as members of communities in relation to others.

Several conditions are necessary for this critical awareness, according to Isasi-Díaz. The first is what she terms a "multi-world view," in which difference is perceived as something besides "other"—where difference is not erased or tolerated but where many differences are seen as comprising the whole. This multi-world view requires an analysis of power and a relational understanding of difference. For white women, this analysis needs to include a thorough understanding of the history of Western oppression of marginalized groups as well as an understanding of the current benefits of white women's privilege, particularly its "invisible package" of unearned assets that white women can count on, to use the terminology of Peggy McIntosh.[14] It involves understanding the ways in which white women consciously and unconsciously contribute to the oppression of women of color. It also involves understanding the ways that privileged white women contribute to the oppression of disabled, poor, and older women of all colors. These understandings are critical for avoiding the paralysis of white women's guilt, a syndrome which may actually serve as a cover up, preventing some white women from engaging in the tough work of multiworld traveling and taking necessary actions to correct injustice.

According to Isasi-Díaz, another condition necessary for reaching critical awareness is advocacy education, a process in which notions of so-called neutral objectivity are demythologized and deconstructed and in which coalitions and structures of solidarity and support are built. For the purpose of discussing the methodology which informs this work, I want to explore Isasi-Díaz's term "advocacy education" and reflect on how we proceed with building the coalitions necessary to demythologize and deconstruct dominant world views. In order to talk about advocacy, I draw upon what Elizabeth Potter has called "the ethics of knowledge." In speaking of the ethics of knowledge, Potter points to a fourth obstacle confronting women as we think about doing theology across the boundaries of cultural difference. This obstacle is what she terms "the temptation to silence."

During a recent presentation to faculty, staff and students of Mills College, Potter began by asking such basic questions as "Can we ever speak for or about someone else? When is it appropriate, if ever, to speak about someone whose identity is in some way different from our own? How? Under what circumstances?"[15] Our ethics, as well as our common sense, have led us to an understanding that we cannot speak for everyone. To universalize is to dehumanize. Yet Potter's question challenges us to think carefully about the issue of advocacy education. She continued her presentation by raising the problem of group identity. If I can speak only for my group, how narrowly is my group defined? Maybe I can only speak for myself. Equally problematic is "the temptation to silence," because to say nothing is safer than entering into the rough waters of a multi-world view. Nevertheless, we have been commissioned to be "world" travelers, in the words of María Lugones.[16] What are our guidelines for when to speak for or about someone or a group whose identity may be quite different from our own?

To speak personally, a few years ago at the annual meeting of the American Academy of Religion in New Orleans, I met a Ph.D. student from Colombia.[17] Together we spoke of the marked absence of Latin American or U.S. Hispanic men and women from the conference program. At that point, she and I wondered together if there were ways that I, as a white feminist liberationist, might make constructive use of my knowledge of Latin American liberation theology in a more public way. But I still had questions about the appropriateness of an Anglo woman speaking on Latin American liberation theology. The questions about the ethics and responsibility of knowledge nagged at me then and continue to do so as I work through my own philosophical and pedagogical issues with advocacy education.

Elizabeth Potter, in her presentation mentioned above, indicated one of the real paradoxes of advocacy education. She hinted that surely one of the requirements for ever speaking for or speaking about another group is that one must understand that group. Secondly, as a non-member of the group, it is impossible to understand the group. This is the dilemma in which I find myself as a student of liberation theologies. While Potter is careful to warn of the dangers of entering the waters of a multi-cultural world view, her observation about the paradox of never being completely able to understand the "other" is not intended to circumvent discussion between those whose circumstances differ. For those of us teaching in small colleges or in small departments, it would be irresponsible to teach only the material of our own experience and background. At Mills College, for example, in an Introduction to Religion class, if I do not teach womanist or *mujerista* theology, they simply will not be taught. Rather than falling into the temptation to be silent, we are offered Potter's suggestion that one must exercise a certain epistemological humility when trying to speak about the "other."

Here Uma Narayan offers two suggestions which may be helpful. First, she suggests that the outsider exercise "methodological humility," in which the outsider conducts herself "under the assumption that, as an outsider, she may be missing something. . . ."[18] Second, she urges "methodological caution," in which the outsider attempts "to carry out her attempted criticism of the insider's perceptions in such a way that it does not amount to, or even seem to amount to, an attempt to denigrate or dismiss entirely the validity of the insider's point of view."[19]

Elsa Tamez offers additional help in designing a means for doing theology across the boundaries of difference. In her 1992 address to the American Academy of Religion in San Francisco, Tamez spoke of the need for the development of indigenous voices within Latin American liberation theology. Tamez, a Mexican of mixed heritage, made the suggestion that it is not the task of mestizos or whites to develop Indian or African American hermeneutics. Rather, her task is to prepare the hearts and minds of those who are not Indian or Black[20] to receive the spiritual practices of others "with joy and equality."[21]

If I understand Tamez correctly, it is my task to try to create an environment in which those of us who are Anglo, and particularly those who are in positions of power, are more ready to receive others' points of view, not with suspicion, but rather with "joy and equality." Tamez' suggestion, then, represents a second possibility for advocacy education, namely, that advocacy education can serve the purpose of educating one's own group about the realities of those whose theological understandings are quite different than one's own.

Rosemarie Tong has suggested another principle which may be helpful for doing theology across the boundaries of difference. The metaphorical "home in which everyone has a room of her own" is key to our future theological endeavors; this metaphor recalls the heavenly mansion in which there are "many rooms." Yet the home that Tong metaphorically constructs is so built as to allow conversations to take place between the people she describes as "a community of friends in virtue, and partners in action."[22] To borrow Tong's analysis, if my teaching and my scholarly, political, and activist work are to be successful, the walls containing my own perspectives as a white, educated woman from a working class background in the United States will be thin enough that the voices of Tamez, Isasi-Díaz, Lapiedra, Cannon, Williams, and Grant, as well as the voices of white feminist women, can be heard.

If we are to begin treading the treacherous waters of advocacy education on the way to critical awareness and a new world order, as Ada María Isasi-Díaz has pointed to, then we must begin to confront the real obstacles inhibiting our progress. We must try to understand something of the lives of those whom we will never completely understand, being open to risk in the process of open dialogue in our theologizing.

We must not think that the task of multi-cultural theological reflection on God will be easy. Again we return to feminist theory for wisdom as to how to proceed. Recognizing the difficulty of the kind of multi-cultural collaboration being proposed, Chela Sandoval offers her wisdom as to how this activity might proceed, saying, "Mistakes must be forgiven. Every day repeats an opportunity for beginning anew."[23] María Lugones offers the following suggestion: "Love has to be rethought, made anew."[24]

Feminist theory clearly has something to say to feminist theology. We must develop an ethic which insists on mutuality and respects difference if we are to engage in multi-cultural work. Likewise, feminist theology has something to say to feminist theorists, for if we pay attention, we will notice that at least some feminist theorists are making use of *theological* language, as noted in the references to the solutions proposed by Sandoval and Lugones. Women doing theology know something about mistakes. We call them sin. We also know something about forgiveness. We surely know about every day repeating an opportunity for beginning anew. We call this hope. These are theological categories. More important, they are the words of our faith. I do not propose that we substitute our words for those of Sandoval or Lugones. Theirs may well be better. However, theologians need to write more about what we know about the Ground of All That Is Sacred making all things new. In the process, new channels of communication between those doing feminist theology and feminist theory may open, particularly if those of us in religious studies make concrete efforts to travel the distance to the world of women's studies and ethnic studies. Indeed, we have evidence that the worlds of women's studies and feminist and liberation theologies may not be nearly so far apart as they once were.[25] It is up to those of us trained in theology to be equipped to speak of the storm that surrounds us as we do womanist, feminist, and liberationist work in the academy and in our communities, and we need to unafraid to speak of the God Who Is Present In The Midst of the Storm.[26] To our sister world travelers in the academy, who like ourselves, may be weary of the constant battle against racism, sexism, and homophobia, we need to make clear that there is a God Who Knows The Truth as together we try to dismantle the lies of patriarchal, racial, class, and sexual oppression so that we can all come to a better place, the home with many rooms, which we might call the realm of God.

Clues for Women's Multi-Cultural Theologizing:
On the Covenanting God

In searching for a biblical image of God to help us in our efforts, one which is woman-centered, liberating, embodied, and relational, the covenant between Naomi and Ruth comes to mind. There is significant evidence that women of very differing cultural contexts are interested in this concept. White feminist Mary Hunt, womanist Delores Williams, and Latin American theologian Tereza Cavalcanti each offers the covenant between Ruth and Naomi as a model for friendship.[27] I believe that within the notion of a Covenanting God and within the covenant between Ruth and Naomi, women theologians have the basis for mutual, shared theological reflection across the boundaries of difference. All of us would do well to hear again the words Ruth said to Naomi: "Do not urge me to abandon you, nor to turn from following you; for where you go I will go, and where you lodge I will lodge; your people shall be my people, and your God my God; where you die I will die, and there will I be buried" (Ruth 1:16, 17a).

Two aspects of this covenant are significant for the proposed model for doing theological reflection on God across the boundaries of difference. First, Ruth promises to accept Naomi's people as her people, altering the usual boundaries of familial and cultural allegiance. If we are to adapt this promise for our own purposes, we will find ways to say to one another, "Your people are my people." These are not words which can be uttered without the praxis of learning another's language and culture and without the commitment of life-long struggle to doing justice and righting relationship. Second, Ruth promises to honor the God of Naomi. In order for women doing theology to make similar commitments to each other, we must make the effort to read and hear each other's theological understandings of God and engage in conversation. Who knows, in our praxis of solidarity, committed Christian womanist, mujerista, Asian American and white feminist liberationist theologians might do well to even worship with each other and pray together.

Two objections must be dealt with concerning this notion of covenant. Jacquelyn Grant brings a hermeneutic of suspicion to notions of reconciliation, community, and covenant:

> All too often, notions of reconciliation, covenantal relationship, unity, and community mirror those in the system of domestic service relationships. The needs of one group (partner) are universalized in such a fashion that those on the topside of history are the beneficiaries of the system; and those on the underside of history are mere victims of the relationship.[28]

Grant prefers the term "discipleship" to describe the hard work of justice making. I want to emphasize that when I use the term covenant, I am not talking about the type of oppressive relationship described by Grant, which might rightly be called pseudo-covenantal. I am referring, instead, to a mutually reciprocal relationship and to an ethic of justice-making which governs the love, friendship, and hard work of those living in covenant with each other.

A second objection has been raised to the use of the Ruth and Naomi story as a good example of covenantal relationship. Several questions are relevant. Is the relationship between Ruth and Naomi mutual and reciprocal, or are Ruth's words to Naomi evidence of a one-sided relationship? Does Ruth give up her own culture, history, family, and God in order to honor those of Naomi? Is this yet another example of the patriarchal God of Israel silencing the god(s) of others? I think it is impossible to answer these questions definitively, for there is no record of Ruth or Naomi directly addressing these questions in the text. However, I want to suggest that within the story of Ruth and Naomi are clues for a model of covenantal love which can lead feminists, womanists, mujeristas and other liberationists toward fruitful dialogue.

While one would wish the narrator had recorded the complete text of all the conversations that ever took place between Ruth and Naomi, a hermeneutics of suspicion tells us that the narrator's own interests, theological and otherwise, may have governed the lines recorded and preserved as sacred text. Naomi does not respond in kind to Ruth's famous words, at least in the version we have in Scripture today. However, we have glimpses of a mutual, reciprocal relationship of love between these two women. Naomi continually addresses her daughter-in-law with the term of endearment, "my daughter."[29] In addition, on several occasions, she refers to the relationship between Ruth and her as one of kinship. For example, in Ruth 2:20 and 3:2, Naomi speaks of Boaz as "our kinsman," a relative "of ours," indicating that she considers Ruth to be part of her family, her "people." Further, it is Naomi who devises the scheme in which Ruth is to ask Boaz to live up to his duty of being the "redeemer." Ruth's prophecy, "Your people will be my people," comes true in part because Naomi wills it to be true by telling Ruth of the existence of Boaz.

As to the question about whether or not as part of the covenant Ruth gives up her own family, culture, and god, I believe it is possible to answer the question in the negative. When Ruth promises Naomi,

"Your people will be my people," we do not have to automatically assume that Ruth gives up her love for her own mother or father or her sister-in-law Orpah, who chooses to stay in Moab. Rather, we are able to imagine that Ruth is able to continue loving her blood family while making the choice to go to Bethlehem and love Naomi and her people. Secondly, we need not automatically assume that Ruth gives up her culture. The text, in fact, continues to refer to Ruth as "the Moabite" after she goes to Bethlehem. Finally, I believe that it is possible that Ruth does not necessarily give up her own God when she vows to honor the God of Naomi. Although it may have been the theological interest of the narrator to demonstrate Ruth's conversion to Yahwist theology (see 1:16), nowhere does Ruth explicitly renounce her Moabite God/s.

In fact, some evidence exists that both Ruth and Naomi understand God to be more than the name Yahweh. According to Louise Pettibone Smith, the God Shaddai of whom Naomi speaks in 1:20 may have been Moabite in origin.[30] What is certain is that Naomi ascribes to God both the names Yahweh and Shaddai. In addition, Smith, Francis Landy, and others have suggested that there is some textual evidence to support the notion that the threshing floor rite, which Naomi suggests Ruth participate in with Boaz, may have had cultic significance and/or perhaps was connected to a barley festival tribute to an ancient grain goddess of Bethlehem.[31] While neither Smith nor Landy make definitive judgements about whether the event has cultic significance or not, it is important for a hermeneutics of remembrance to know that at least at the level of folk culture and folk religion, a syncretistic understanding of God may well have survived at the time. What I am suggesting, for only a suggestion is possible based on the text as it has been preserved, is that perhaps Ruth and Naomi were able, in their own wisdom, to honor a multitude of Gods simultaneously, or perhaps they understood God to have many names.

In sum, in answer to the question of whether or not Ruth gives up her own family, culture, God, and identity, I do not believe we have any explicit textual evidence to suggest a renunciation of her heritage. Naomi's travel to Moab does not entail giving up her heritage from Judah. Likewise, I believe it is entirely possible that Ruth is able to travel to Naomi's "world" without giving up her own. In fact, the two women seem to be making every effort to forge a culture of their own, demonstrating a kind of cultural and theological flexibility that allows these women together to engage in the serious business of working out their salvation.[32] In the prophetic words of covenant which Ruth says to Naomi, we may have an early glimpse of the "multi-world view" which Ada María Isasi-Díaz believes is a key to liberation.

The covenant between Ruth and Naomi is important because it provides a relational link between God and these two women. Its covenantal formula harkens back to the covenantal formula which God has consistently used, "I will be your God and you will be my people." These two women of very differing cultural backgrounds make a commitment to each other to relate to one another just as God makes a relational commitment to humanity. The model I offer is that Ruth and Naomi's relatedness in friendship across the boundary of difference *is* the embodiment of the Covenanting God.

This essay has attempted to suggest a means for moving us closer to the home suggested by Tong, a home with many rooms, a home in which the walls of our own agendas, perspectives, and biases are thin enough to permit a conversation. If we are to begin building a theological home together, we will need to confront the obstacles to its construction described in this essay. We will need to speak in our distinct theological dialects and we will need to all become multi-lingual so that we can understand each other. We will need to speak our anger, listen in patience, and learn from each other. We will need to develop world-traveling skills and form multi-world views. We will need to speak of each other's lives in those places where it is appropriate and keep silent on other occasions. These are some of the conditions for us being able to enter into covenant together to relate to each other in mutually loving and liberating ways. In Kentucky, where my family lives and my roots are, when we speak of "our people," we mean our kin. Perhaps if we accept the invitation of the Covenanting God to enter into life-long, committed covenant with each other to work out our salvation together, as did Ruth and Naomi, we will find ways to become more human, literally to become "people," to one another.

Notes

[1] This essay is a revised version of a paper given at the College Theology Society Fortieth Annual Convention, Saint Mary's College, Notre Dame, Indiana, May 27, 1994. I am grateful to CTS readers for the *Annual Volume*, to CTS participants in

the joint session on Women and Religion and Psychology and Religion, and to Elizabeth Say for their helpful comments and suggestions.

[2] Rosemarie Tong, *Feminist Thought: A Comprehensive Introduction* (Boulder: Westview Press, 1989), 7.

[3] See Toinette M. Eugene et al., "Special Section on Appropriation and Reciprocity in Womanist/Mujerista/Feminist Work," *Journal of Feminist Studies in Religion* 8, no. 2 (Fall 1992), and Katie Geneva Cannon and Kristine A. Culp, with an introduction by Emilie M. Townes, "Appropriation and Reciprocity in the Doing of Feminist and Womanist Ethics," *The Annual of the Society of Christian Ethics* (Boston: The Society of Christian Ethics, 1993).

[4] Here I have consciously chosen the term "women doing theology" in recognition that some women prefer not to use the term "feminist" to describe the cultural context for their work, given that the term "feminist" has often been used to describe the cultural context of white women. See Chela Sandoval, "Feminism and Racism: A Report on the 1981 National Women's Studies Association Conference," first published in 1982 by the Center for Third World Organizing, Oakland, California and Washington, D.C. In *Making Face, Making Soul: Haciendo Caras: Creative and Critical Perspectives by Women of Color*, ed. Gloria Anzaldua (San Francisco: Aunt Lute Foundation Books, 1990), 55. See also Chela Sandoval, "Comment on Krieger's 'Lesbian Identity and Community: Recent Social Science Literature,' " *Signs: Journal of Women in Culture and Society* 9, no. 4 (1984), 728.

[5] Elizabeth Spelman, *Inessential Woman: Problems of Exclusion in Feminist Thought* (Boston: Beacon Press, 1988), ix.

[6] Ibid., 187.

[7] Audre Lorde, *Sister Outsider* (New York: The Crossing Press Feminist Series, 1984), 130.

[8] Alison M. Jaggar, "Love and Knowledge: Emotion in Feminist Epistemology," in *Gender/Body Knowledge*, ed. Alison Jaggar and Susan Bordo (New Jersey: Rutgers University Press, 1989), 157.

[9] Ibid., 160.

[10] Ibid.

[11] Ibid.

[12] Ibid., 162.

[13] Ada María Isasi-Díaz, "Educating for a New World Order," paper presented at the annual meeting of the National Association of Women in Education, Seattle, Washington, March 6, 1993.

[14] Peggy McIntosh, "White Privilege: Unpacking the Invisible Knapsack," *Independent School* (Winter 1990), 31. For further discussion of white privilege, see her article "White Privilege and Male Privilege: A Personal Account of Coming to See Correspondences Through Work in Women's Studies," in *Race, Class and Gender*, ed. Margaret Andersen and Patricia Hill Collins (Belmont, California: Wadsworth, 1992), 70-81.

[15] Elizabeth Potter is Chair of Women's Studies at Mills College, Oakland,

California. This discussion took place at a faculty seminar given on March 15, 1993.

[16] See María C. Lugones and Elizabeth V. Spelman, "Have We Got a Theory for You! Feminist Theory, Cultural Imperialism and the Demand for 'The Woman's Voice.' " *Women's Studies International Forum* 6, no. 6 (1983) and María Lugones, "Playfulness, 'World'-Traveling, and Loving Perception," in *Making Face, Making Soul.*

[17] I am thankful to Marta Inés Castillejo C. for the conversation which led to these observations.

[18] Uma Narayan, "Working Together Across Difference: Some Considerations on Emotions and Political Practice," *Hypatia: A Journal of Feminist Philosophy* 3, no. 2 (Summer, 1988), 38.

[19] Ibid.

[20] I have followed the recommendation of Emilie M. Townes that she and other womanist scholars prefer that the word "Black" be capitalized. For stylistic purposes, parallel use of the words Anglo and Hispanic are also capitalized throughout.

[21] Elsa Tamez, "Quetzalcoatl Challenges the Christian Bible," paper presented at the Annual Meeting of the American Academy of Religion and Society for Biblical Literature, November 1992, San Francisco, California.

[22] Rosemarie Tong, *Feminist Thought*, 7.

[23] Chela Sandoval, "U.S. Third World Feminism: The Theory and Method of Oppositional Consciousness in the Postmodern World," *Genders* 10 (Spring 1991), 71.

[24] María Lugones, "Playfulness, 'World'-Traveling, and Loving Perception," in *Making Face, Making Soul: Haciendo Caras*, ed. Gloria Anzaldua (San Francisco, Aunt Lute Foundation Books, 1990), 393.

[25] Evidence for the bridging of gaps between women in women's studies and religious studies is clear in recent publications. *Women and Values: Readings in Recent Feminist Philosophy*, ed. Marilyn Pearsall (Belmont, CA: Wadsworth Publishing Co., 1986) contains a chapter on Philosophy of Religion. *The Cross Cultural Study of Women*, ed. Margot I. Duley and Mary I. Edwards (New York: The Feminist Press at the City University of New York, 1986) contains a chapter on Women and Religion. *A Reader in Feminist Knowledge*, ed. Sneja Gunew (London and New York: Routledge, 1991) contains a chapter on Religion. *The Women's Studies Quarterly* 21, no. 1 and 2 (Spr/Sum 1993) is a thematic issue on Spirituality and Religion.

[26] The image of God in the Midst of the Storm is derived from a story told in Katie Geneva Cannon, "Surviving the Blight," in *Inheriting Our Mothers' Gardens: Feminist Theology in Third World Perspectives*, ed. Letty Russell et al. (Philadelphia: Westminster Press, 1988), 88.

[27] See Mary E. Hunt, *Fierce Tenderness: A Feminist Theology of Friendship* (New York: The Crossroad Publishing Company, 1992), 74; Delores Williams, "Breaking and Bonding," *Daughters of Sarah* (May-June, 1989), 20, 21; Tereza

Cavalcanti, "The Prophetic Ministry of Women in the Hebrew Bible," in *Through Her Eyes*, ed. Elsa Tamez (Maryknoll, New York: Orbis Books, 1989), 127.

[28] Jacquelyn Grant, "The Sin of Servanthood," in *A Troubling in My Soul: Womanist Perspectives on Evil and Suffering*, ed. Emilie M. Townes (Maryknoll, New York: Orbis Books, 1993), 215.

[29] Phyllis Trible concurs as to the significance of this term of endearment. See Phyllis Trible, *God and the Rhetoric of Sexuality* (Philadelphia: Fortress Press, 1978), 176.

[30] Louise Pettibone Smith, "The Book of Ruth: Introduction and Exegesis," in *The Interpreter's Bible*, Volume II (New York: Abingdon-Cokesbury Press, 1953), 838.

[31] Louise Pettibone Smith, "The Book of Ruth," 844, 845, and Francis Landy, "Ruth and the Romance of Realism, or Deconstructing History," *Journal of the American Academy of Religion*, 62, no. 2 (1994), 287-289.

[32] Phyllis Trible agrees with this interpretation in her summation, "All together they are women in culture, women against culture, and women transforming culture." Phyllis Trible, *God and the Rhetoric of Sexuality*, 196.

Ecclesial Discernment: Women's Voices, New Voices, and the Revelatory Process

Ann O'Hara Graff

For some time it has seemed clear to me that all key decisions which guide the life and teaching of the Roman Catholic church, universal, regional, and local, should entail an explicit institutional practice of discernment which would reflect contemporary theological insights about revelation as disclosed within the events of human experience. Thus the first concern in this essay is the meaning of starting with experience. The second is to ask what we learn about revelation when we start with experience. The third issue is to suggest what this implies for ecclesial discernment.

Karl Rahner re-taught this generation of Catholics that it is precisely in our human experience that we can be hearers and bearers of the word of God. It is only in exploring our experience that we come to understand ourselves, and so to understand, as Augustine learned so long ago, that to find our authentic selves is to find the indwelling presence of God. To avoid who we are is to avoid access to the Divine. To grapple with ourselves is to break open the way for the revelation of God. The familiar theological phrase, that the Divine is disclosed in and through the human, is not mere epistemology. It creates an insistent political demand within the *ecclesia*. At the very least it requires that we think about discernment in close connection to human experience.

Yet I wish to examine this more specifically. Attention to experience as a locus of revelation marks many twentieth century Catholic theologies. Here I will explore what we learn about revelation when women's voices, and other new voices of previously silent/silenced people, enter the conversation of Christians. Then I will argue that this learning about revelation indicates the need for new ecclesial structures for discernment that can attend to this revelatory process.

Discernment is an effort to recognize revelation in the present. It is the effort to seek the presence and guidance of God in the ambiguity of human life.[1] Whether implicitly or explicitly, a church claims a discernment process whenever it trusts that in its major decisions it is acting and speaking in accord with its sense of God's presence and guidance. This may be cast in the language of "when the bishop speaks, Christ speaks," or in that of following the Holy Spirit, or trust in the providence of God, or similar formulations. However, the claim is that the wisdom of the decision-makers bespeaks the will of God. Such a claim of its very nature entails a theory of revelation and a congruent practice of discernment. It is my claim that what we are learning from women and other recent participants in the public conversation called theology indicates that experience is our necessary and best starting point for recognizing revelation and practicing discernment.

Experience as Located

The attention of Karl Rahner, and many others today, to experience as a starting point, and indeed, the context for our recognition of the revelation of God, demands that we take account of those factors which are our own situation's major informants. Experience is always located. At the present time in the North American Catholic church, our situation is constantly qualified by issues that shaped modernity, and now shape our post-modern era. Modernity is marked by the rise of scientific consciousness, and later historical consciousness, the attention to the individual and the development of the notion of the social contract, and the epistemological turn to the subject, and the consequent explorations of the limits as well as the multi-faceted dimensions and designs of human knowing and experiencing. In the post-modern era, the relativities of history have been added to by the increased recognition of the relativity of cultures as humanly constructed worlds, and of social locations within cultural worlds that further define and separate people. The Enlightenment's attention to the processes that constitute experience and knowing have intersected with this recognition of the ways in which people are shaped by culture, social location, historical moment. One result is that from our differing social locations, defined (in part) by the intersections of gender, race, class, age, and sexual orientation, we have learned that we interpret the world differently even when we share a larger culture and historical moment. It is precisely this problem of locally diverse interpretation that becomes interesting for an understanding of revelation.

The way that these issues impinge on revelation may be more visible if I follow a thread of emerging insights in feminist theology. Similar threads could, no doubt, be traced in black theology, or in the work of Latin American liberation theology, or in the recent contributions of Asian and African theologians to the international conversation. I attend to the feminists because I am a white, middle class feminist, and I have found that this path has led me toward the others.

The "second wave" of American feminism was an outgrowth of the civil rights movement of the 1960s. In Catholic theology, Mary Daly and Rosemary Radford Ruether were two of the formative early voices. In 1968 Mary Daly published *The Church and the Second Sex*.[2] In 1972 Ruether published *Liberation Theology*,[3] and in 1975, *New Woman, New Earth*.[4] These texts were primarily efforts to name the misogyny and injustices of the Christian tradition and the practice of the church. This was possible because women had begun to recognize that not only was their experience not encoded in the public tradition, but women had persistently suffered oppression and violence at the hands of a male dominated church. The insight into women's different situation and our oppression has necessitated ongoing work to name and deconstruct those elements of the tradition.

However, the insight into difference has also led to a steady effort to name what constitutes women's experience. This had already been initiated in European feminist theory, in a book that was very influential among American feminists, Simone de Beauvoir's *The Second Sex*.[5] However, as the work of feminist theory and feminist theology grew, white feminists were called to account by African American women, notably Audre Lorde and Katie Geneva Cannon.[6] White women did not and could not simply refer to women's experience as if it included every woman. The issue of differences among the different was apparent. This concern has been re-echoed by Latina women, Asian women, and Native American women.[7]

This conversation among women theologians is now paralleled by the international conversation about the nature and symbols of Christian theology. Many people from Latin America, Africa, and Asia, both men and women, whose voices were rarely heard in the public arena are now speakers. Each and all are quite clear that their experience is unique, and that no one else can speak for them. What we experienced in North America since the mid-sixties has become a global phenomenon, as more and more of the world's culturally and socially diverse peoples command attention in our multi-lateral public conversation.

This international conversation and within it, the coming to voice of many diverse women, concretizes the modern and now post-modern recognitions that experience is historically, culturally, and socially located. It also suggests that the contours of experience specify Rahner's abstract pursuit of the transcendental turn to the subject initiated in the Enlightenment. If the revelation of God is disclosed in and through our experience, it must be within the specific experiences we have as culturally, historically, socially located people. Or taken from the other side of the type of theological endeavor Rahner proposed, the incarnation itself directs us into the specificities of human lives in the world. Moreover, as Asian feminist Kwok Pui-lan, as well as C. S. Song and Robert Hood each argue, a God who chooses incarnation, and who is the very definition of truth and love cannot be confined to one cultural stream, but must, necessarily, embrace us in all our diversities, and so be discoverable within our cultural, historical, social worlds.[8]

The Event of Revelation within Located Experience

If we cannot but deal with the realities of our diverse experiential locations, then it behooves us to examine what we learn concretely when we move from location to location and engage in the interpretation of Christian narratives and symbols. At the outset I want to name that wherever we are located, one anchor we share is the narrative tradition of the Scripture, another is the ritual dramas of the sacraments. While Christians have named Word and sacrament as revelatory for two millenNia, what we are grappling with today is the way we experience the event of revelation within the specific contexts in which we live. Moreover, we also recognize the narratives of Scripture and the forms of ritual to encode socially, culturally, historically located experience themselves. However authoritatively these function for us, they remain within the category of located experience. Thus they are certain definitive, touchstone experiences with which we engage our own experience in order to name the sacred in our midst.

In what follows I offer several examples in recent theology that illustrate the dynamic of revelatory events as we engage the central symbols and narratives of Christianity from our diverse locations. Two recent examples of white middle class feminist theological interpretation of God illustrate the way that the symbol of God can be re-examined in terms of analogies drawn from female experience.[9] Sallie McFague opens up the mystery of the Trinity as mother, lover, and friend. As an example of her project, she uses mother love as an interpreter of Divine *agape*, which is not disinterested, but passionately engaged in the welfare of all her children. Female birthing and feeding are also used as metaphors for creation and providence; the mother gives life and cares for the child. McFague links generativity and justice as a mother's care desires justice for every child.[10]

Elizabeth Johnson's acclaimed book, *She Who Is,* explores the realm of analogies drawn from female experience, as well as from the wisdom tradition, to explore the Trinity under the rubric of Sophia. In each case the persons of God, and the Trinity as a whole are depicted through the metaphors of a lively and enlivening relational Divine nature. She argues that God is ultimately "She Who Is" intimately and empoweringly among us, providing for and sustaining human life from moment to moment.

Both of these women take us on a journey into the more of God, and they do it in a way that provides new life for Christian women, including us in the Divine Mystery in a way that has not been written about before. Yet other feminist theologians illustrate that the depths of our Christian symbols carry conflictual interpretations.

One ready-to-hand example is that of the interpretation of Jesus the Christ as servant. This interpretation may be wholly appropriate as a prophetic gospel message when the hearers of the word are people with access to powerful positions of influence in the church itself, as well as in our institutions both public and private. However, as Elisabeth Schüssler Fiorenza pointed out in her article on the subject, this proclamation of Jesus as one held up for our emulation can simply serve to reinforce the subordinate and self-effacing roles women are induced to play in patriarchal cultures.[11] Thus it is not gospel, but rather functions as an ideological reinforcement of women's diminution as subjects. For Schüssler Fiorenza, to transform Jesus' practice of a discipleship of equals, struggling together for love and justice, into charitable service, does a serious disservice to the Gospel.

To take this one step further, womanist theologian Jacquelyn Grant has noted that while the role of Jesus as servant, especially suffering servant, was one which slave women could identify with and which helped them in their need, it is not an interpretation of Jesus which should be maintained for contemporary black women, as it has the function of restricting rather than enlarging the growth of black women into their own full humanity.[12]

For Grant, this interpretation of Jesus is problematic on the basis of her social location, but differently than for Schüssler Fiorenza. Fiorenza turns to the images of Jesus as the one who proclaimed and practiced a discipleship of equals as a helpful way to relate to Jesus. For Grant the clue is in the incarnation. The fully human Jesus who is the Christ enables the journey of black women toward their full humanity. My point is to illustrate that the interpretation of Jesus as servant, which could function as a prophetic call to imitation among people in social locations in which they wield power, may only diminish the humanity of people in quite different social locations. This raises a question about what interpretations of our polyvalent symbols and narratives serve as Gospel, in what situations. Or in the context of this essay, what is a revelatory event?

This same insight is the one pressed by many theologians whose work is being done in other cultural bases than those of the North and West. In a brilliant series of essays in *Voices From the Margin*, editor R. S. Sugirtharajah demonstrates that the towering symbol of the Exodus, used in so many liberation theologies, can also function as a powerful instrument of terror and harm when people experience their position as Canaanites and not as children of Israel.[13] However redemptively this symbol may function for the poor of Latin America or the *minjung* of Korea, it has been a terrible weapon used against Palestinians and Native Americans. Again, what is a central retrieval of the gospel as a pathway for liberating praxis in some situations can in other contexts be a militaristic ideology which masks the humanity of others and wreaks destruction on them. Examples of this type could be multiplied. Again, the meaning of the Word of God is at stake.

Yet even to say this is already to indicate that the symbols and narratives, indeed the doctrines and theologies, which fund the Christian tradition, are multivalent. At the least we may learn more about what is revealed when people from different social locations appropriate the symbols. Feminists like Sallie McFague or Elizabeth Johnson demonstrate that explorations of the identity of God can yield rich new fields of symbols which do not so much negate older interpretations as add to our insight into the Divine. Tied to this is the way in which they also make women visible and honored partners in the sacred mystery among us. Yet, as the examples about the servant or the Exodus symbols indicate, we may confront conflictual interpretations, and thus that they require a discernment process in the church in order that we might affirm together the event of Jesus the Christ and his good news in our midst.

From Revelation in Diversity to Discernment

The recognition that the gospel is borne and received under the conditions of diversity, like the recognition of historical conditionedness in the last century, is challenging,—exhilarating for some, and frightening to others. How do we mediate this ecclesially? I have suggested that we must attend to a process of discernment that could aid us in becoming an international church of local churches, a communion of communions. I would like to see the realization of the church as a catholic church of diverse and authentic local churches, whose unity is incarnated in the common conversation to discern, affirm, and challenge multiple forms of evangelical praxis in local churches around the globe. My vision is that local churches might come together in regional areas to discern together, and that the Vatican might become a center of international ecclesial discernment, challenge and support. It is precisely the discernment process itself as a center of conversation among the local churches that would allow us to be both one and catholic. Or, in the language of this essay, it would allow us to name and practice the gospel differently, as our locations require, yet to mediate our diversity in the commerce of conversation about the narratives and symbols we all share.

While this cannot be the place to attend to the fullness of what might be required in an adequate discernment process in the church,[14] I can indicate that the process of discernment is centered in conversation. This is already evident from the examples offered about the exploration of key Christian symbols above. We see that the Exodus symbol operates as a beacon of liberating hope, and a demand to work for social justice when the experiences with which the symbol is in dialogue are those of the poor of Latin America, Asia, especially the *minjung* of Korea, or of Black America. Yet, as we noted, the Exodus can be terrifying if one is placed in the category of the Canaanites as Palestinians or Native Americans have been. What is clear is that people in different social locations are conversing with the narrative, and in fact working with it, or, painfully experiencing its negative effects. To begin to discern the revelation of God in these contexts would start with conversation about the experience of the situations and the power of the symbol/narrative within them. What is potent about Sugirtharajah's editing of the texts so that we see successively how the Exodus functions in different contexts is equally important for the church. When we bring our experience of living Christian symbols into dialogue with each other we have the opportunity to learn from beyond our own perspective, to meet our own limitations, and be challenged, as well as to be affirmed in our efforts to live out of Scripture and tradition in our own situations.

In a thought-provoking article, Roberto Goizueta refers to the present ecclesial reality in the language of Johann Baptist Metz as the "epoch of a culturally polycentric genuinely universal church."[15] Goizueta takes up three issues in relation to such a polycentric church and its differing theological perspectives that I find helpful here, and I will reflect on these in terms of my concern for enacting a discernment conversation for a church of local churches. The first is that diversity not be misunderstood as individualism, bereft of institution and tradition. The second concern is that authentic pluralism demands that all contributors to the common conversation be full partners, not voices already interpreted by groups in dominant positions. The third issue is tied to the first and has already been hinted at in this essay, namely how do we have conversation, and not sheer equivocity? I will weave these concerns into the comments which follow.

Goizueta's second point offers an important qualifier about the character of an ecclesial discernment conversation. A polycentric church must really mean that all groups give up the claim to be the center. There is no center with margins anymore;[16] rather local churches are genuinely centers which can engage each other. It also means that conversation entail what Goizueta calls a "methodological attentiveness," to the ways in which we are truly open or closed to one another.[17] I would suggest this calls for ecclesial structures that would institutionalize practices of attention to all contributors to a common conversation.

This apparently obvious concern is truly radical, in the sense that its implementation would subvert and transform the power relations of groups as they exist in present social arrangements. Both Elisabeth Schüssler Fiorenza and Sharon Welch are clear that to admit diversity, even to celebrate it, must also always entail the political awareness that our diverse social locations, based on gender, race, class, ethnicity, age, and the like, are shaped, in no small part, by the interstructuring of oppressive power relations.[18] People join the conversation from different economic, political, social, cultural, gendered positions of power. For those who have had dominant public voices to yield to those who are now also speaking, as equals, is a major step, as is the step to own one's voice when it has been denied or suppressed. In the context of her work on communities acting for justice, Welch reminds us that we must examine the very language we use which encodes power when we speak about our own experience. Other feminists, psychologists and literary critics, are also teaching us how to hear and speak even though our voices and experiences have been repressed or silenced.[19] Voice and power go together. Surely one meaning of the preferential option for the poor is exactly this, that those who have held voice and power recognize both the partial and powerful, even oppressive character of their own voice and position, and begin to speak and to hear with that in mind. Similarly, those who have not had voice or power must become speakers who can also do what Nelle Morton taught us, namely, "hear one another into speech."[20]

These angles of vision on the contemporary church, and the recognition that we are a church of local churches, mean we are a church of multiple interpreters and practicioners of the gospel. Moreover, if the local churches are truly the bearers of ongoing, incarnate events of revelation when their experience interacts anew with the gospel borne in scripture and the traditions, then these churches, each and all, have an authority in the overarching ecclesial search for the best ways to proclaim and live the gospel in each present situation. In David Tracy's language, these churches could be understood as our chief interpreters of the classics of Christianity.[21] And it is the classics themselves—Jesus the Christ, the New Testament, the great doctrines, theologies, rituals, etc.—that provide the ground for the common Catholic Christian struggle for understanding and practice.

This concern brings us back to the related issues Goizueta raises about recognizing the traps of individualism and equivocity, and insuring conversation in relation to community and tradition. To discern is not simply to name everyone's viewpoint and value it. The danger of our post-modern situation is precisely the sheer fragmentation of all conversation into personal experience and convictions. If every "I" is only extrinsicly related to every other "I" and each island "I" has only his/her own convictions, then we are left with little absolutist individuals, and no way to learn from and with each other.

Catherine Keller's brilliant book, *From a Broken Web: Separation, Sexism and Self*,[22] argues that we belong to each other through the relations out of which we continuously build ourselves. We create ourselves in relationship to one another. Keller uses process thought as well as psychological insight to formulate this insight into our fundamental relatedness. She thoroughly debunks the notion of the separated individual self. This work is supported and complemented by the recent work of feminist psychologists at Wellesley College who propose that women (and probably men too!) grow in relations to others, both past and present, and that we create ourselves in terms of our relations to others all our lives.[23]

In his complex and careful analysis of our post-modern situation, Mark Kline Taylor supports and broadens this recognition. He is clear that even in this era which is so conscious of our pluralism and even our fragmentation, we still belong to socially located groups. These groups are carriers of tradition, handing on a past and able to shape a future, however particular that may be.[24] Although we cannot easily claim a great tradition which shapes us all and functions as authority for us, nevertheless some elements of tradition, myth, and ritual form us from within our social groups. Tradition and pluralism interact. We are not sheer individuals. Moreover, the struggle to resist domination in all its forms is woven into the discourses, politics, and practices of difference which attend pluralism. Again, the dangerous memories of the socially located groups may be key in shaping resistance in a fragmented, but not atomized, world.

Created in a tradition and ecclesial institutions, we may selectively articulate, practice and transform elements of these in ways that transcend and challenge both. We may also find ourselves challenged by values within these traditions and institutions, however much we may want to reject or change them. If these insights are correct, individualism as we experience it in North America is an illusion, albeit a powerful one.[25] Moreover, it affirms that when we discern together, our diversity is not about mere individualism, but about the necessary mediation of our constructed cultural and social worlds, which continue to interpret, and be interpreted by, the central narratives and symbols of Christianity.

Much of this essay has implicitly argued against the univocity of Roman or other dominant theologies, ecclesial or academic. It has also argued against sheer equivocity, whether of individuals or of groups, because this simply fragments the absolutist claims of one dominant voice into the absolute claims of many.[26] To struggle with the truth claims of a tradition, including its legitimate diversity, is not the same as simply claiming the truth of one's own experience and living it—or thinking one does. Tracy, Goizueta, and Dussel, and in another context, Elizabeth Johnson, all recognize that as Christians, however differently located, we claim a common tradition and our interpretations of it make claims on each other.[27] In that sense, we work analogically, we interpret analogically. This means we struggle with similarities-in-difference. To return to the examples of the servant interpretation of Christ, or the Exodus as both liberating and terrorizing, to recognize that a particular symbol may hold both hope and terror, may give life or take it, is to recognize that our symbols function in a range of ways in a range of contexts. Only the conversation among the practitioners of the gospel, particularly those who live and proclaim the experience of the local churches, can assess, challenge, and affirm one another as we all seek to practice the common faith. This deliberately moves us from diverse interactions with a symbolic tradition to grapple with the effort to do this in a polycentric, analogous way, such that the criteria of challenge and affirmation, thus the criteria for discernment, are disclosed in the function of the living, practical interpretation of the symbols in the lives of the people who are the churches and the church.

If we could truly be a church of local churches, with a common mission to proclaim and live the gospel of Jesus Christ, the center of our common life might well be ongoing conversation to do the work of discernment together, to challenge, affirm, understand, and help one another for the sake of our world. The unity of such a church of particular churches would be based in the shared classics, the common conversation supporting common witness to the gospel, however diverse the forms, and in the love of the Holy Spirit shed abroad in our hearts.

The argument of this essay has been to suggest that we need to begin to identify the specific structures of ecclesial discernment as an international conversation among the members of local churches precisely because we have learned from women, and other marginalized people, that only when we take our experiential starting places into account can we recognize Divine revelation in our midst. To take this seriously means that we are not simply interested in the diversity of forms of revelation, but that we are committed to the practice of the gospel for the sake of all people. Therefore, to the extent that revelation tells us who we are and how to live, we must, as a global church of local churches, engage in discernment so that we can do our best throughout the world to live the gospel as a Catholic church.

Notes

[1] For a lengthy study of discernment in the tradition and its implications for ecclesial decision-making see Ann O'Hara Graff, *Vision and Reality: Discernment and Decision-Making in Contemporary Roman Catholic Ecclesiology* (Ph.D. Dissertation, University of Chicago, 1986).

[2] (New York: Harper & Row, 1968).

[3] (New York: Paulist Press, 1972).

[4] (New York: The Seabury Press, 1975).

[5] Trans. and ed. by H. M. Parshley (New York: Alfred A. Knopf, Inc., 1952). Originally published in France in 1949.

[6] One important example of this is Audre Lorde's well-known letter, "An Open Letter to Mary Daly," *Sister Outsider* (Trumansburg, New York: The Crossing Press, 1984), pp. 66-71. Another example is the 1982 correspondence of Katie Geneva Cannon and Carter Heyward excerpted in *God's Fierce Whimsey: Christian Feminism and Theological Education*, ed. The Mud Flower Collective (New York: Pilgrim Press, 1985), pp. 36-59.

[7] See Letty M. Russell, et al., *Inheriting Our Mothers' Gardens: Feminist Theology in Third World Perspective* (Louisville: Westminster Press, 1988) offers one sense of the dialogue among feminist theologians. Another excellent example is Carol P. Christ and Judith Plaskow, eds., *Weaving the Visions: Patterns in Feminist Spirituality* (San Francisco: Harper & Row, Publishers, 1989).

[8] See Kwok Pui-lan, "Discovering the Bible in the Non-Biblical World," in *Lift Every Voice: Constructing Christian Theologies from the Underside*, eds., Susan Brooks Thistlethwaite and Mary Potter Engel (San Francisco: Harper & Row, Publishers, 1990), pp. 270-282; C. S. Song, *Tell Us Our Names: Story Theology from an Asian Perspective* (Maryknoll: Orbis Books, 1984); Robert E. Hood, *Must God Remain Greek: Afro Cultures and God-Talk* (Minneapolis: Fortress Press, 1990).

[9] Sallie McFague, *Models of God: Theology for an Ecological, Nuclear Age* (Philadelphia: Fortress Press, 1987); Elizabeth Johnson, *She Who Is: The Mystery of God in Feminist Theological Discourse* (New York: Crossroad, 1992).

[10] McFague, pp. 97-123.

[11] " 'Waiting at Table': A Critical Feminist Theological Reflection on Diakonia," *Concilium* 198 (August 1988): 84-94.

[12] "Subjectification as a Requirement for Christological Construction," in *Lift Every Voice*, pp. 201-214; see also her unpublished paper, "Jesus and Servanthood: Re-imaging Redemption," for the Women's Seminar in Constructive Theology, Catholic Theological Society of America, June 16, 1991.

[13] (Maryknoll: Orbis Books, 1991), pp. 227-295.

[14] See Graff, *Vision and Reality,* for one construction of a larger picture of ecclesial discernment.

[15] Metz, "Theology in the Modern Age, and before Its End," *Different Theologies, Common Responsibility,* Claude Geffré et al., eds. (Edinburgh: T&T Clark, 1984), p. 16; quoted in Goizueta, "United States Hispanic Theology and the Challenge of Pluralism," *Frontiers of Hispanic Theology in the United States,* ed. by Allan Figueroa Deck (Maryknoll: Orbis Books, 1992), p. 1.

[16] Goizueta, p. 14, citing David Tracy, "On Naming the Present," in *On the Threshold of the Third Millennium* (London: SCM Press, 1990), 67.

[17] Ibid., p. 13.

[18] Schüssler Fiorenza, *Discipleship of Equals: A Critical Feminist Ekklesialogy of Liberation* (New York: Crossroad, 1993), esp. pp. 344-45; Welch, *Communities of Resistance and Solidarity: A Feminist Theology of Liberation* (Maryknoll: Orbis Books, 1985). Welch's work engages Michel Foucault throughout on these issues.

[19] As examples see Lyn Mikel Brown and Carol Gilligan, *Meeting at the Crossroads: Women's Psychology and Girl's Development* (Cambridge: Harvard University Press, 1992); Sidonie Smith and Julia Watson, eds., *De/Colonizing the Subject: The Politics of Gender in Women's Autobiography* (Minneapolis: University of Minnesota Press, 1992).

[20] *The Journey Is Home* (Boston: Beacon Press, 1985), pp. 127-131; however this is a key theme in the entire text.

[21] *The Analogical Imagination: Christian Theology and the Culture of Pluralism* (New York: Crossroad, 1981).

[22] (Boston: Beacon Press, 1986).

[23] Judith V. Jordan, et al., *Women's Growth in Connection: Writings from the Stone Center* (New York: The Guilford Press, 1991).

[24] *Remembering Esperanza: A Cultural Political Theology for North American Praxis* (Maryknoll: Orbis Books, 1990), esp. pp. 23-45. This book is a liberation theology that carries explicit feminist concerns.

[25] This is further supported by Robert Bellah, et al., *Habits of the Heart: Individualism and Commitment in American Life* (Berkeley: University of California Press, 1985).

[26] Goizueta, pp. 15-16; Enrique Dussel, "Historical and Philosophical Presuppositions for Latin American Theology," *Frontiers of Theology in Latin America*, Rosino Gibellini, ed. (Maryknoll: Orbis Books, 1979), esp. pp. 185-96.

[27] Note that I am not implying that each of these people works out the meaning of analogy in exactly the same way. However, I am saying that the tradition that affirms analogy is critical to our common discourse.

Beyond Mere Gender:
Transforming Theological Anthropology

Jane Kopas

Trudy, a "bag lady" who narrates Jane Wagner's *The Search for Signs of Intelligent Life in the Universe*, concludes her commentary on life by describing the spectators at a play. "I forgot to tell 'em to watch the play; they'd been watching the *audience*!"[1] What her companions find in watching the audience is that the audience itself becomes art as they sit together in the dark, laughing and crying about the same things. In shifting its attention, the audience re-writes the script.

In the Christian tradition women have often been the audience—witnesses to theology, but not active shapers of it. Like Trudy's audience, women today are probing their experience and reshaping many areas of theology, taking on roles as actors and writers not just audience. Even as audience, women observe one another's experience and find new resources in their stories for the interpretation of their own human identity. One area affected by this new self-understanding is theological anthropology.

Theological anthropology offers a theme that calls for a new script, one that allows for the participation of a greater diversity of voices and new possibilities for improvisation. The unfinished character of feminist efforts to re-write theological anthropology makes it difficult to delineate its form clearly or to evaluate its success. Yet it can be examined as a work in progress. This article pulls together ideas not located in a single place and examines critical and constructive dimensions of the project. Thus it seeks to clarify some issues that will set the future agenda.

The movement of women from audience to scriptwriters in theological anthropology is especially evident among Catholic feminists. They, more than others, have had to confront the difficulties in traditional anthropology. Because of the emphasis on theological anthropology in the Catholic tradition, this article gives considerable attention to Catholic feminist theologians. The Catholic tradition has focused consistently on systematic issues related to doctrines about human beings. In the last several decades the hierarchical interpreters of tradition have drawn on a dualistic theological anthropology to support traditional teaching about women and ordination. They have attempted to limit the imagination by reiterating the exclusion of women from the great symbolic act of presiding over worship. A limiting theological anthropology has been used to justify this exclusion.

But as Catherine LaCugna so perceptively pointed out, the exclusion of women from presiding at the central act of worship has proven to be an opportunity to develop other strengths that might not have been developed.[2] Instead of focusing their energies on ordained ministry, Catholic women have focused their energies on theology and on other ministries. This has proven to be revolutionary in its own way because it means that women have taken the opportunity to revise our view of being human. As a result a new stage is being set in theological anthropology.

The first part of this article deals with several critical areas: the discipline of theological anthropology, the place of gender in theological anthropology, and the emergence of a feminist theological anthropology. The second part of the article highlights several major issues that characterize an emerging feminist theological anthropology, issues that both incorporate gender more explicitly and critically into theological anthropology and that signal a movement beyond gender. The article concludes by identifying tensions that underlie the emerging vision.

Raising the Curtain on the Debate

Theological anthropology is a relatively new term, although its elements have been present for a long time. Because notions like the person as creature, sinner, and image of God have been present for a long time, Christian theological anthropology appears settled and timeless. Another reason the elements of theological anthropology appear to present a universal and unchanging picture of the nature of human beings is that theologians have helped to create the impression by the method of their analyses.

Contemporary theologians like Paul Tillich, Wolfhart Pannenberg, and Karl Rahner present theological anthropologies that systematize human experience. They look for fundamental universal experiences or human characteristics that can provide a basis for the relation of all human beings to God. Feminist theologians question the extent to which these insights can be systematized as well as the validity of applying the insights universally. They also question how gender identity and roles have and have not functioned in the interpretation of human nature.

According to Edward Farley, we can speak of a vision of the human being that arose in connection with the faith of Israel and of Christianity, but this vision is "not so much a piece of timeless dogma resting above history as a loosely connected collection of insights that continually calls for reformulation."[3] Farley insists that theological anthropology is flexible not only because of the historical development of theological anthropology but also because contemporary challenges to Christian views of the person require that theology is able to continually reinterpret its insights in new and different contexts.

From the perspective of feminist theologians, too, understanding the relation of human beings to God is a theological work in progress; the insights that characterize our understanding of human beings and their connections with one another must be criticized and reformulated. And yet, feminist theologians have demonstrated a certain reluctance to reconstruct theological anthropology in a fully systematic way for several reasons associated with the enterprise as it has been traditionally defined.

A good number of feminist theologians are wary of the systematic development of theological anthropology because of the tendency of such analyses to be essentialist and ahistorical, to rely too heavily on abstract reasoning, and to rely on a single taxonomy that obscures human complexity. First, contemporary versions of theological anthropology have emphasized the essentialist character of what it means to be a human person. Christine Gudorf notes that theological anthropology traditionally assumes fixed discernible structures in people. These fixed structures predetermine character and behavior. They set expectations for the roles of particular groups and hint at the limits of their possibilities. Most feminist theologians reject this concept and incorporate the view of social sciences that differences between the sexes are largely learned.[4]

Second, many feminist thinkers have questioned the dominance of abstract reasoning in theological anthropology. Abstract reasoning separates experience from reason, and thought from action. It tends toward the building of a system of thought into which experience is expected to fit. Marjorie Reiley Maguire points out that feminist theology does not have the goal of building an abstract edifice but of identifying areas that call for social transformation. In this regard she and other feminist thinkers challenge a traditional approach to theological anthropology that disengages it from ethics.[5]

Traditional theology's reliance on abstract reasoning obscures the "thickness" and "texture" of human existence. For a number of feminist theologians, using philosophical frameworks, even contemporary ones, distances analysis from the concrete.[6] Feminist theologians find that contextualizing analysis leads to greater concreteness and the acknowledgement of limits, especially the limits of their own theological perspectives. Thus they are cautious about any theological anthropology that makes abstract universal claims.

Third, a number of feminist theologians resist the identification of a single taxonomy as providing a key to the human. They believe this identification draws us away from the complexity and mystery of the human. Ann O'Hara Graff notes there is no unified body of women's experience on which theological anthropology is to be based, but only multiple forms and dimensions that can be "mapped."[7] This approach departs from not only the abstract theorizing characteristic of Augustinian and Thomistic theology, but even from much of the subject based theology that generalizes from "human experience." The taxonomy of identifying the human as a rational animal, a symbol making animal, or a questioner creates a situation that reinforces the power of the one who names.[8] Likewise, theories of religious experience that identify the experience of finitude, openness to the world, or conversion as the common ground for apprehending God generalize the fears and hopes of one group to all. They canonize one group's values and restrict the value of other perspectives.

A sharpened awareness of gender accompanies the reluctance to systematize in theological anthropology. Until recently systematic approaches to theological anthropology have tended to overlook gender and diversity in the interest of universality.[9] Though past generations have not been keenly aware of it, gender (especially male gender) has played a significant role in theological anthropology. Its role has been obscured, however, because gender was considered a given and not distinguished from sex. Social scientists today offer a distinction that enables us to appreciate the flexibility of roles that were previously seen as unchanging. They define sex as a set of biological characteristics that mark human beings as male and female, although perhaps not in as watertight a way as usually presumed. Gender, on the other hand, represents a set of characteristics a particular culture judges to be masculine or feminine.[10] When the terms are understood as interchangeable, as theology has understood them in the past, human possibilities are clearly confined.

Nowhere is the failure to distinguish sex and gender more evident than in the theological anthropology that has dominated Christian and Catholic thought. Feminist responses to Vatican documents on ordination and on women reveal not only a conflict regarding the interpretation of scripture and tradition; they indicate a basic difference in understanding the relation between sex and gender. A brief summary of the response of American theologians to the Vatican position on women's ordination makes this evident.

Inter Insigniores, the Vatican "Declaration on the Question of the Admission of Women to the Ministerial Priesthood," set forth the official position on the possibility of ordination for women.[11] The Vatican based its position on the need for the priest to stand in the place of Jesus (who was male), on the absence of women among the twelve apostles, and on the lack of a tradition of ordaining women. A careful analysis of this position, however, revealed assumptions about "human nature" which are as important as reasons based on tradition.

A committee of the Catholic Theological Society of America prepared a response which analyzed the role of theological anthropology in the official document.[12] The committee identified two basic approaches to theological anthropology, the "two-nature" and "one-nature" approaches.[13] According to the two-nature approach, each sex embodies different possibilities for the development of humanness. These possibilities suggest a kind of biological determinism or unchanging pattern for each sex. That is, sex and gender are not distinguished. This view, though similar to that of classical writers like Augustine and Aquinas, tries to avoid the idea that women are inferior to men. In an effort to avoid the appearance of inferiority in one of the "natures," contemporary proponents of the dual approach often speak of them as "complementary." The characteristic traits of one sex "balance" or complement traits in the other sex. Inherent differences in sex translate into inherent differences in gender. The research team found a tendency on the part of those who argued against ordination of women to assume a "two-nature" view of humanity.

An approach to women and men based on a "one-nature" anthropology differs from the dual nature approach which relies on unchanging, stereotypical qualities like activity/passivity, reason/emotion, or logic/intuition. The single nature approach emphasizes similarity rather than differences and proposes that either sex can develop qualities traditionally associated with the other. A common humanity is the starting point for the one-nature approach. Male or female sex is part of that humanity but does not determine gender. The committee observed that the one-nature approach lends itself more readily to support for the ordination of women.

Both approaches have their strengths and weaknesses. The two-nature approach recognizes the importance of the body by highlighting the significance of sex in shaping identity. However, in equating sex and gender it overlooks the role that culture plays in shaping human behavior and expectations. It also overlooks the way that human potential is defined by those in positions of power who dictate what are masculine and feminine qualities. A major strength of the one-nature approach lies in its recognition of historical and cultural influences on our understanding of persons. It better distinguishes between the biology of sex and the sociology/psychology of gender. At the same time, it has been criticized for not taking sufficient account of the body and for its tendency to define the one nature in terms of an agenda shaped by men.

The analysis of anthropology introduced a new dimension into the discussion. Though the committee did not use the language of sex and gender, it was undoubtedly influenced by the findings of human sciences and present historical circumstances. As a result, the committee concluded that the single nature model of theological anthropology provides a more adequate understanding of human commonality and difference, as well as providing support for the ordination of women.[14]

Church documents since *Inter Insigniores* make it clear that original attitudes regarding sex and gender still prevail. John Paul II's "Mulieris Dignitatem" attempted to affirm the value and gifts of women.[15] Unfortunately, it promoted an asymmetrical human model of complementarity based on stereotypical qualities. Stereotypical feminine qualities appear to have ontological status without reference to social influences. The U.S. bishops struggled to bring forth a document that would address the concerns of women but found it hard to do so without assuming certain elements of a theological anthropology that were unacceptable to a large number of U.S. Catholic women.[16] Their eventual abandonment of the project testifies to their delayed good judgment in realizing that as a body of men, they were not in a position to reflect adequately on women. More recently, the Apostolic Letter, "Ordinatio Sacerdotalis" which reiterates the inadmissibility of women to holy orders, has drawn on earlier descriptions of women's dignity and "vocation" as expressions of a continuing theological anthropology.[17]

It is evident that despite discussions of alternative anthropologies, little has changed to suggest a critical understanding of sex and gender in official Church documents. Yet something has changed with regard to women's discussion of theological anthropology. Feminist theologians have put aside discussion of one- and two-nature anthropologies, which became a dead end, and have moved from a critical to a constructive phase. In this present phase, still very much in process, the issue of gender is important but the agenda has expanded beyond gender and beyond a sectarian agenda.

Experiencing/Transcending Gender

Contemporary theology has been marked by a turn to the subject and, with the turn, to a greater concentration on experience. Theologians like Paul Tillich or Karl Rahner, who have turned to the subject, look to universal experiences such as finitude or transcendental experience, to illuminate the human condition. While their analyses of experience allow them to see the limits of historical contexts on theological reflection, they do not suggest limits to their own insights in other areas. In particular, they usually do not make explicit the limits of their gender, race, or western perspective on their analyses of experience.

As women began to theologize, they initially directed their attention to the difference between their own experience and that of men who dominated theology.[18] In early discussions women stressed the need to draw on their own experience instead of basing their theology on men's experience which had been generalized to women. But frequent references to "women's experience" eventually met with challenges both from mainstream women and from women of diverse cultures.[19] Some women criticized the tendency of white middle class women to generalize from their experience to all women because it reflected a kind of imperialism. Feminists were charged with falling into an approach like the one they reacted against that deprived them of their own distinctive voice.

In response to these criticisms, feminist theologians are growing wary of falling into a new attitude of privilege. For this reason, they often state explicitly that they speak from a particular perspective of being white, middle class, Christian, and so forth.[20] As women turn more deeply to their own experience as subjects, they are refining their ideas of experience in relation to specific local contexts.

Appreciation of concrete local situations allows doors to be opened between women of different ethnic groups, racial identities, and social classes. As these doors are opened, it becomes impossible to develop a cohesive and systematic theological anthropology that is universally applicable. Yet sensitivity to diversity itself represents an increasingly important element in developing theological anthropologies. The theme of diversity signals a broadening of feminist concerns beyond gender. By discovering a wider range of influences on experience, feminist theologians have begun to set an agenda and write a script that is more catholic and global.

Issues in Feminist Theological Anthropology

Against the backdrop of the recent history of feminist theological anthropology, some new models are beginning to emerge in theological anthropology; but they are at an early stage of their formation so that their parameters cannot be clearly defined. Despite the inability to define these nascent models with any precision, it is possible to identify issues in several areas that suggest some contours. In identifying these areas it will become apparent that the role of gender itself is likely to be transformed.

Feminist theologians are already in some sense transcending gender issues as they reflect critically on their experience in relation to class or race. Interaction among women who interpret their experience through the prism of race or class as well as gender provides one example of a stimulus to transcend gender. Such interaction can prompt feminist theologians to move beyond the correction of gender neglect to altering the way we think about gender. Another way feminist theologians are moving beyond gender shows itself in the specific areas of theological anthropology with which they are concerned.

Five issues in theological anthropology illustrate distinctive elements in women's perspectives on persons. These include developing a more holistic approach to the body; affirming the formative influence of culture on persons, especially on the gendering of persons; rethinking autonomy and relations as interactive rather than separate; refusing to separate theology and ethics; and incorporating the metaphor of transformation into an understanding of persons in process.

1) The body has come into greater prominence in a number of areas of theology, including women's theological reflection on God.[21] In the area of theological anthropology, the significance of the body has always been noted, though often with negative overtones. The dualistic attitude that focused on the fragility and dangers of the body relegated it to a place of lesser importance, but women are re-claiming its value. Rosemary Ruether's pioneering challenge to dualism set the stage for the analyses of a generation of women.[22] Ruether's work, unlike some other women's response to dualism, does not turn to a mystical sort of unity. Instead her critique of dualism focuses on matters of justice. Her objections to dualism highlight the effects of violence that result from dualistic attitudes and distorted characterizations of the other. Her justice orientation counteracting negative attitudes toward the body (and women as representative of the earth and body rather than culture and spirit) is evident in her critiques of racism, imperialism, and sexism. Violence and injustices toward women can be seen as a primary mode of acting out fear or hatred of the body.

The call for justice toward the body echoes in concerns with bodily woes—hunger, sexual violence, infanticide, genital mutilation. One approach to recovering the value of the body to deal with these woes is to give attention to the doctrine of the Incarnation. Paula Cooey notes that this doctrine, though used to reinforce patriarchal values, can be recovered as a liberating metaphor.[23] While the body has served as a battleground in the exercise of power and often serves to define those whose power a culture limits, the body can still be redeemed as the site for God's groaning creativity.

In a similar vein Susan Ross seeks to recover the notion of sacramentality as a resource for feminist theological anthropology.[24] Ross observes that while sacramentality has often served to idealize the male body and has, at the same time, dealt ambivalently with the body, a more adequate sacramental approach to the body can contribute to a more adequate theological anthropology. Feminist concerns for interconnection, relation, and context are part of an approach that sees the self as inconceivable apart from the body.

A more integral incorporation of the body into theological anthropology can help to deal with the issues raised in the one-nature vs two-nature debate in anthropology. The body is always situated in historical, cultural, and social environments with their own assumptions about gender. Dealing with the body as a biological and relational reality can ground discussion concretely before stereotypical value judgments are made. Understanding the body more holistically and concretely puts discussions of "nature" into cultural and relational settings that qualify the meaning of nature and the body.[25]

2) Feminist theologians have widely recognized the influence of culture on the formation of sexual identity and have generally challenged the notion that women are born with a unique female "nature."[26] The view that gender is largely determined by culture and based on cultural expectations has taken a firm hold in feminist theology.[27]

While cultural definitions of gender may be judged as negative and limiting (especially by white women), the role of culture is clearer when viewed in terms of dominant culture and marginal cultures. From one perspective the dominant group in a culture may name the qualities that are characteristic of each sex and thereby limit opportunities; from another perspective those who are not part of a dominant group may be prompted to clarify their cultural identity and thereby bring the dominant group to greater awareness of the influence of culture. Recognition of this broader influence of culture has opened up possibilities of moving beyond gender, especially in terms of appreciating diversity.

The contribution of women from cultural positions other than white feminists is instructive here. For example, the mujerista theology of Ada María Isasi-Díaz draws upon the social analysis of gender but goes beyond conventional treatments.[28] Isasi-Díaz notes the differences in the occurrence of sex-role socialization according to historical time and culture. This results in different understandings of appropriate gender behavior and also in different experiences of gender oppression. Thus Hispanic women's experiences of oppression will differ from those of Anglo women and will result in a different theological anthropology.

Mujerista theological anthropology is based on the lived experience of Latinas who struggle to survive. Emphasis is placed on struggle more than on suffering. *La lucha*, the struggle, requires the praxis of reflective action and a grounding in community rather than the individual. Thus mujerista theological anthropology differs from that of North American feminists because it emerges from a different relationship to culture. Culture functions positively to provide a deep sense of community, respect for the elderly and children, religiosity, and respect for the worth of individuals as well as functioning negatively when it calls for a critique of *machismo*. Mujerista theology offers a lesson that awareness of differing possibilities for cultural conditioning can relativize the role of gender itself.

3) Another area of feminist thinking that has affected theological anthropology concerns the tension between autonomy and relations. Here the influences of the social sciences are again evident. The work of Nancy Chodorow, Jean Baker Miller, and Carol Gilligan has highlighted differences in male and female development of a sense of self, seeing men's development as occurring primarily through separating and women's development through connecting. While feminist theologians in general have neither taken over the analysis without question nor offered a great deal of critical analysis, they have addressed the role of the self in a theological anthropology.

Anne Carr speaks of the need of all human beings to develop virtues associated with both autonomy, traditionally regarded as a male strength, and relatedness, traditionally regarded as a female strength.[29] She addresses the need to balance or integrate these qualities as part of a holistic spirituality. In response to a dualistic approach that juxtaposes independence and connection, Carr offers a framework that promotes the development of human character through human freedom and self-creation, qualities essential to women's self-determination of their future position in society and the Church.

Likewise, Elizabeth Johnson reflects on the structuring of the self through the interaction of autonomy and relations. The self is formed through mutuality rather than through a dualistic opposition between persons.[30] A genuine and healthy independence does not require isolation but develops instead through relationships that the person integrates and balances. Johnson refers to this integration as relational autonomy. As with Carr's view, relational autonomy represents an ideal, but it also reflects the dialectic in mature caring relations. When two persons act out of their own centers and respond to one another freely while affirming the freedom of the other, they are neither isolated nor absorbed into one another. Whether women possess the qualities necessary for relational autonomy already or whether their reflection on the need for liberation without sacrificing connections prompts the desire for them, relational autonomy represents a condition for full human development. It is critical for a feminist theological anthropology.

The attempt to integrate autonomy and relationality signals another instance where feminists are working to transform categories based on socially assigned gender characteristics.[31] Concern for the kind of character that is formed by a vision of mature persons represents another hallmark of emerging feminist anthropology. An approach to the person that involves an ongoing interaction between relationality and autonomy leads predictably to a more integrated role for ethics.

4) The inseparability of theology and ethics has become a recurrent theme in feminist theology. Margaret Farley offered an early development of this theme in connection with gender patterns of relation.[32] The patterns of domination and subordinance that characterized relations between women and men in the past have slowly been giving way to new patterns. These new patterns, which replace hierarchy in male-female relationships with mutuality and responsibility, represent a moral revolution, according to Farley. It is a revolution that mirrors our changing understanding of what it means to be a person. That understanding, the foundation of theological anthropology, not only sees relationships as frameworks of mutual responsibility, but also includes critical praxis as an expression of responsibility.

The relationship of ethics to theological anthropology is not merely a theoretical relationship based on the connection between disciplines. Ethics is built into feminist theological anthropology in that whatever shape its understanding of the human takes, it requires critical praxis. The theological anthropology implicit in a variety of forms of feminist theology includes this ethical dimension as an expression of the ongoing need for liberation.

As is characteristic of many other forms of liberation theology, feminist theology sets its sights clearly on theology's implications for behavior. Rather than evaluating a theological argument solely on the basis of whether it is consistent and logically sound, many feminist theologians direct their attention beyond simple coherence to the effects of theology on the disenfranchised and oppressed and on the formation of persons. In so doing, they construct a liberation theology that includes liberation from sexism but goes beyond it as well. Gender equality is one concern, but not the only one. It is part of a complex cluster of concerns that makes up the ethical component intrinsic to a theological vision of the person.

The work of Rosemary Ruether exemplifies this connection as does the work of a significant number of other feminist theologians.[33] Ruether's theological anthropology, even when it is implicit rather than spelled out, signals the essential role of ethical activity through critical praxis. The connection between theological anthropology and ethical activity is also borne out in the symbol of transformation that characterizes ongoing expectations for personal and social development.

5) Finally, the metaphor of transformation has proven to be central for feminist theologians. Margaret Farley's discussion of the transformation of relations between women and men as a moral revolution, Mary Buckley's proposal of a transformative model of human nature that goes beyond unitary and dualistic models, Anne Carr's exploration of contemporary feminist theology as a transforming grace, all signal interest in the profound alterations in the interpretation of human existence and self-understanding.[34] Transformation for these theologians does not mean a change from one essentialist understanding of persons to another essentialist understanding. It means, rather, that the basis for understanding persons rests on a relational view of existence that is open to future transformations.

Relational concerns shape feminist theological anthropology which understands the person as embedded in and constantly transformed by a network of relations. Though not all feminist theologians emphasize the same aspects of relations, relations play a central role in their theological anthropologies. The metaphor of transformation appropriately describes the vision of persons in process, and at the same time describes theological anthropology itself as conversation in which dialogue partners are changed in the process of hearing/relating to others.

The five issues that have been highlighted above represent dominant themes in emerging feminist reflection on theological anthropology. But in each of the areas, there is evidence that feminist thought is moving beyond gender. Some concluding reflections attend to the ramifications of this movement.

Conclusion

As a review of issues in theological anthropology has revealed, feminist theologians have, in some respects, moved beyond mere gender issues. They have envisioned the body more holistically, have recognized that culture creates gender, have challenged the sharp distinction between male autonomy and female relationality, have re-integrated theology and ethics, and have gravitated toward the metaphor of transformation as a sign of inclusivity.

Elizabeth Johnson summarizes the need for a more comprehensive approach to the issue of gender in theological anthropology. Johnson has observed that it is time to "re-order the two-term and one-term systems into a multiple term schema, one which allows connection in difference rather than constantly guaranteeing identity through opposition or uniformity."[35] Johnson proposes that this need for a new schema emerges from a realization that all persons are constituted by a variety of anthropological constants including bodiliness, sex, race, relation to the earth and other persons, economic, political and cultural locations, age, and other aspects of concrete historical existence.[36] This realization allows us to move beyond gender in our own self-understanding as well as in our responses to others for whom gender is not the main category of analysis.

I believe that Johnson is right in calling us to situate our theological reflections on the human within a larger, more complex framework of factors that constitute us. The five issues I have discussed regarding feminist theological anthropology as well as the anthropological constants Johnson notes add up to a multi-faceted approach to the human that transcends analysis through one factor such as gender.

Awareness of the role of gender has been critical in helping women to find their own voice. Analysis of the pervasive and subtle influence of gender has introduced new dimensions into theological anthropology. But in some respects gender has been overemphasized as an individual trait.[37] Some feminist theologians like Elizabeth Johnson recognize that the next phase of work in theological anthropology will involve moving beyond gender to more inclusive sets of categories.

There is some evidence that women may already be pre-disposed to see beyond gender to a range of other issues that must be considered. According to some research women have a propensity to look at things as a whole, resulting in decision making styles that include more factors and pay more attention to context.[38] The ability to see beyond gender differences represents the strength of inclusivity and resourcefulness. Yet there is also a risk in that we can lose focus and intensity necessary to address gender issues that require a sustained and continuing critique. The challenge for theologians who want to develop more adequate theological anthropologies will be to look at human life as a whole, reflecting ethical sensitivity to a wide range of factors, while maintaining constant vigilance toward issues such as gender that demand the fullest attention at particular times.

The pattern I have identified in feminist approaches to theological anthropology only hints at models still in the process of being formed. As women reinterpret gender and even transcend it in the interests of a wider, more complex understanding of human experience, we need to be careful not to deny or minimize gender so as to lose the insights that have been gained.

As feminist theologians convinced of the rightness of our concerns we need to continue to write our own scripts with a finely tuned sensitivity. We need to remain aware of the role that gender can play in distorting human equality. Preserving the intensity of commitment to gender justice and recognizing the diverse range of influences on human thought and behavior should occupy us for some time. While it does, the setting for the theological anthropology that guides us may be best described by Jane Wagner's "bag lady," Trudy, "sitting together in the dark, laughing and crying about the same things" and carefully watching the audience.

Notes

[1] Jane Wagner, *The Search for Signs of Intelligent Life in the Universe* (New York: Harper and Row, 1986), 212.

[2] Catherine Mowry LaCugna, "Catholic Women as Ministers and Theologians," *America*, October 10, 1992, 248.

[3] Edward Farley, "Toward a Contemporary Theology of Human Being," *Images of Man: Studies in Religion and Anthropology*, ed. J. William Angell and

E. Pendleton Banks (Macon, GA: Mercer University Press, 1984), 59.

[4] This and several other references are drawn from ongoing theological anthropology seminars at the annual meetings of the Catholic Theological Society of America. In this instance see *Catholic Theological Society of America Proceedings* (1986): 157. Referred to hereafter as *CTSA Proceedings*.

[5] She presented these ideas in the seminar on theology and the social sciences, *CTSA Proceedings* (1984): 87.

[6] Susan Brooks Thistlethwaite raises the issue in *Sex, Race, and God: Christian Feminism in Black and White* (San Francisco: Harper San Francisco, 1988), 87-88. She concludes that metaphysics is a male enterprise and should be avoided even when it seems it might be free from traditional biases. I do not share her distrust of philosophy on the basis of its having been developed by males.

[7] *CTSA Proceedings* (1991): 194. See also, Ann O'Hara Graff, "The Struggle to Name Women's Experience: Assessment and Implications for Theological Construction," *Horizons*, 20 (Fall 1993): 215-233.

[8] For a variety of these definitions see Erich Fromm and Ramon Xirau, eds., *The Nature of Man* (New York: Macmillan, 1968).

[9] Part of the reason for feminist distrust of traditional theological anthropology lies in its association with philosophical positions which seem to dictate what is singled out as important.

[10] See John Money, "Gender Role, Gender Identity, and Core Gender Identity: Usage and Definition of Terms," *Journal of the American Academy of Psychoanalysis* (1973): 1:397-402 and John Money and Anke Erhardt, *Man and Woman, Boy and Girl* (Baltimore,: Johns Hopkins University, 1972).

[11] Paul VI, "Declaration on the Question of the Admission of Women to the Ministerial Priesthood," *Origins* 6, 33 (February 3, 1977).

[12] *Research Report on the Status of Women in Church and Society: Considered in Light of the Question of Women's Ordination*, ed. Sara Butler (Bronx, NY: Catholic Theological Society of America, Manhattan College, 1978). The committee that prepared the report consisted of Sarah Butler, M.S.B.T., Anne Carr, B.V.M., Frederick Crowe, S.J., Margaret Farley, R.S.M., and Edward Kilmartin, S.J. Elisabeth Schüssler Fiorenza and Joan Range, A.S.C., served as consultants.

[13] The study cites as a resource for its analysis the categories of "two-nature" and "one-nature" articulated by Mary Aquin O'Neill in "Toward a Renewed Anthropology," *Theological Studies* 36 (1975), 734-736.

[14] Mary Buckley, proposed a third model, a transformative model, in "The Rising of the Woman Is the Rising of the Race," *CTSA Proceedings* 34 (1979), 48-63. This model of theological anthropology built on the unitive model but emphasized the need to critique social systems that shape human beings. It did not substantially alter the notion of a common humanity.

[15] John Paul II, "Mulieris Dignitatem," *Origins* 18, 17 (October 6, 1988): 262-283.

[16] The bishops worked through four drafts without arriving at a satisfactory document.

[17] John Paul II, "Ordinatio Sacerdotalis (Apostolic Letter on Ordination and Women)," *Origins* 24, 4 (June 9, 1994): 50-52.

[18] Valerie Saiving's article "The Human Situation: A Feminine View," *Journal of Religion* 40 (April 1960): 100-112, represents a pioneering effort in this regard though she later came to see the limits of her initial approach to experience.

[19] For a mainstream criticism of generalizing experience see Sheila Greeve Davaney, "The Limits of Appeal to Women's Experience," *Shaping New Vision: Gender and Values in American Culture*, ed. Clarissa Atkinson, Constance Buchanan, and Margaret Miles (Ann Arbor, MI: UMI Research Press, 1987). There are numerous examples of questioning the category of "women's experience" from diverse cultural perspectives. Some representative examples can be found in Jacquelyn Grant, *White Women's Christ and Black Women's Jesus: Feminist Christology and Womanist Response* (Atlanta: Scholars Press, 1989); Rita Nakashima Brock, *Journeys by Heart: A Christology of Erotic Power* (New York: Crossroad, 1992); Marina Herrera, "Who Do You Say That Jesus Is?" Christological Reflections from a Hispanic Woman's Perspective," in *Reconstructing the Christ Symbol: Essays in Feminist Christology*, ed. Maryanne Stevens (New York: Paulist, 1993), 72-94.

[20] For examples of this see Anne Carr, *Transforming Grace: Christian Tradition and Women's Experience* (New York: Harper and Row, 1990), 3; Elizabeth Johnson, *She Who Is* (New York: Crossroad, 1993) ; Karen Lebacqz, *Justice in an Unjust World* (Minneapolis: Augsburg, 1987); Brock, *Journeys by Heart*, xv.

[21] Grace Jantzen, *God's World, God's Body* (Philadelphia: Westminster, 1984); Sallie McFague, *Models of God* (Philadelphia: Fortress, 1987) and *The Body of God: An Ecological Theology* (Minneapolis: Fortress, 1993).

[22] Rosemary Radford Ruether's works are too numerous to cite. Her *Sexism and God Talk: Toward a Feminist Theology* (Boston: Beacon, 1983) and *To Change the World: Christology and Cultural Criticism* (New York: Crossroad, 1983) are representative of her insights on dualism. Her *Gaia and God: An Ecofeminist Theology of Earth Healing* (San Francisco: Harper and Row, 1992) extends her insights into cosmic concerns.

[23] Paula Cooey, "The Redemption of the Body: Post Patriarchal Reconstruction of Inherited Christian Doctrine," *After Patriarchy: Feminist Transformations of the World Religions*, ed. Paula Cooey, William Eaken, and Jay McDaniel (Maryknoll, NY: Orbis, 1992), 106-130.

[24] Susan Ross, "Then Honor God in Your Body (1 Cor. 6:20): Feminist and Sacramental Theology on the Body," *Horizons* 16, 1 (Spring 1989): 7-27.

[25] Aquin O'Neill, "The Mystery of Being Human Together," *Freeing Theology*, ed. Catherine LaCugna (San Francisco: HarperSanFrancisco, 1993), 150, now observes that the issue is not a one-nature or two-nature anthropology but how one imagines the unity underlying the sexes.

[26] For a good discussion of this topic see Katherine Zappone, " 'Women's Special Nature': A Different Horizon for Theological Anthropology," in *The Special Nature of Women?*, ed. Anne Carr and Elisabeth Schüssler Fiorenza,

Concilium 6 (1991): 87-97. Zappone believes that the praxis of living with difference introduces questions at the heart of feminist theological anthropology.

[27] There are some women (see for example, Penelope Washbourn, *Becoming Woman: The Quest for Wholeness in Female Experience* (New York: Harper and Row, 1977) who accent the uniqueness of female experience based on bodily experience somewhat in detachment from culture. For the most part, however, feminist theologians accept the evidence of social sciences that gender is inculcated through the roles and characteristics that society attributes to women and men.

[28] Ada María Isasi-Díaz, *En La Lucha: Elaborating a Mujerista Theology* (Minneapolis: Fortress, 1993), 18-20.

[29] Carr, *Transforming Grace*, 208.

[30] Johnson, *She Who Is*, 68.

[31] Nancy Veeder in *Women's Decision-Making: Common Themes . . . Irish Voices* (Westport, CT: Praeger, 1992), 127, refers to this quality as "individuated attachment" or "connected autonomy."

[32] Margaret Farley in "New Patterns of Relationship: Beginnings of a Moral Revolution," *Theological Studies* 36, 4 (December 1975): 627-646 maintains that patterns of relationships need to change because the older patterns reflect an inadequate understanding of persons.

[33] From her early work, *New Woman, New Earth: Sexist Ideologies and Human Liberation* (New York: Seabury, 1975) to the recent *Gaia and God*, Ruether presents a view of human beings that focuses on their ethical character to a greater extent than on metaphysical issues. A similar ethical emphasis is present in the scriptural studies of Elisabeth Schüssler Fiorenza. The respective works of Anne Carr and Elizabeth Johnson, *Transforming Grace: Christian Tradition and Women's Experience* and *She Who Is*, reflect a theological anthropology integrating ethical dimensions, though philosophical concerns are more central to their writing.

[34] See also, Maria Riley's *Transforming Feminism* (Kansas City, MO: Sheed and Ward, 1987) which identifies the possibilities for feminism as a pluralistic, transformative influence in the Church.

[35] Johnson, *She Who Is*, 156.

[36] Daniel Callahan observes that the difficulty of defining the human species according to one basic criterion should instruct us in the importance of attending to the widest possible diversity. Callahan says we should find genetic criteria more adequate than morphological criteria, but that we need to take account of both genetic and cultural factors in defining the human species. See Daniel Callahan, "The 'Beginning' of Human Life: Philosophical Considerations," in *What Is a Person*, ed. Michael Goodman (Clifton, NJ: Humana Press, 1988), 42-43.

[37] Myra Marx Ferre and Beth Hess, eds., *Analyzing Gender: A Handbook of Social Science Research* (Newberry Park, CA: Sage, 1987), 16, propose that gender should not be seen as an individual trait but as a system that divides people into distinct, non-overlapping categories despite their natural variability.

[38] See for example, Nancy Veeder, *Women's Decision-Making: Common Themes . . . Irish Voices.*

Kristeva and the Cross: Rereading the Symbol of Redemption

Phyllis H. Kaminski

At the cross her station keeping,
Stood the mournful mother weeping,
Close to Jesus to the last.
                    Jacopone da Todi

But you too, good Jesus, are you not also a mother?
Are you not a mother who like a hen gathers her
            chicks beneath her wings? . . .
And you, my soul, dead in yourself,
run under the wings of Jesus your mother
and lament your griefs under his feathers.
Ask that your wounds may be healed
and that, comforted, you may live again.
                    Anselm of Canterbury[1]

Women occupy a central place in the Christian story of redemption. All four Gospels mention women at the cross and tomb of Jesus. Women are also the first witnesses of the resurrection. Yet the history of women in Christianity has not always been good news. It has in fact been at times a sorrowful tale. One way feminist theologians have attempted to expose patriarchal distortions in Christian history has been to examine why the Word of God on which the Christian community is founded became "a Word which excludes woman from direct access to the heart of the community and secures the link of Word and man by allowing only men the representative activity of speaking for God".[2] Another strategy, not unrelated to the first, has been to study the central theological symbols of creation and redemption. The Word became flesh, dwelt among us, and died in abjection on the cross that we might live. But again, the theological history of redemption has conceived the embodied Word of God in Jesus over against and separate from women's bodies, even the body of his mother. Moreover, the cross has been used historically to justify and even glorify suffering in ways that are damaging and ethically dangerous to women.[3]

Though feminist theologians have addressed the misuse of the symbol of the cross, they have not been as successful in their constructive attempts.[4] Interest in the dialogue between feminism and theology naturally leads to a figure like Julia Kristeva, a theorist and critic of culture whose views of religion and of the cross suggest hidden sources for the transformation of theological discourse.

Born in Bulgaria in 1941, Kristeva emigrated to Paris in 1965. A brilliant student of linguistics she quickly made her mark on the French university scene. With her fluent Russian and Eastern European education, she had first-hand knowledge of the Russian formalists and the great Soviet theorist of dialogue, Mikhail Bakhtin. She also had a solid grounding in Marxist theory and experience of communist practice. A foreigner, at home on the Left Bank, Kristeva combined her prolific writing and her interest in the politics of the late sixties with the study of psychoanalysis and the status of the subject in language. She first learned, but then transcended Lacan's reading of Freud. Now a practicing psychoanalyst herself, Kristeva continues to move back and forth across borders as she engages in the task of healing patients, theorizes about the development of personal identity and the workings of social systems, and reflects on psychoanalytic, literary, and religious conceptions of love. In 1974 Kristeva married Philippe Sollers and in 1976 she bore a son, a fact which is not irrelevant to her theory or to the questions of this essay.[5]

Kristeva's religious roots remain enigmatic. Léon Roudiez says, "She received her early education from French nuns."[6] Kristeva herself adds that she was raised in a "family of believers" and recalls kneeling as an adolescent before an icon of the Virgin, contemplating its "Byzantine iconography."[7] Whether Kristeva was Catholic or Orthodox is less important than where she first experienced religion. As Marilyn Edelstein notes, in a Communist state like Bulgaria, where religion was strictly regulated, religious discourse became a "real repressed other."[8] At present, from her vantage point in the secular environment of the University of Paris, Kristeva has turned more and more to analysis of religious discourse. She sees "the crisis of modernity and the failure of both religion and reason as a historical moment not only of danger but of opportunity," a moment in which we can imagine new ways of relaying the operations of power and the forces that have supported them.[9] Throughout her work, religion remains "a two edged sword." It is capable of infantilizing us to the point where we cannot make proper use of the tools it offers. It also offers profound ways of negotiating the struggle of human maturation in society.[10]

The complexity and scope of Kristeva's relationship with western culture, Anglo-American feminism, and her critical but appreciative consideration of religion make her a splendid resource for theology whose full value has not yet been realized. Although references to Kristeva have been appearing since the late 1980s, sustained conversation between Kristevan theory and theology is only beginning.[11] I want to enter that conversation by exploring how Kristeva's essay "Stabat Mater"[12] can further feminist reflections on the cross as symbol of redemption. Kristeva's understanding of the speaking subject, her reading of the abject, and her "herethics of love" as maternally embodied, "dialogically constituted sites (or processes) of encounter between subject and other,"[13] broaden understanding of the self in relation. Kristeva helps us understand not only why traditional theologies are inadequate but also how we can begin to create new ways of speaking about women, women's bodies, and redeeming love. This love always involves an *other* and, in Kristeva's scheme, the other is within as well as without.

Written in 1977, under the title "Héréthique de l'amour," "Stabat Mater" situates Kristeva's interest in the discourses of motherhood, love, the avant-garde, and religion.[14] The essay also indirectly illustrates her complex understanding of the politics of discourse and apparently non-political aspects of human life—like love and desire.[15] Traditional religious accounts no longer adequately interpret motherhood for Kristeva. The myth of the Virgin Mary, in particular, she claims, covers up the unsettling aspects of both maternity and the mother-child relationship. We need a new discourse on motherhood, one that liberates the logic of the maternal body and that in so doing is creative of "new and more mobile subjective and cultural identities."[16] Kristeva combines the strategies of language acquisition and symbolic function to explore the paradox of Christianity's entrenchment of the patriarchal order guarded by the sorrowful mother.

Pergolesi's "Stabat Mater," a baroque rendition of the Latin hymn on the agony of the Virgin Mary at the crucifixion of her son, provides Kristeva with a multidimensional focus (historical, devotional, poetic, iconographic) for her reflection: "At the cross her station keeping, Stood the mournful mother weeping, Close to Jesus to the last."[17] Like the composer whose work she uses, Kristeva's primary interests are secular. She finds in the Latin text and its two-voiced setting new ways to disclose the symbolic value of Mary's body. The music allows her to show how the very discourse that represses and oppresses women can be split open to reveal "a Word beyond and beneath the Word of governance, command, and law, a Word of plurivocity, embodiment and connection."[18]

Most theologians, like psychoanalytic theorists, focus on the mother as an object of reflection and analysis. As Edelstein points out, however, Kristeva "emphasizes the mother as *subject,* the mother's own experience of her maternity and of her relation to her child and her own body (and to her own mother)."[19] Kristeva's maternal subject uncovers the human body of a woman which is hidden in Christian theological language. At Calvary, therefore, the figure of Mary reveals how birth and death cross and are crossed in women's experience.

Traditional iconography centers on the dead or dying crucified Jesus flanked by John, the disciple whom he loved, and his mother Mary. Some images include the two thieves crucified on either side of Jesus and/or Mary Magdalene and the other women watching from a distance. The hymn "Stabat Mater" refers only to the dying son and the weeping mother. Kristeva's essay focuses on that mother and where she stands symbolically and in reality. To that end Kristeva requires that we look not only at the Mother but also at the space between the mother and the son. In her text, which destabilizes traditional spaces visually and conceptually, Kristeva shows that mothers stand in many places. Her analysis moves beyond traditional gender constraints in language and in social relations to expose the paradox of motherhood as "the *consecrated* (religious or secular) representation of femininity."[20] Kristeva's "Stabat Mater" helps us understand what's wrong with traditional theological interpretations of Mary at the cross and what's wrong with the alternatives the suffering mother image has imposed on women. Kristeva also offers a constructive interpretation of maternal space in ways that show how "[b]odiliness opens up the mystery of God to the conditions of history, including suffering and delight."[21]

The Split Subject

Building on her previous work in linguistic theory and language acquisition, Kristeva uses the history of Christian discourse on the cult of Mary[22] to develop a theory of identity and difference that negotiates the extremes of totalitarianism and chaos. While elsewhere she works with the discourse of poetry and psychoanalysis, in "Stabat Mater" she focuses on maternality as a material model of the reformulated subject, the *sujet-en-procès* (subject-in-process/on trial). This Kristevan term conveys the dynamic nature of language and human personhood as well as indicating that the identity of the speaking subject is always divided, in a position which is at once free of, yet dependent on, the "Law of the Father."[23] Since identity is necessary to the social realm, it is important to Kristeva that alterity or difference exists without being repressed or annihilated and at the same time without completely breaking down identity.

Signification, the process of meaning in language and society, is driven by a "dialectic oscillation" between semiotic drive forces and symbolic stases. Although she draws on Lacan's distinction between the Symbolic and the Imaginary, Kristeva makes her own distinction between *le symbolique* and *la dimension symbolique*. One difficulty in reading her in English is that symbolic refers not only to the symbolic order, the social realm composed of both semiotic and symbolic elements, but also to a specifically symbolic element within the symbolic order that she opposes to the semiotic. Oliver's distinction using the upper case Symbolic for the symbolic order and the lower case for the symbolic element helps clarify why for Kristeva revolutions within the Symbolic order are possible. Although the symbolic, the element of stasis, resists the semiotic, the element of rejection, both are crucial to signification. The semiotic moves both within and beyond the Symbolic. Because of the interaction of the semiotic and the symbolic, the Symbolic order is not just the order of Law; it is also the order of resistance to Law. For Kristeva, the infusion of semiotic elements within signification can actually change the structure of discourse.[24]

More pertinent to this essay is that Kristeva's semiotic serves as a strategy to bring the body back into the very structure of language. From a psychoanalytic perspective, the semiotic refers to the basic pulsions that are linked to pre-Oedipal primary processes. These are "predominantly anal and oral"; "simultaneously dichotomous (life v. death, expulsion v. introjection) and heterogeneous."[25] The endless flow of pulsions is gathered up in the *chora* (the Greek word for enclosed space, womb), a concept that Kristeva appropriates from Plato and redefines. The *chora* is "constituted of movements and their ephemeral stases. . . . Neither model nor copy, it is anterior to and underlies figuration and therefore also specularization, and only admits analogy with vocal or kinetic rhythm."[26] Oliver points out that Kristeva associates the semiotic chora with "a law before the law, a distant space, the maternal body, the feminine, and woman." The *chora* is not a univocal principle of identity but rather a principle of multiplicity.[27] Its meaning and function shift throughout Kristeva's writings, but this fluid concept which points to a "subject-in-process" is a rhythmic space and a process by which meaning is constituted.[28]

This theoretical background helps to clarify why in reading Kristeva we have to simultaneously look at a traditional image of Calvary, listen to the Latin hymn, and read the cross flow of her reflections. In "Stabat Mater," Kristeva focuses primarily on Mary, though by so doing, she uses Marian theology to explore the intimate relations between the maternal and the speaking subject, the actual bodies of mothers, and possibilities for a new ethos of speaking and reading the world.[29]

As Kristeva "theorizes about mothers, others, and the love and space between and within them,"[30] she starts with a question: "If it is not possible to say of a woman what she is (without running the risk of abolishing her difference), would it perhaps be different concerning the *mother*, since that is the only function of the 'other sex' to which we can definitely attribute existence?" (161). Kristeva answers her question by analyzing what the figure of Mary, Virgin and Mother, has signified within Western Christian discourse. In her reading, Christianity has taken a "translation error" (the Greek *parthenos*, young unmarried woman) "projected its own fantasies into it, and produced one of the most powerful imaginary constructs known in the history of civilizations" (163). Presented as unique "alone among women" and as our human link with God through her motherhood, Mary has become a spiritualized mother goddess who is also the guardian of paternal power, the arch-symbol of obedience to the Law of the Father. Kristeva substantiates her claim by uncovering the body of the woman hidden in Christian logocentric discourse on Mary.

Although "Stabat Mater" begins with conventional typography, in a **"FLASH"** the text splits and a second column, in bold typeface, is brought forth on the left. It seems to offer an account of the speaker's physical and psychic impressions of the birth of her son. This personal poetic narrative of motherhood continues as a counter voice to the text that traces the development of Marian doctrine. At times the left-hand column disappears and the analytical discourse on the right becomes the sole "voice": for example, "Freedom with respect to the maternal territory then becomes the pedestal upon which the love of god is erected" (162). At other times the voice on the left seems to mimic the one on the right:

Laugh. Impossible **Flash on the unnamable** **weavings of abstractions to** **be torn. Let a body venture** **at last out of its shelter** **take a chance with meaning** **under a veil of words. WORD** **FLESH. From one to the** **other, especially, broken up** **visions, metaphors of the** **invisible.**	And yet, the humanity of the Virgin mother is not always obvious, and we shall see how, in her being cleared of sin, for instance, Mary distinguishes herself from humankind. But at the same time the most intense revelation of God, which occurs in mysticism, is given only to a person who assumes himself as "maternal" (162).

Like Pergolesi's hymn, Kristeva's "Stabat Mater" is "a duet as well as a juxtaposition of two solo voices."[31] As Barbara Johnson suggests the typographical use of two columns calls "the reader's attention to the syntactical function of spacing in the act of reading."[32] The split text obliges the eye to cross the space between the columns in order to grasp the whole. From a feminist perspective, the full page reproduces visually the split/whole folds of the labia. The two-columns that form one essay thus produce meaning that cannot be understood by a reader who seeks only the message of the words. As Edelstein points out, Kristeva's narrative strategies and construction of both speaking and reading subject(s) are as constitutive of the essay's content as its propositional statements.[33]

This experimental form is Kristeva's first venture out of the technical style of her early writing on semiotics. Building on her insights into the link between the literary/linguistic limits, identity, and women's bodies,[34] Kristeva explores "the most radical and problematic aspects of the relationship" between motherhood and language.[35] While she rejects the *écriture féminine* of writers like Cixous or Irigaray, here Kristeva borrows their style. The unsayable breaks through the dominant discourse as Kristeva breaks open the traditional format of the printed page. Kristeva's left hand column with its semiotic sensuousness and pulsing rhythm does not take over, nor does it stand alone. Kristeva puts the irrupted voice of the semiotic (what's left out of traditional discourse) into a dialogic relationship with the symbolic voice on the right. The tactic is effective: "The text is concretely transgressive, as words, images and ideas cross over from one column to the other. It may be transgressive, too, in Kristeva's positive sense of confounding the limits of the symbolic through the incursions of the semiotic."[36]

The symbolic realm of language and culture represents the law of the Father. Kristeva's semiotic is the realm of the body, the drives, the unconscious, the maternal, yet for Kristeva "bodily drive force already includes the logic and prohibition of the Symbolic and that bodily drive force is never completely repressed within signification."[37] Subjectivity is always in process/on trial. The split page concretizes the ever present dialogue between the symbolic and the semiotic. In Kristeva's understanding of the dialogic, the movement is not towards transcendence or dominance of one voice over the other. Difference and relation strive towards harmony "all the while implying an idea of rupture . . . as a modality of transformation."[38] At times, for example, when Kristeva discusses the theme of death in Christian discourse, the analytical voice on the right enters into the left hand column and overtakes the sensual first person voice on the left. The irruptive voice returns, however, speaking about the impotence of language, the **"difficult experience of the Word"** and **"the reassuring wrapping in the proverbial image of the mother."** The voice on the right links man's attempt to overcome death with maternal love and, while yearning for the liberative power of linguistic expression, suggests listening to Pergolesi's music, the "subtle gamut of sound, . . . older than language . . ." (176-177). As the essay progresses, the columns begin to sound more like each other. The left column which early in the essay is lyrical: **"Head reclining, nape finally relaxed, skin, blood, nerves warmed up, luminous flow"** (166), intones its last intervention with a proposition: **"The love of God and for God resides in a gap"** (184). At the end of the essay, the gap remains. The subject-in-process/on-trial has become visible and Kristeva will not cover over the dilemma of alterity in human life or language. [39]

In order to see in "Stabat Mater" how the voice of the left column changes the meaning of the right column and questions the hegemony of the patriarchal Marian model, we need to remember that both voices are Kristeva's. She embodies the divided speaker even as she theorizes about Mary and the split subject-in-process/on trial. The reader too is divided, struggling with both columns. Do I constantly move back and forth? Do I read a section, a paragraph in one column and then switch to the other? However individual readers solve the problem, "Stabat Mater" offers theologians an experience of the tension between the Logos and those voices which threaten to disrupt it— "the voice of the woman as other, the voice of the poet, the voice of the body or the unconscious, the voice of the semiotic." [40]

Further insights into Kristeva's understanding of the mother come in the largest section of "Stabat Mater" with her discussion of love. On one level her analysis agrees with Christian discourse. Maternal love is a form of sacrifice. Yet on another level Kristeva exposes a fundamental lack in the Marian symbol, the mother has no sex. There is no talk of pleasure in the virginal conception nor of painful labor in the virgin birth. Juxtaposing Marian doctrine with what happens in real mothering, Kristeva reclaims "the feminine fate of being the source of life" (175). She demonstrates textually and visually how "word meets flesh," [41] and suggests that Christian discourse on Mary, with its splitting of maternal generativity from sin, from sex, and from death, spiritualizes motherhood in a way which hides the violence and sacrifice at the origin of ordered social life. [42] Drawing on traditional iconographic representations of Calvary, Kristeva forces us to ask which figure is despised and rejected. Her answer requires that we look at what she means by the "abject maternal."

The Abject Maternal

The figure of Mary at the cross allows Kristeva to bring together her theoretical perspectives on sexuality and death by exploring maternal *jouissance*[43] and the abject maternal. In her analysis, the process of pregnancy, birthing, and mothering produces "an acute sense of both identification and separation, of narcissism and masochism, of pleasure and pain."[44]

Within the discussion of love and the Marian cult in Western Christianity, Kristeva splits the text as she speaks of "the ideal totality that no individual woman could possibly embody" (171). The voice on the left expresses the intense joy of mothering: **"I hover with feet firmly planted on the ground in order to carry him, sure, stable, ineradicable, while he dances in my neck, flutters with my hair . . . sweetness of the child . . ."** (171). But that same voice has already spoken through the labor of birthing: **"a mother is always branded by pain"; "My body is no longer mine, it doubles up, suffers, bleeds . . . the pain . . . inflames me at once without a second's respite"** (167). As the text on the left pulses with sensuality and a blending of bodily experience of the mother, her mother, and her son, the voice on the right coolly traces the spiritualization of Mary "immaculately conceived" and born *"praeredemptio"* without the stain of original sin (167). Not only is Mary free from sin, however, her role in redemption also puts singular boundaries on her sexual relations. From the virginal conception of Jesus to the climax of her role in redemption as the Mater Dolorosa, Mary knows no masculine body save that of her dead son(175). Making explicit the parallel between Mary the redeemed and Jesus the redeemer, Kristeva writes in the left column that mothers **"live on that border, crossroads beings, crucified beings"**(178). Although other texts suggest that all (split) subjects exist at this border between pain and pleasure, lack and plenitude, sameness and difference, here Kristeva locates such "crucifixion" in mothering.[45]

This connection between her semiotic approach to meaning and the empirical process of child bearing and rearing suggests a second way in which Kristeva revisions discourse on the symbol of redemption. What's wrong with the Christian picture is that patriarchal discourse presents us with a double bind.[46] It celebrates the symbolic motherhood of Mary yet deprives us of the reality of her maternal body: "We are entitled only to the ear of the virginal body, the tears and the breast. With the female sexual organ changed into an innocent shell, holder of sound, there arises a possible tendency to eroticize hearing, voice or even understanding. By the same token however, sexuality is brought down to the level of innuendo" (173). Despite the spiritualization of Jesus' birth in religious discourse, Mary's semiotic reality continued to speak to women. The milk and tears that were "the privileged signs" of the sorrowful mother's body, "never ceased to fill the Marian visions of these, men or women (often children), who were racked by the anguish of a maternal frustration" (173-74).

Besides what the virginal breast suggests to Kristeva of infantile regression, she highlights that "this should not conceal what milk and tears have in common: they are the metaphors of non-speech, of a 'semiotics' that linguistic communication does not account for. The Mother and her attributes, evoking sorrowful humanity, thus become representative of a 'return of the repressed' in monotheism" (174) The Virgin Mother functions for Kristeva to redeem the Christian God: "She adds to the Christian trinity and to the Word that delineates their coherence the heterogeneity they salvage" (175). She also provides the link that moves from death to life. The Mater Dolorosa sheds tears over the corpse of her son, because she has borne him to life (175).

Kristeva carefully probes the "paranoid logic" that the law of the Father imposes on Mary as Mother of God—faith in the resurrection of her son, and ultimately her own escape from the finality of death through her "dormition" and assumption into heaven. Yet the right column admits that the immortality postulated by the "name of the Father" does not succeed in overcoming the unthinkable of death except by "postulating maternal love in its place—in the place and stead of death and thought" (176). Kristeva adds from the left:

Belief in the mother is rooted in fear, fascinated with a weakness—the weakness of language. . . . I want to believe— that there is someone who makes up for that weakness, Someone, of either sex, *before* the id speaks, before language who might make me be by means of borders, separations, vertigos. In asserting that "in the beginning was the Word", Christians must have found such a postulate sufficiently hard to believe and, for whatever it was worth, they added its compensation, its permanent lining: the maternal receptacle, purified as it might be by the virginal fantasy. . . . Every God, even including the God of the Word, relies on a mother Goddess. Christianity is perhaps also the last of the religions to have displayed in broad daylight the bipolar structure of belief: on the one hand, the difficult experience of the Word—

a passion; on the other, the reassuring wrapping in the proverbial mirage of the mother—a love. (176)

The power of birth and reassurance of maternal love represent the positive aspects of the maternal function. As Kristeva reads the mother's body, she cannot ignore the dark side of maternal milk and tears. How does the process of birthing speak of death, of rupture in the body and ultimate threat to identity?

For Kristeva the relationship between fetus and mother invokes the dynamic oscillation between the semiotic and the Symbolic. Just as *semanalyse* challenges the binary oppositions which support the logic of the Symbolic, so does the pregnant woman defy discrete categorizations between self and other. Gestation, birth, and lactation break through the physical and psychic boundaries between mother and child.[47] Motherhood gives expression to a form of existence rooted in the crossing of already unclear boundaries. The maternal function thus negates traditional presuppositions of the subject's unicity. In the words of Jane Gallop, it represents "a permanent calling into question" of language, culture, and human subjectivity.[48]

As Caputi argues, this subversive blurring of distinctions and the eradication of discrete boundaries are disturbing. The maternal threatens to disrupt and challenge from within the very limits of the Symbolic. As such the "maternal receptacle" (176) is not only repressed and excluded, it is made abject.[49] Although Kristeva will develop her notion of the psychic state of abjection in *Powers of Horror*, in "Stabat Mater" she already probes the trauma of birth and the primitive terror of maternal engulfment that is hidden in the Christian construct of the Virgin Mother.

The music behind (beneath, and around) the poem "Stabat Mater" recalls the memory of an existence which precedes acculturation, an existence relived through various forms of expression which are immediate, bodily, and unstructured by language. In the maternal body of Mary, something primal and "abject" threatens the logocentrism of Christian discourse. A creative force, the semiotic realm of the maternal is unpredictable, disruptive, something to be scared of. It is deeply unsettling.[50]

While Christian theology and iconography focus on the abject body of Jesus, Kristeva looks at the body of the savior's mother. It is as if she senses the unspoken implications of the early Christian aphorism, "what is not assumed is not redeemed."[51] The Kristevan text assumes the body of the mother in both columns. Why does the patriarchal Marian myth hide the maternal body? As Kristeva reflects on the mother goddess in the left column, in the right she asks us to listen to the dying Pergolesi's musical cry to Mary facing her son's death: *"Eia Mater, fons amoris!"* (Hail mother, source of love, 176).

The mother in Kristeva's disruptive column does what the avant-garde authors she analyzes elsewhere do. She works against traditional prose and strives to carry the reader to language's other side (*elle traverse les frontières*). In theological terms, the mother moves subversively from the sorrowful mystery of Jesus' death to the joyful mystery of Jesus' birth. Birth is violent, disruptive, and bloody. Kristeva's first person account emphasizes the shocking discovery of the abyss between the mother and her child. There is a death inherent in birth. The laboring woman engages in a process of separation in which the only continuity between mother and child remains the paradoxical "continuity" of love and pain:

> **What connection is there between myself, or even more unassumingly between my body and this internal graft and fold, which, once the umbilical cord has been severed, is an inaccessible other? My body and . . . him. No connection.** (178)
>
> **My body is no longer mine, it doubles up, suffers, bleeds, . . . the pain, its pain—it comes from inside, never remains apart, other, it inflames me at once without a second's respite. As if that was what I had given birth to and, not willing to part from me, insisted on coming back, dwelled in me permanently. One does not give birth in pain, one gives birth to pain: the child represents it and henceforth it settles in, it is continuous. Obviously you may close your eyes, cover up your ears, teach courses, run errands . . . think about objects, subjects. But a mother is always branded by pain, she yields to it.** (166-167)

For Kristeva the theorist, this pain, a response to the wound within the maternal body, implies not merely a separation of the mother and the child but also an inscription of alterity and distance into every identity and linguistic practice: "A mother is a continuous separation, a division of the very flesh. And consequently of language—and it has always been so" (178). Birth overwhelms and terrifies in its ability to recall the archaic and unmediated in the face of cultural law and order.

Yet the terrible pain of separation in birth is also marked by love. In Kristeva's terms, it is like the negativity of *jouissance,* inseparable from joy and laughter as a certain overflowing of identity and difference. From the mother's perspective, the creative force of birthing, with its excruciating pain, is also natural, welcome, exultant. For all the otherness of the newly expelled infant, the mother knows the child as flesh of her flesh. For all the distance that can and will occur, the trace of the mother-child bond never ends.

In the fluidity of this moment, however, the maternal voice on the left also recalls her earliest sense of her mother. She has only **"spatial memory."** There is no language to describe the daughter's birth and childhood: only **"connections between atoms, molecules, wisps of words, droplets of sentences"** (180, 181). She remembers the "*corps-à-corps*, the forgotten body relationship with her mother as a **"strange feminine see-saw that makes 'me' swing from the unnamable community of women over to the war of individual singularities, it is unsettling to say 'I' "** (182). She muses that great ancient matriarchal civilizations avoided personal pronouns. She also charges Christian patriarchal discourse and its spiritualized sexless Virginal Maternal with having attempted to **"freeze that see-saw,"** to **"tear women away from its rhythm"** (192-93).

The voice on the right agrees and adds that Christian discourse has been constructed to keep watch over the primacy of the Father God. Western patriarchal representation of Mary works against both sexes. In psychoanalytic terms, "The Virgin obstructs the desire for murder or devoration by means of a strong oral cathexis (the breast), valorization of pain (the sob) and incitement to replace the sexed body with the ear of understanding" (180-181). The symbol of Mary limits men and women through her virginal conception, her power as mother of God, queen of heaven, and her assumption (which fosters the fantasy that humans can escape the bodily limits of time and death). The symbol of Mary Immaculate especially militates against women because she repudiates the other woman (the woman's mother). The sinless one becomes "A Unique Woman: alone among women, alone among mothers, alone among humans since she is without sin"(181).

What remains hidden in the symbolic construct of such discourse is the rejection of the maternal receptacle. Birthing precedes subject-object relations and is indeed the ground from which they rise. From the perspective of the child, the subjective condition resulting from being born is initially one of discomfort, unease, and dizziness. It is an experience of abjection: "Kristevan abjection afflicts a troubled and unformed entity that knows itself as an I only though the sense of having been thrown out or repulsed from an Other. This trauma precedes the incest struggle and the murderous impulses between child and father both temporally and analytically."[52] Marian doctrine spiritualizes the trauma. Virginal conception and maternity cover over the bodily connection between mother and father, between mother and child. The virgin birth hides the traumatic separation of child from mother. This elimination of "the maternal fold between the biological and the cultural" domesticates the mother's power and brings it under paternal control.[53]

Although Kristeva will fully develop her theory of the abject maternal only in *Powers of Horror,* in "Stabat Mater" she already discloses how the oedipal triangle fails because it ignores the dilemma of the mother. In Sophocles' play Jocaste is forced to choose the son over the father. In the Christian drama Mary is forced to face the death of her son in obedience to the Father. Traditional psychoanalytic and Christian discourses thus hide the sacrificed maternal body on which the symbolic and social order is founded.

As Kearns points out, abjection becomes Kristeva's point of reference for "considering the meaning and function of law, defilement, purification, and atonement in the history of religion." The body of the mother is rejected, controlled, dominated by culture because pregnancy always threatens the stability of the Symbolic order. Abjection helps her further Freud's insights into the relationship between the sacred and the abject: the incest taboo and violence. It offers her a single principle to tie together the motifs of maternal incest and paternal murder. "Her ultimate concern . . . is to demonstrate both how abjection is represented in society and how it is mediated, purged, and healed by the mediations of language—in religious discourse, undeniably, though as it were accidentally and in spite of itself, but more recently and preeminently in art and psychoanalysis."[54]

In "Stabat Mater" Kristeva uncovers the violence and sacrifice hidden beneath the pure white and blue folds of Mary's virginal robes. The traditional Marian symbol proposes an ultimate model of self-sacrificing maternal love. At the same time, the symbol exults the mother and robs her of her sexuality, her son, and her death. It also leaves out the relation of the mother to herself, to her mother, and to other women; it offers no language for "the war between mother and daughter"(183). If, for Kristeva, Freud has offered "only a massive nothing . . ." (178-79) to help understand the complexities and pitfalls of maternal experience, Christian discourse similarly fails to provide "any discourse of the Other Woman—of women's relationship both to their own mothers and to Woman as an abstraction and collectivity."[55] Although Kristeva acknowledges that the Virgin Mary construct has in some ways served "women's wishes for identification," it has primarily functioned to stabilize society, mediating between the "unconscious needs of primary narcissism" and a society requiring "the contribution of the superego and . . . the symbolic paternal agency" (182). Nonetheless the symbolic construct has never obliterated the driving power of the semiotic pulse. Pergolesi's musical cry sounds the possibility of a transformation of consciousness: "*Eia mater, fons amoris!* Hail mother, source of love!"[56]

A "Herethics" of Love

A discussion both of maternal passion (love and hatred) and the repudiation of the other sex (the masculine) implied by Marian doctrine leads to Kristeva's final suggestion and the concerns of the essay's original title "Héréthique de l'amour." Kristeva suggests that with her experience of enfolded alterity, the mother's experience of pregnancy and birth provides a new model for human agency. The mother-child dyad provides a foundation for all social relations.[57] So Kristeva proposes an *herethics,* "an heretical ethics separated from morality" (185). Morality for her seems to involve an abstract set of principles while ethics is grounded in relational dialogic practice.[58] The maternal serves as the basis for this ethics that has to operate outside the Law of the Father yet also within the Symbolic order.

Kristeva imagines the mother's love for the child, which is a love for herself but also the willingness to give herself up (185). The very image is metaphor for one who relates to another through love. Elsewhere she writes that "maternity is a bridge between singularity and ethics."[59] Kearns reminds us that Kristeva offers two practical strategies to cross that bridge: analytic listening and aesthetic practice. Transformation of the maternal symbol demands that we listen to women and their struggles, with a disciplined attention, informed by psycho-analysis but not confined to the analytic situation.[60] Only thus can we recognize the unspoken which yearns to be born (and which threatens the established powers).[61] Aesthetic practice is the complement to analytic listening for it requires that we communicate in ways that bridge semiotic and symbolic discourse.[62] Here, as "Stabat Mater" ends, Kristeva simply suggests that we listen to the mother and her music, "all the music" (185). Kristeva, the theorist, suggests that motherhood needs the support of a mother's mother (even in the person of a father, or imaginary father). Kristeva, the mother, points to her mother present in her own motherhood. The love that founds herethics is a daughter's love through identification with her mother. A mother's love seeks reunion with her own mother, not only as a third party, but also as herself.

Inherent in Kristeva's imagining of the mother as metaphor for the ethical agent is "the possibility—but not the certainty—of reaching out to the other" (182). We are all, as her recent work suggests, *Strangers to ourselves*. While she admits the difficult move from imagining to realizing such an herethics (185), Kristeva provides her own contribution to the effort. "Stabat Mater" offers a concrete way in which the maternal can ground transformed ethical practice. Playing with language as she is wont to do, Kristeva writes that "herethics is undeath [*a-mort*], love [*amour*], (185). And as Edelstein reminds us, for Kristeva a mother is "she who (or that which) produces life, undeath as well as exposes and loves the otherness of even ourselves."[63] Unlike patriarchal theological discourse which copes by denying death, covering it over in the myth of resurrection and the symbol of the Virgin Mother's unfailing love, Kristeva faces death in all its abject reality. Her humble tentative hope suggests that a herethical response is "perhaps no more than that which in life makes bonds, thoughts, and therefore the thought of death, bearable" (185).

Kristevan herethics thus "challenges rather than presupposes an autonomous ethical agent." Maternal love "sets up one's obligations to the other as obligations to the self and obligations to the species. This ethics binds the subject to the other through love and not Law."[64] As Oliver suggests, Kristeva's is at times "an outlaw ethics." It is also an ethics-in-process based on the power of erotic justice: "It is a matter of embracing the return of the repressed other, the foreigner, the outcast, the woman, the Unconscious, *jouissance* in all of its manifestations."[65]

I agree with Ewa Ziarek that in "Stabat Mater" Kristeva argues for "a new, and a specifically feminist, understanding of the maternal."[66] Kristeva is not seeking a romantic recovery of the myth of the archaic mother. She denounces nostalgia for the presence of the maternal body as a utopian "belief in the omnipotence of an archaic, full, total englobing mother with no frustration, no separation, with no break-producing symbolism."[67] As Edelstein points out, Kristeva does not naively assume "that all mothers are inherently ethical, in their relations to others or even to their own children." They are capable of infanticide and hate. Yet, the maternal in all its complexity offers a compelling root metaphor for a particular kind of transformative ethical practice.[68] Kristeva's concern for a new ethics based on the logic of the maternal body is profoundly social and looks to transformed relationships between all subjects-in-process and the other within and around them.

Toward a Theological Re-articulation of Redeeming Love

By the end of "Stabat Mater," Kristeva's crossed voices suggest new possibilities for redeeming love. The right hand discourse calls us to the music. The left asserts **"The love of God and for God resides in a gap (*un hiatus*)."** (184) The gap is the broken space which sin on the one side and transcendence on the other explicitate, clarify. "Stabat Mater" with its split text and double voices suggests that redemption occurs where God is found, in that gap, that broken space. Kristeva asks us to transgress boundaries that would limit the full signification of the love of God and the space of women. Such transgression is not a sinful breaking of the Law; rather it bridges unspoken depths and opens new possibilities for including women in constructing an inclusive theology of redemption. If Christian discourse has failed women, it also has, by Kristeva's own demonstration, remarkable capacity to sustain the semiotic in its theological symbols.

Kristeva's theory can help us move toward transformed discourse within the Christian community. She has brought the speaking body back into language by putting the logic of language into the body.[69] As Ziarek demonstrates, not only does Kristeva provide conceptual tools for "diagnosing the limitations of what counts as discursive," she also provides the ground for renegotiating the position of the feminine speaker by demystifying the "nature of the symbolic bond" that places women in a subordinate position.[70] The strength of her position and its ethical potential is that Kristeva's analysis of the maternal body inscribes "alterity into *the* very site of domesticated normalcy (or what is perceived as such) and into the construction of every subject."[71]

Kristeva's psychoanalytic view of the embodied relational process thus goes beyond Mary Grey's metaphoric reimaging of the cross in terms of "at-one-ment" and "birth."[72] Kristeva stands at the limits of language and culture and creates an intersection, a crossroads of possibility. Convinced that transformed language can lead to transformed practice, Kristeva articulates the construction of the maternal function in order to reconceive of ethics and sociality. Her ethics, as Oliver says, oscillates between Law and love, and, significant for theology, it probes the mystery of love beneath the Law. The maternal body enfleshes the Word (162) as love and speaks in new ways of autonomy, intimacy, life, and death.

Contemporary political, liberation, and feminist theologies have long since repudiated interpretations of Jesus' death on the cross as required by God in repayment for sin. Yet feminist theologies still struggle to articulate the relationship of the historical suffering and death of Jesus, the redemptive mystery of God's love, and women's experience. Elisabeth Schüssler Fiorenza effectively integrates feminist theological discussions of the cross with early Christian rhetoric about the meaning of the cross.[73] But Kristeva can add to these discussions. Further study is needed to free her from charges of essentialism.[74] As Oliver successfully argues Kristeva resists facile categorization. Her theory confronts the double bind of identity (equality and conformity/ difference and marginality).[75] As feminist theologians work with the emerging voices of the heretofore other and the multiple forms of oppression, Kristeva can be a strong ally. Her theory points to the profound psychic, social, and cultural sources of violence against women and all who are viewed as "other." Her view of the speaking subject, of the abject maternal, and ethical practice rooted in maternal love confirms that the story of redemption has not yet been fully told.

"Stabat Mater" subverts traditional theological discourse and iconography. The essay helps understand the recent papal letter which says the ordination of women cannot even be discussed.[76] It also helps understand the threatening power of the women's movement with all its diverse voices and the struggle of women with each other. The essay does not suggest how herethics might deal with concrete dilemmas in sexual morality, reproductive technology, or medical and social ethics. Yet Kristeva opens a space in which women and men can work towards transformed practice. She offers a constructive theoretical framework from within which feminist theologians can continue to re-interpret the cross as "part of the larger mystery of pain-to-life, of that struggle for the new creation evocative of the rhythm of pregnancy, delivery, and birth so familiar to women of all times."[77]

Notes

[1] Jacopone da Todi "Stabat Mater," as translated in the *St. Gregory Hymnal and Catholic Choir Book* (Philadelphia: The St. Gregory Guild, Inc., 1941), 30; from the "Prayer to St. Paul," *The Prayers and Meditations of St. Anselm*, trans. S. Benedicta Ward (New York: Penguin Books, 1973), 153-156; emended for inclusivity, and cited by Elizabeth A. Johnson, in *She Who Is* (New York: Crossroad, 1992), 150.

[2] Rebecca S. Chopp, *The Power to Speak: Feminism, Language, God* (New York: The Crossroad Publishing Company, 1991), 26.

[3] See Sally B. Purvis, *The Power of the Cross: Foundations for a Christian Feminist Ethic of Community* (Nashville: Abingdon Press, 1993), 14; also Joanne Carlson Brown and Caroie R. Bohn, eds., *Christianity, Patriarchy, and Abuse: A Feminist Critique* (New York: The Pilgrim Press, 1989).

[4] For one such attempt, see Elisabeth Moltmann-Wendel and Jürgen Moltmann, *God His and Hers* (New York: Crossroad, 1991), 77-91. Elisabeth Schüssler Fiorenza provides an excellent critical overview of feminist perspectives on the theology of the cross in *Jesus: Miriam's Child, Sophia's Prophet* (New York: Continuum, 1994), 98-107.

[5] See Léon Roudiez, "Introduction," in Julia Kristeva, *Desire in Language*, trans. Thomas Gora, Alice Jardine, and Léon Roudiez (New York: Columbia University Press, 1980), 1-20; and "Introduction," in Toril Moi, ed., *The Kristeva Reader* (New York: Columbia University Press, 1986), 1-22.

[6] "Introduction," in Julia Kristeva, *Desire in Language*, 1f.

[7] Julia Kristeva, *In the Beginning Was Love: Psychoanalysis and Faith*, trans. Arthur Goldhammer (New York: Columbia University Press, 1988), 23

[8] Marilyn Edelstein, "Metaphor, Meta-Narrative, and Mater-Narrative in Kristeva's 'Stabat Mater' " in *Body/Text in Julia Kristeva: Religion, Women, and Psychoanalysis*, ed. David Crownfield (Albany: State University of New York Press, 1992), 47, note 6. I am grateful to Marilyn Edelstein for her careful reading of an earlier draft of this essay. Her work on "Stabat Mater" and her bibliography have been invaluable to my project.

[9] Suzanne Clark and Kathleen Hulley, "An Interview with Julia Kristeva: Cultural Strangeness and the Subject in Crisis," *Discourse* 13.1 (Fall-Winter 1990-1991), 154.

[10] Cleo McNelly Kearns, "Kristeva and Feminist Theology," in *Transfigurations: Theology and the French Feminists*, ed. Susan M. St. Ville, C. W., Maggie Kim Susan M. Simonaitis (Minneapolis: Fortress Press, 1993), 61.

[11] For the relation of Kristeva to theology see *Body/Text in Julia Kristeva: Religion, Women, and Psychoanalysis*, David Crownfield, ed. (Albany: State University of New York Press, 1992) and *Transfigurations: Theology and the French Feminists*, ed. C. W. Maggie Kim, Susan M. St. Ville, and Susan M. Simonaitis (Minneapolis: Fortress Press, 1993). Both of these also provide references to earlier use of Kristeva in religious reflection. For an excellent introduction and critical analysis of the Kristevan corpus see Kelly Oliver, *Reading Kristeva: Unravelling the Double-bind* (Bloomington: Indiana University Press, 1993).

[12] First published as "Héréthique de l'amour" in *Tel Quel*, 74 (Winter 1977, 30-49), this essay on the cult of Mary and its implications for the Catholic understanding of motherhood and femininity was reprinted as "Stabat Mater" in *Histoires d'Amour* (Paris: Denoël, 1983); translated as *Tales of Love* by Léon Roudiez (New York: Columbia University Press, 1987). Citations in this paper are from the Roudiez translation in *The Kristeva Reader*, Toril Moi, ed. (New York: Columbia University Press, 1986), 160-186.

[13] Edelstein, 29.

[14] Edelstein, 28.

[15] See Toril Moi, "Introduction" in the *Kristeva Reader*, 8. The on-going evolution of Kristeva's thought is significant. Alice Jardine argues that there are three Kristevas: the sixties Kristeva who developed the new science of *semanalyse*; the seventies Kristeva who tried to describe a subject that has been repressed in Western history within the limits of totalitarianism and delirium; and the eighties Kristeva who explored the deep logics of psychic phenomenon (Jardine 1986). Kelly Oliver suggests that a fourth Kristeva is developing, the nineties Kristeva who turns back to politics through psychoanalysis and fiction. In her most recent work, Kristeva probes the psychic structures of social ostracism and suggests a new ethics and politics that grow out of psychoanalysis (Oliver, 1993, 14).

[16] Kearns, 63.

[17] Jacopone da Todi, "Stabat Mater." See note 1.

[18] Chopp, 29.

[19] Edelstein, 29.

[20] "Stabat Mater," 161. Italics Kristeva's.

[21] Elizabeth A. Johnson, *She Who Is* (New York: Crossroad, 1992), 168. Although Johnson does not use Kristeva in her interpretation of the incarnation and redemption Johnson's theological understanding of embodiment is not incompatible with Kristeva's psychoanalytic one.

[22] Kristeva draws on the work of Marina Warner, *Alone of All Her Sex: The Myth and the Cult of the Virgin Mary* (New York: Alfred A. Knopf, 1976).

[23] See Toril Moi, "Introduction," in *The Kristeva Reader*, 12-15; also Toril Moi, *Sexual/Textual Politics: Feminist Literary Theory* (New York: Methuen & Co., 1985), 11-13.

[24] Oliver, 8-12. Oliver's fuller explanation is helpful on this extremely technical point.

[25] Moi, *Sexual/Textual Politics*, 161.

[26] "Revolution in Poetic Language," *The Kristeva Reader*, 93, 94.

[27] Oliver, 48.

[28] See Oliver, 48ff, for a discussion of the divergent responses of feminist critics to Kristeva's *chora* and its association with the maternal.

[29] Edelstein, 29ff. The remainder of this section relies heavily on Edelstein's textual analysis, 29-36.

[30] Edelstein, 32.

[31] Edelstein, 30. See also 48, note 10, where Edelstein comments that such a two-column essay reflects in a subversive way the theological tradition of textual/ scriptural commentary with glosses written in the margins. While traditionally such marginal notes comment on others' texts, here both left and right hand voices are Kristeva's. Neither of her columns is reducible to gloss.

[32] Barbara Johnson, "Translator's Introduction " to *Dissemination*, by Jacques Derrida (Chicago: University of Chicago Press, 1981), xxviii.

[33] Edelstein, 29.

[34] Edelstein, 30. See also "Women's Time," in *The Kristeva Reader* and Moi, *Sexual/ Textual Politics*, 163.

[35] Julia Kristeva, "Postmodernism?" in *Romanticism, Modernism, Postmodernism*, ed. Harry R. Garvin, spec. issue of *Bucknell Review* 25 (1980), 139-140.

[36] Edelstein, 30-31; citation from 31.

[37] Oliver, 19.

[38] "Word, Dialogue and Novel," *The Kristeva Reader*, 58. As Edelstein notes, Kristeva inherited her notion of the dialogic from Mikhail Bakhtin, yet as with so much of her borrowing she appropriates and redefines the meaning of the term (Edelstein, 31-32).

[39] Cf. Edelstein, 36. Also Oliver, 12-13.

[40] Edelstein, 39.

[41] Diane Jonte-Pace, "Situating Kristeva Differently: Psychoanalytic Readings of Women and Religion," in *Body/Text in Julia Kristeva*, 9.

[42] Kearns, 59.

[43] *Jouissance* is the French word for enjoyment, delight, sensual pleasure; it also refers to orgasm. For Kristeva the sensuality of nursing and fondling the new born can provide intense pleasure for the mother. *Jouissance* is also a highly theoretical concept referring to the subject's experience of mastery of meaning as well as passage through it. See *Desire in Language: A Semiotic Approach to Literature and Art*, trans. Léon S. Roudiez (New York: Columbia University Press, 1980; also Jean Graybeal, "Joying in the Truth of Self-Division," in *Body/Text in Julia Kristeva*, 129-138.

[44] Edelstein, 33

[45] Cf., Edelstein, 33, last paragraph.

[46] I borrow this term from Kelly Oliver yet here I use it as a metaphor for the problems specific to theological discourse on Mary.

[47] These dyadic processes invoke the "wandering or fuzziness" of the negativity which Kristeva celebrates ("the semiotic activity . . . introduces wandering or fuzziness into language and . . . stems from the archaisms of the semiotic body"). Ann Rosalind Jones, "Julia Kristeva on Femininity: The Limits of a Semiotic Politics," *Feminist Review*, No. 18, (November 1984), 59. See Mary Caputi, "The Abject Maternal: Kristeva's Theoretical Consistency," in *Women and Language* Vol. XVI, No. 2 (Fall, 1993), 35. I am grateful to Mary Caputi whose essay introduced me to Kristeva and whose many discussions of her work have helped clarify my thinking.

[48] See Caputi , 35, quoted from Gallop, *The Daughter's Seduction*, 122.

[49] "A fluid haze," "an elusive clamminess," a "violent nausea," abjection afflicts a troubled and unformed entity that knows itself as an I only through the sense of having been thrown out or repulsed from an Other. *Powers of Horror*, (New York: Columbia University Press, 1982), 6. Cf. Caputi, 35.

[50] See *Powers of Horror*, 15: "Abjection is a resurrection that has gone through death (of the ego). It is an alchemy that transforms death drive into a start of life, of new significance." The maternal resonates with the repressed, the unconscious, and—outside of language—is made abject and assumes violent and terrifying connotations in the narcissistic crisis of the one being born. (See also Caputi, 14-15).

[51] See Johnson, 153, for a feminist discussion of the christological implications of the maleness of Jesus.

[52] Kearns, 58.

[53] See Oliver, 51.

[54] Kearns, 58.

[55] Edelstein, 34.

[56] Cf. Edelstein, 34.

[57] Kristeva postulates the process of interruption and increase by grafts and folds of otherness in the construction of every identity. "This process could be summarized as an interiorization of the founding separation of the socio-symbolic contract, as an introduction of its cutting edge into the very interior of every identity whether subjective, sexual, ideological, or so forth" ("Women's Time," *The Kristeva Reader*, 210).

[58] Edelstein, 34. See also the essay by David Fisher, "Kristeva's *Chora* and the Subject of Postmodern Ethics," in *Body/Text in Julia Kristeva*, 91-106.

[59] "A New Type of Intellectual," in *The Kristeva Reader*, 297.

[60] Kearns, 68.

[61] See "About Chinese Women," in *The Kristeva Reader*, 156.

[62] See "Women's Time," in *The Kristeva Reader*, 210.

[63] Edelstein, 35.

[64] Oliver, 183.

[65] Oliver, 189. For a theological presentation of justice in mutual sexual relations see Carter Heyward, *Touching Our Strength: The Erotic and the Power of God* (New York: Crossroad, 1990).

[66] Ewa Ziarek, "At the Limits of Discourse: Heterogeneity, Alterity, and the Maternal Body in Kristeva's Thought," *Hypatia* 7 (2, 1992), 100.

[67] "Women's Time," *The Kristeva Reader*, 205.

[68] Edelstein, 50, note 23.

[69] Oliver, 3.

[70] Ziarek, 105.

[71] Ziarek, 104. (Italics Ziarek's.)

[72] Mary Grey, *Feminism, Redemption, and the Christian Tradition* (Mystic, CT: Twenty-Third Publications, 1990), 160.

[73] See her argument in *Jesus*, 119-128.

[74] See for examples of feminist theologians' reading of Kristeva as essentialist, Elisabeth Schüssler Fiorenza, *But She Said: Feminist Practices of Biblical Interpretation* (Boston: Beacon Press, 1992), 106-108; and Paula M. Cooey, *Religious Imagination and the Body: A Feminist Analysis* (New York: Oxford University Press, 1994), 20-25.

[75] Oliver, especially 163-180.

[76] John Paul II, "Apostolic Letter on Ordination and Women," *Origins*, vol. 24, no. 4 (June 9, 1994).

[77] Johnson, 159. See also, "Final Document: Intercontinental Women's Conference," in *With Passion and Compassion: Third World Women Doing Theology* (Maryknoll, NY: Orbis, 1988), 188; Ursula King, ed. *Feminist Theology from the Third World: A Reader* (Maryknoll, NY: Orbis, 1994), 271-302; and Elizabeth A. Johnson, "Redeeming the Name of Christ," in *Freeing Theology: The Essentials of Theology in Feminist Perspective*, Catherine Mowry LaCugna, ed. (San Francisco: Harper SanFrancisco, 1993), 115-138.

AFTERWORD

Presidential Address

Joan A. Leonard

We have come together in this elegant setting to join Saint Mary's College in celebrating its sesquicentennial as well as the 50th anniversary of its School of Theology. At the same time we celebrate the 40th anniversary of the College Theology Society, and the 20th anniversary of our journal *Horizons*. On this occasion of remembering the roots of the college and the Society the theme of this year's convention, "Women and Theology," is especially appropriate. We are delighted for the opportunity to develop the theme through our convention deliberations and presentations. It is especially significant that we hold our scholarly exchange about this crucial area for contemporary theological studies on this campus which is one of the first two Catholic colleges recognized to offer baccalaureate degrees to women. The college has long been noted for its pioneer efforts in offering the opportunity for women to study theology. We in the College Theology Society are pleased to be part of the festivities here in South Bend.

For our part, as we have just heard in the tribute to one of our founding members, Gerard Sloyan, we, too, have played a significant role in encouraging scholars and teachers of religion. We continue to grow, having over 900 members who share in a vigorous intellectual life by participating in annual and regional meetings, and serving on the Board, and standard and ad hoc committees. We also write for *Horizons* and produce papers for the annual volume of each meeting. From its early days, the CTS has put a high premium on pedagogical concerns and the fostering of community in its approach to scholarship.

There is also a place for community in this process of remembering that occurs on anniversaries. Educator and theologian Parker Palmer reminds us that to "remember" means literally to re-member the body, to bring the separated parts of the community of truth back together, to reunite the whole. The opposite of re-member is not forget, but dis-member. This is what we do when we forget truth: we are dismembering the relationship between us and the rest of reality, between us and the knowledge we need to take our part in the community of truth. Memory allows us to enter dialogue with other beings who are distant in time and space. As our memory deepens and expands, our network of face-to-face relationships grows richer and more complex. We can call upon memory to introduce third parties, and (more to the present task) to invoke voices too distant in time and space to speak easily for themselves.[1]

And so tonight we remember with gratitude and deep appreciation our founding members, past presidents, officers, board members, those who served on standing committees, or gave leadership to directing conventions, publications, or editing *Horizons*. We also are grateful to those who served as local chairs of conventions, regional officers, those who presented papers, and those loyal members who swelled the crowds at annual meetings. Most of all, we are thankful for former and present colleagues and faithful friends.

Anniversaries are times of remembrance and reflection on where we have been, occasions of currently assessing where we are now, and moments of looking ahead to the challenges of the future. To take a glance back after reaching a milestone is always a sobering, even humbling experience and one appreciates more keenly T. S. Eliot's lines in "Gerontion": "History has many cunning passages, contrived corridors and issues."[2]

In this address I wish to do three things. First I will describe in general the world background against which the challenges of women doing theology arise. Next I assess some of the issues that are currently raised by feminist theology and, third, I suggest some of the strengths of CTS that may sustain us in the struggle for more just communities. I want to keep in mind some of the questions that have been raised this weekend in the context of hospitality. My observations are not exhaustive, nor will they be radically new or revolutionary.

I would like to situate the context for our future work in terms of some statistics that give urgency and substance to our task. Hans Küng's work *Global Responsibility; In Search of a New World Ethic*, grounded in the critical issues of the world, begins with these stark words:

> Every minute, the nations of the world spend $1.8 million on military armaments. Every hour, 1500 children die of hunger-related causes. Every day, a species becomes extinct. Every week during the 1980's, more people were detained, tortured, assassinated, made refugees, or in other ways violated by acts of repressive regimes than at any other time in history. Every month, the world's economic system adds over $7.5 billion to the catastrophically unbearable debt burden of more than $1,500 billion now resting on the shoulders of third world peoples. Every year, an area of tropical forest three-quarters the size of Korea is destroyed and lost. Every decade, if present global warming trends continue, the temperature of the earth's atmosphere could rise dramatically (between 1.5 and 4.5 degrees Celsius) with a resultant rise in sea levels that would have disastrous consequences, particularly for coastal areas of the earth's land masses.[3]

The heart of Küng's concern is expressed in his introduction:

> It has become increasingly clear to me in recent years that the one world in which we live has a chance for survival only if there is no longer any room in it for spheres of differing, contradictory and even antagonistic ethics. This one world needs one basic ethic. This one world society certainly does not need a unitary religion and a unitary ideology, but it does need some norms, values, ideals and goals to bring it together and to be binding on it.[4]

According to Küng what we need is a world order in partnership.[5]

Certainly these days we have been reminded of the pain and suffering, as well as the commitment and serious toil borne by many women and men scholars as they attempt to make significant contributions to theology, society, and the globe. During this convention we have pondered the dilemmas raised up for us by our plenary speakers and presenters.

The CTS has also been known for widening its circle of hospitality to current members, fledging professors, graduate students, ecumenical participants, guests and friends alike. Hospitality means receiving each other, our struggles, and our newborn ideas with openness and care.

First as to hospitality and the asking of questions: We have provided a space for celebration and have insured freedom in the asking of some thorny questions In the words of Henri Nouwen,

> Hospitality means primarily the creation of a free space where the stranger can enter and become a friend instead of an enemy. Hospitality is not to change people, but to offer them space where change can take place. . . . Hospitality is not a subtle invitation to adopt the life style of the host, but the gift of freedom for the guest to find her own.[6]

In her volume of poetry, *Revolutionary Petunias*, Alice Walker examines the nature of love and of revolution. She exposes herself as one who must question, feel, and pursue the mysteries of life. I would like to cite a part of her poem "Reassurance," because it articulates women's need to sustain ourselves in our persistent questions which are crucial for our future. Walker writes:

> I must love the questions
> themselves
> as Rilke said
> like locked rooms
> full of treasure
> to which my blind
> and groping key
> does not yet fit.[7]

Feminist writers and theologians explore the questions of women in a male defined culture and patriarchal society. They seek a new voice, a new common language that can express the meaning and significance of women's lives and make us visible and central in culture, society, and theology.

Mary Collins in speaking of the blessing that feminist theological discourse is for the Church says: "One of the best gifts for the critical mind and for a living tradition is the gift of a new question."[8] Before proceeding I want to frame the discussion with two questions that are often neglected. They are: 1) Who is asking the question and 2) To whose advantage is it that the questions are asked? These are questions that orient us and ground us as we link contemporary issues to a real life context.

The question of feminist theology is very recent. Only within the past twenty-five to thirty years have women gained enough of a foothold in theological education to begin to question the androcentric bias of the tradition. It is not surprising, therefore, that women do not yet have all the answers, and indeed are only beginning to formulate the questions. What is surprising is the enormous amount of solid work in all fields from biblical studies to history to theology to ethics, pastoral psychology and ministry that has already been accomplished.

A key question that surfaced in many sessions this weekend was not whether patriarchal tradition and feminism have a future together. Rather, a number of voices from very different perspectives asked whether feminist theology will sufficiently transform theology as it is taught in colleges and universities so that we no longer have a patriarchal theology? In other words, will we achieve a theology that has the potential to bring about a renewed community of women and men in church, society, and academy where women from diverse classes and cultures bear an equal share of responsibility to men at all levels and where they can freely contribute their gifts, insights, values, and experiences?

Or will another scenario be in place? Will patriarchal theology succeed in confining feminist theology to the margins of the theological enterprise, so that the next generation of students will no longer be able to raise feminist questions, but also will not be able to imagine the possibilities such questioning unfolds for the revision of theology because the questions and the possibilities both have been ruled out-of-bounds by guardians of theological orthodoxy?

Painfully, we have heard that at the heart of feminism is women's experience of being marginalized with all the suffering this entails. Being marginal has become a key category for interpreting women's experience. It identifies women as accessories to men rather than active subjects of history in their own right. It is an inhospitable place of systematic devaluing where one is overlooked, does not have much importance, isn't able to shape symbols, or decide significant matters for the whole community.

This has been clarified for me by two very different examples. First, two years ago I attended a conference on women faculty teaching in Catholic colleges and universities held at Boston College. Addressing some difficult issues of women at Catholic institutions, Patricia Weltzel O'Neill from Trinity College, Washington, D.C., used the host-guest metaphor to nods of recognition. She certainly identified a different kind of hospitality than the one that we have been advocating.

She pointed out that women faculty and administrators often feel like guests, committed to a certain protocol of etiquette toward their hosts, their male colleagues, especially in institutions that have previously been all-male. Women are guests as well, she noted, in the area of knowledge. Women were taken in late to a university owned by men who think they own the knowledge. Australian feminist scholar, Dale Spender, confirms O'Neill's point in her book, *Women of Ideas (And What Men Have Done to Them)*. Spender argues that the absence of women's voices and their invisibility in intellectual history—as well as the experience that every feminist work has been received as if it emerged from nowhere—is fundamental to the perpetuation and hegemony of patriarchal power in the academy.[9]

The second example is the experience documented in S. Francis Bernard O'Connor's book, *Like Bread, Their Voices Rise: Global Women Challenge the Church*. She refutes the assumption that Catholic women's desire for full participation in the life and mission of the church is only a North American "problem." The author collected data from Catholic women in Bangladesh, Brazil, Uganda, and the United States, spending one to three months in each country. In her book, O'Connor documents the range of church experience from the liberation approach one finds in Brazil to the traditional and even ultra-traditional theology of Bangladesh and Uganda.

The survey focused on determining how women are awakening to the reality of their place in the church, what they are doing to challenge the church in order to live the message of the Gospel and what they claim for themselves as equal members of the church. O'Connor reports that, when she first met with the various groups of women, the initial reactions to her questionnaire were skepticism and suspicion, on the one hand, and interest and excitement on the other.[10] The universal comment was, "No one has ever asked us what we think about the church before." (Again, who is asking the question? and to whose advantage is it that the questions are being asked?)

According to United Nations statistics, while forming about one-half of the world's population, women work two-thirds of the world's working hours, own one-tenth of the world's wealth and one-hundredth of the world's land, and form two-third's of the world's illiterate people. Over three-fourths of starving people are women with their dependent children.[11] Surprisingly, there are more men in the world than women, who numbered 2.63 billion out of the total population of 5.3 billion in 1990. The greatest difference is in the developed regions, where the ratio is 106 women to 100 men. In Asia and the Pacific, there are only 95 women for every 100 men.[12] Explaining the discrepancy, the report notes that in many areas, girls and women are denied equal nutrition, health care and other support. Other suggested reasons include widow-burning, dowry deaths, female infanticide, and abortion based on male preference.

As Canadian author, Margaret Atwood notes, "To see the world clearly is to see the world through tears."[13] We are beginning to understand that we will only experience the hospitality of community when those at the center and those at the periphery come together. As we start to work toward this goal, we need to listen to the admonition of Sharon Welch who warns that "Just as slavery and the treatment of women were for centuries not even recognized by sensitive theologians and people of faith as oppressive, it is possible that my thought and actions share in the perpetuation of as yet unrecognized forms of oppression."[14]

By contrast, women's experience bears out again and again that the most life-giving exchange occurs when bonds are reciprocal or mutual. It involves a hospitable climate of concomitant valuing of each other, a give and take according to each one's strengths and weaknesses, and a common regard marked by trust, affection, and respect for differences—all this in contrast to competition, domination or assertions of superiority. In the words of Elizabeth Johnson:

> Feminist thinking prizes dialectical connectedness that flourishes in a circle of mutuality. . . . if the self is defined by a dialectic of friendly, constitutive relation, then it becomes possible to reconcile previously dichotomous elements: self and other, most basically, and consequently matter and spirit, body and soul, passions and mind, embodiedness and self-transcendence, women and men, humanity and earth. . . . Oppositional, either-or thinking which is essential to the hierarchical dualistic pattern of real-

ity is transformed by a new paradigm of both-and. Regarding humanity's connection to the earth, women's wisdom suggests that the relation is not one of "over against" and "superior to" but "together with," moving in an interactive circle of mutual kinship.[15]

Our era of planetary destruction and inhospitable behavior brings to the fore the question Küng mentioned earlier: how should we relate to the earth? Scientific journals, ecologists and theologians decry the rapid dissection of whole species of plants and animals, loss of topsoil, and pollution of air, water, and ozone layer. The ultimate tragedy, the scholars such as Rosemary Ruether, Sallie McFague, Elizabeth Johnson and Thomas Berry perceptively point out is that this devastation is caused by human domination, an "over against" mentality. In the introduction to *Gaia and God: An Ecofeminist Theology of Earth Healing*, Rosemary Ruether writes:

> Ecology and feminism, brought together in the unified perspective of ecofeminism, provide the critical perspective from which I seek to evaluate the heritage of Western Christian culture. The goal of this quest is earth healing, a healed relationship between men and women, between classes and nations, and between humans and the earth. Such healing is possible only through recognition and transformation of the way in which Western culture, enshrined in part in Christianity, has justified such domination.[16]

I have unfolded the background against which the challenges have arisen, focussed on hospitality, and assessed the questions of women's marginalization, connectedness and relationship. These give ample warrants for working collaboratively on issues of ecology and peace and justice. A flourishing humanity on a thriving earth is the vision that shapes the College Theology Society Agenda for the future. As I turn now to imagining this future, I draw on six strengths of the CTS:

1) Given our tradition of expansive hospitality, let us widen our circles to include a more diverse membership—particularly among women, peoples of diverse cultures, younger professors, graduate students, and scholars in other traditions who are seeking a home base and dialogue partners. Would a collaboration with Baptist professors or Islamic scholars enrich our group and broaden our horizons?

Let us offer that free space to voices that ask the penetrating questions that most people do not want to hear about. Let us hear the complexities that feminist critique has raised up. Let us also stand with younger colleagues and students who struggle to reconcile an alternative vision with institutional commitment.

2) Understanding theology as the interpretation of tradition and the interpretation of contemporary experience, let us encourage more interdisciplinary work. Let us forge bonds with those who carry out the analyses of both tradition and contemporary experience in other fields. Let us redouble our efforts in the professions and ethics, notably in health and medicine. Let us expand our work in science and theology, especially in ecology and theology. Let us join forces with academic colleagues in economics and political science as well.

3) As a professional society that values teaching and participation in a community of relationships with other persons, things and ideas, let us incorporate the viewpoints and writings of women and persons from other cultures in our courses and professional meetings. Let us encourage the development of cooperative learning styles and explore diverse ways of related knowing and then mine the depths that a study of the new cosmologies and epistemology yields. As educator and theologian Parker Palmer observes: "The shape of our knowledge becomes the shape of our living: the relation of the knower to the known becomes the relation of the living self to the larger world, the way we interact with the world in knowing it becomes the way we interact with the world as we live in it. . . . Our epistemology is quietly transformed into our ethic."[17]

4) In academic settings challenged by professionalism, political correctness, competition, Vatican assaults on academic freedom, Cartesian dualism, objectivism, and business management-style administrators, let us offer the best of what we have learned from our experience in cooperative, mutual ways of leading our society and organizing our classes. Not only in our departments and institutions, but also among professional societies, let us continue to model communal, cooperative ways of leadership. Many of us have learned that the old hierarchical ways of doing things just don't hold.

5) Aware of the growing pluralism of our institutions, and many of our members' ecumenical expertise, let us embrace the challenge for ecumenical and interfaith dialogue. Even as specialists elaborate on the definitions of dialogue and the new insights gained from an understanding of

pluralism, let us have the vision to foster the increasing role of women as participants and leaders. Frequently the situation of women in these circles is problematic as they are consistently underrepresented in leadership and all too often ignored for their contributions.

Catholics especially must converse intellectually and spiritually with many other communities of meaning in our culture. As individual persons and as communities we need to understand how Christianity distinguishes itself from other world religions—to make the journey into another viewpoint so that we can return home with new insight. Several years ago Bill Shea challenged Catholic universities to establish a genuinely major ecumenical faculty of theology.[18] To date no one has picked up on his suggestion.

6) How will our commitment to peace and justice be evidenced? Both students and teachers in religious studies and theology have a special mandate to develop and use our knowledge and the skills of the field to do what we can to make real the biblical vision of justice and shalom. Let our clearly focused vision of a renewed spirituality be the basis of what we teach and learn and of how we enable students to understand and make decisions both in the classroom and outside. Such an understanding of the tradition enables all of us to live rooted in reality even as we seek to transcend it. It expands our shriveled consciousness to incorporate the best of the tradition.

In this address I have asked whether we will achieve a theology that has the potential to bring about a renewed community of women and men in church, society, and academy where women bear an equal share of responsibility to men at all levels and where they can freely contribute their gifts. In the context of hospitality we have considered issues of women's questions, marginality and relatedness. We then considered six strengths of the CTS: hospitality, theological expertise, pedagogical innovation and flexibility, mutual, cooperative leadership, openness to dialogue, and commitment to peace and justice. These provide warrants for remaining with the issues and sharing in struggle and faith with others. As these strengths operate they interact with the sufferings of women and men sensitive to injustice, and become catalysts for an interdependent, relational way of acting and living.

Reinforcing the relational mode, Rosemary Ruether uses the metaphor of dance: "We must start thinking of reality as the connecting links of a dance in which each part is equally vital to the whole, rather than the linear competitive model in which the above prospers by defeating and suppressing what is below."[19] With festivity and hospitality, let us go forth to continue the dance.

Notes

[1] Parker Palmer, *To Know as We Are Known: A Spirituality of Education* (San Francisco: Harper and Row, 1983), p. 103.

[2] T. S. Eliot, "Gerontion," in *Collected Poems 1909-1962* (New York: Harcourt Brace and World, Inc., 1963), p. 30.

[3] Hans Küng, *Global Responsibility: In Search of a New World Ethic* (New York: Crossroad, 1991), p. 2.

[4] Ibid., xvi.

[5] Ibid., p. 68.

[6] Henri Nouwen, *Reaching Out: The Three Movements of the Spiritual Life* (New York: Doubleday, Inc., 1975), p. 51.

[7] Alice Walker, *Revolutionary Petunias* (New York and London: Harcourt, Brace, Jovanovich, 1973), p. 33.

[8] Mary Collins, "Naming God in Public Prayer," *Worship* 59 (1985), 292.

[9] Dale Spender, *Women of Ideas (And What Men Have Done to Them)* (London: ARK Paperbacks, 1983) cited in *Discipleship of Equals: A Critical Feminist Ekklesia-logy of Liberation,* Elisabeth Schüssler Fiorenza (New York: Crossroad, 1993), p. 4.

[10] S. Francis Bernard O'Connor, *Like Bread Their Voices Rise: Global Women Challenge the Church* (Notre Dame, Ind.: Ave Maria Press, 1993).

[11] "Women's World Data Sheet" (Washington, D.C.: Population Reference Bureau in collaboration with UNICEF). Report of the World Conference to Review and Appraise the Achievements of the United Nations Decade for Women, Equality, Development and Peace (New York: United Nations, 1985).

[12] Ibid.

[13] Cited by Lois Wilson at the "Reimaging Community Conference," Minneapolis: November, 1993.

[14] Sharon Welch, *Communities of Resistance and Solidarity: A Feminist Theology of Liberation* (Maryknoll, NY: Orbis Books, 1985), pp. 85-86.

[15] Elizabeth A. Johnson, *Women, Earth, and Creator Spirit* (New York: Paulist Press, 1993), pp. 27-28.

[16] Rosemary Ruether, *Gaia and God: An Ecofeminist Theology of Earth Healing* (San Francisco: Harper and Row, 1992), p. 1.

[17] Palmer, *To Know as We Are Known*, p. 21.

[18] William Shea, "Beyond Tolerance: Pluralism and Catholic Education," in *Theology and the University,* John Apczynski, ed. (Lanham, Md.: University Press of America, 1989), p. 264.

[19] Rosemary Ruether, *To Change the World: Christology and Cultural Criticism* (New York: Crossroad, 1981), p. 67.

Contributors

María Pilar Aquino is assistant professor of theology and religious studies at the University of San Diego. She is the author of *Our Cry for Life: Feminist Theology from Latin America* (Orbis Books, 1993) and editor of *Aportes para une teología desde la mujer* (Madrid: Biblia y Fe, 1988).

Regina A. Boisclair is Head of Reader Services at the Jesuit-Krauss-McCormick Library, Chicago, IL. An *Elève Titulaire de l'École Biblique*, she is completing a dissertation on the hermeneutics of the contemporary lectionaries at Temple University.

Helen Marie Ciernick is a doctoral student in Church History at the Catholic University of America. Her field of study is the American Catholic Church.

M. Shawn Copeland is associate professor of theology at Marquette University, Milwaukee, Wisconsin. She is the author of more than thirty articles, reviews, and commentary in professional journals and books, and co-editor with Elisabeth Schüssler Fiorenza of *Concilium: Violence Against Women.*

Mary Rose D'Angelo is associate professor of theology at Notre Dame University and a member of the editorial board of the Journal of Biblical Literature. Her articles include feminist and historical critiques of claims about the titles "abba" and "father" and studies of women's partnerships in the New Testament, women in Luke-Acts, women and resistance in the context of Jesus and the divorce sayings as evidence of sexual politics in ancient Christianity.

Ann O'Hara Graff is assistant professor of theology at Seattle University. She edited *In the Embrace of God: Feminist Perspectives in Theological Anthropology,* published by Orbis Books.

Dana Greene serves as professor of history and associate provost of faculty at Saint Mary's College, Saint Mary's City, Maryland. She is the author of *Evelyn Underhill: Artist of Infinite Life* (Crossroads, 1989).

Mary Ann Hinsdale, I.H.M., is associate professor of theology in the Religious Studies Department of the College of the Holy Cross, Worcester, MA. Her publications include *Faith that Transforms* (Paulist Press, 1987) and *"It Comes from the People": Community Development and Local Theology* (Temple University Press,1995).

Phyllis H. Kaminski is assistant professor in the Department of Religious Studies at Saint Mary's College, Notre Dame, IN. Her most recent article, "Claiming Our Voices: A Teaching/Learning Experiment," appeared in the *Journal of Feminist Studies in Religion* 10/1.

Jane Kopas is a professor of theology at University of Scranton and a member of the Franciscan Sisters of Allegany, N.Y. Author of *Sacred Identity* (Paulist Press, 1994), she edited the CTS Annual Volume, *Interpreting Tradition: The Art of Theological Reflection* (1983), and has published numerous articles.

Joan Augusta Leonard, O.P. (1941-1995) was professor of religious studies at Edgewood College, Madison, WI. Joan published "Teaching Introductory Feminist Spirituality" in the *Journal of Feminist Studies in Religion* 6/2 and was a regular religion columnist for the *Capital Times* newspaper in Madison.

Susan Marie Maloney is chair of the M.A. Program in Feminist Spirituality at Immaculate Heart College Center in Los Angeles, California. She coordinates a cross-cultural summer program entitled *Working for Solidarity: Women Doing Faith-Based Social Analysis* and is a member of the Sisters of the Holy Names of Jesus and Mary.

Caritas McCarthy, S.H.C.J., teaches at Rosemont College, PA. She is the author of *The Spirituality of Cornelia Connelly* (Edwin Mellen Press, 1986) and has done extensive archival work on Cornelia Connelly and the Society of the Holy Child Jesus.

Linda A. Moody works as chaplain at Mills College, Oakland, CA. Her articles have appeared in *Christian Century*, the *Journal of Woman and Religion*, and *TESOL Quarterly*. She is currently writing *Hearing God Calling,* forthcoming from Orbis Books.

Kwok Pui-lan is associate professor of theology at the Episcopal Divinity School, Cambridge, MA. She is the author of *Chinese Women and Christianity, 1860-1927* and *Discovering the Bible in the Non-Biblical World* (Orbis, 1995).

Anne E. Patrick, S.N.J.M., is professor of religion at Carlton College, Northfield, MN, and a past president of the Catholic Theological Society of America. She is currently completing a book entitled *Liberating Conscience: Feminist Explorations in Catholic Moral Theology.*

Mary T. Rattigan teaches in the Religious Studies Department at Caldwell College, NJ. Her articles on christology and God in process thought have appeared in *Encounter* and *The Irish Theological Quarterly.*